Cancan and Barcarolle

Cancan and Barcarolle

The Life and Times of Jacques Offenbach

ARTHUR MOSS & EVALYN MARVEL

GREENWOOD PRESS, PUBLISHERS
WESTPORT, CONNECTICUT

Library of Congress Cataloging in Publication Data

Moss, Arthur, 1889-
    Cancan and barcarolle.

    Reprint of the ed. published by Exposition Press, Ne
York, in series: A Banner book.
    Bibliography: p.
    1. Offenbach, Jacques, 1819-188(. I. Marvel,
Evalyn, joint author. II. Title.
[ML410.O41M7 1975]   782.8'1'0924 [B]   75-8716
ISBN 0-8371-8045-7

Originally published in 1954 by Exposition Press, New York

Reprinted with the permission of Exposition Press, Inc.

Reprinted in 1975 by Greenwood Press,
a division of Williamhouse-Regency Inc.

Library of Congress Catalog Card Number 75-8716

ISBN 0-8371-8045-7

Printed in the United States of America

Authors' Note

The authors in writing this biograph, have in the main used a narrative treatment, because it is their sincere belief that this is the best method of giving life to Offenbach and his times. It is also their feeling that the average reader does not want to be bogged down with the assaying of probabilities and possibilities. In the case of Jacques Offenbach there is such a plethora of material and detail on which to draw that very little is left to conjecture. Although certain scenes have been constructed on probabilities, the incidents on which they are based are always factual. There is scarcely a line of dialogue which cannot be accounted for by the memoirs of a contemporary. Those conversations that seem most unlikely are taken from verbatim reports of Halévy, Houssaye, or the recollections garnered by Offenbach's grandson. Finally, Offenbach's own letters give ample evidence of both his mode of thought and manner of speaking. The authors have at all times conscientiously tried to avoid tampering with the facts and believe that they can be accused of no more serious offense than transposing a conversation or minor incident to a different date or setting in order to preserve the continuity of the story. Their hope is that they have succeeded to some degree in bringing to life not only Offenbach but his epoch.

A. M.
E. M.

Contents

Cancan and Barcarolle

CHAPTER ONE

Paris Is the Promised Land

1

The huge diligence lumbered to a final stop in the cobble-stoned courtyard of its terminal in the eastern outskirts of Paris. Only three passengers were left and they clambered down from the upper deck, the cheaper seats.

A thin, middle-aged man and two rather scrawny boys in their teens, they had the marks of long and uncomfortable travel on their cheap and obviously foreign clothes. To the hostlers in the courtyard, these three were merely the usual weekly stragglers into France from that outlandish region on the other side of the Rhine, speaking only a few words of French and that with a horrible guttural accent. Had not the elder of the trio remarked:

"C'est le derminus, n'est-ce-bas? C'est Baris, même?"

To the father and his sons, for such was manifestly the relationship, this dingy courtyard, with its slimy, manure-cluttered cobbles, was the Gateway to Paradise, the Mecca of their Hegira.

The father inquired as to how they could go on to their ultimate destination and mentioned a street in the Marais, the Jewish quarter of Paris proper. The gruff French hostler at first pretended he did not understand a word the stranger said, a stalling device employed against foreigners by Frenchmen from time immemorial. However, he finally relented, being a family man himself, and remarked that it would be a long walk for the trio, if that was really their intention. ᵢor only five francs, he suggested, he would drag out a two-wheeled handcart and take them to their goal.

After a worried consultation in German with his sons, the father decided to dip into their meager funds. After all, they did have several valises, not to mention the various musical instruments with which they were burdened. Young Jakob had a cello almost as big as himself. Julius, the elder boy, carried a violin case.

Everything was heaved into the handcart, and with the hostler in the shafts, they trundled their way out of the courtyard and into the twisting streets.

The East End streets of the French capital in that year of 1833 were teeming with traffic. The country was relatively prosperous under the dull and niggardly reign of Louis-Philippe. Market carts laden with produce, huge carryalls holding as many as two dozen passengers, occasional private coaches returning from the countryside, bumped and clattered over the cobbles of the Boulevard du Temple. This was not the most attractive section of Paris, but to the Offenbach trio it was indeed the Promised Land. For Isaac Offenbach and his two boys, the eighteen-year-old Julius and the fourteen-year-old Jakob, had come from a far more stultifying scene, the somber Jewish ghetto in the German city of Cologne. Not that they had been unduly oppressed there, but anti-Semitism in Germany even then was something to be reckoned with. True, in Paris there was a Jewish quarter, but Jews were not herded into it, not forced to live in it. There were no official residential restrictions for them in France, no restrictions except those self-imposed for economic reasons or because they themselves had the herd instinct.

Actually in Cologne the Offenbachs had not been too badly

off. They had lived in a small house in a courtyard known as
the Street of the Bells in the Judengasse. They were favorably
known even beyond the ghetto as a musical family. Father not
only was a cantor in the synagogue—which supplied them their
home—but gave lessons in singing, the violin, the flute and the
guitar. Also, when Julius and young Jakob were old enough and
sufficiently proficient with their chosen musical instruments, he
had organized a family trio, hiring out in the various restaurants
and taverns of Cologne. All this, however, brought barely enough
to defray the expenses of a family of fourteen, and now that
the boys were moving to Paris to study, it was more necessary
than ever to conserve funds.

Of the three Offenbachs following the hand-drawn cart across
town, only young Jakob displayed more than passing curiosity
in the scene. Isaac, his mind busy with the problem of settling
his sons, observed little of the movement around him. Julius,
while an intelligent enough youth, was too phlegmatic and docile
to exhibit any great enthusiasm for anything. If his father had
unaccountably suggested that they should turn around and return to Cologne, he would dutifully and unprotestingly have
followed him.

But Jakob, a scrawny boy who looked even less than his fourteen years, was already a far more positive person than his older
brother. He was mischievous, precocious, and quite capable of
taking care of himself. He had an intense curiosity, a love of people and excitement, and an absolute certainty of his own successful destiny. Not that he was a thoughtless, selfish boy—far
from it. He had the greatest respect and admiration for his
father, who was his hero, and he adored his mother. Perhaps
he was her favorite child. In any case, she had done her utmost
to spoil him. For that matter, his hard-headed father had done
his share along that line since his young Jakob, born in the
midst of a family already endowed with talent, had shown early
signs of outstripping them all. The trip to Paris had been originally planned mainly on the younger boy's account, and Jakob
knew it.

Jakob's face was thin and pointed, almost ratlike, and he

would have been impossibly ugly if it had not been for his
bright, eager eyes. They, together with his quick, shy smile,
gave his face such animation as to make one overlook its intrinsic homeliness. Now, as he trudged along the Boulevard du
Temple into the Rue des Filles du Calvaire, they darted ceaselessly from side to side taking in the spectacle of the busy streets.

It was growing dusk on that late November day of 1833 and
the candles were already lit in some of the shops. People were
hurrying home before darkness set in, along the tree-shaded
walks, occasionally darting across the cobblestone streets in front
of a lurching carryall or a team of four of some presumably
wealthy nobleman. Jakob was enchanted. During the four-day
trip he had had twinges of homesickness, of sadness at parting
from his mother and sisters. The towns and villages along the
way had all seemed frighteningly strange and in his heart he
had yearned for the familiarity of the little house on the Street
of the Bells. But this—this was different. There were no beautiful tree-lined streets like this in Cologne, none of the gaiety
and excitement he was seeing all around him. From down the
street came the strains of an orchestra playing a *galop,* and as
they came abreast of the café, Jakob glimpsed in the candlelight
the high-hatted gentlemen and exaggeratedly dressed young
women grouped around the tables. Alongside the café, back of
a picket fence, he could see the tree-shaded little garden where
the *café-concerts* were held in the summer, closed now that the
weather had turned cold. He grinned to himself and continued
on his way, following the hostler and his cart, completely oblivious of his tired, aching body.

Herr Offenbach observed the café-concert too, mentally noting
that one of these places might afford a livelihood for his young
sons until they had finished their schooling. The first thing to
do tomorrow was to visit Cherubini at the Conservatoire. A col-
league in Cologne had provided him with a letter of introduction to the great composer who was the director of that famous
institution. Whether Julius could be placed in the Conservatory
was somewhat doubtful, but there was no question in his mind

about Jakob. He had absorbed all that his teachers had been
able to impart to him and only in Paris could he secure the
training commensurate with his talent.

And there was that other thing too. In Germany so many ob-
stacles were put in the way of a Jew, so many prohibitions, that
it was next to impossible to rise beyond the ghetto. France, as
everybody knew, was the land of liberty, of freedom, where a
man, no matter what his race, was accepted on his merits. Even
now, in this period of the reign of the dour Citizen-King, the
ideas of liberty handed down from the Revolution still per-
meated the atmosphere. Some day, here, Jakob would win recognition.

2

Herr Offenbach and Jakob sat in the Maestro's private music
room. The father's face was distorted with misery and in his
quiet, guttural voice he was searching for words in French with
which to plead his case. For once, young Jakob was motionless,
his eyes fixed on the face of the elderly Cherubini, the great
Italian composer and Director of the Conservatory.

Once again the latter cut Herr Offenbach short.

"I regret," he said with finality, "but rules are rules. We accept only Frenchmen as students."

Isaac Offenbach had been warned back in Cologne that Maître
Cherubini was a stickler for exactitude. He had a mania for
punctuality, taking out his watch frequently to prove it, and
he also believed that rules were rules, to be kept scrupulously.
One of the regulations of the Conservatory was that no foreign
students were permitted within its hallowed walls. Maître Cherubini himself, of course, had long ago become a French citizen.

Herr Offenbach realized that, for once, the dictum did not
arise from the fact that he and his son were Jewish. It was because they were Germans—foreigners. That too he had learned
in Cologne. He knew of a case about ten years previously when
a twelve-year-old boy named Liszt had been turned away be-

cause he was Hungarian. But Herr Offenbach had counted on his letter of introduction, and now it had failed. He decided to make one final effort.

"I beg of you, *Maître*," he pleaded, "at least hear my boy play. Tell me frankly, as a great musician, what you think of his ability."

Cherubini hesitated. He was bored and anxious to end the interview. He glanced again at his watch. Perhaps this was the best way to get rid of these importuners after all.

"All right," he said with a peculiar smile, "I will give him something to play."

Jakob reached for his cello case. Taking out the instrument, he set to work tuning it, while Cherubini rummaged through a pile of sheet music on his desk. There were plenty of interesting concertos and sonatas already humming through Jakob's head, but since the *Maître* preferred to test him with something new it was not the moment to protest.

In a few minutes Cherubini came up with the work he was looking for. It was an almost unknown Italian cantata and there was a satisfied little smile on the old man's face as he passed it to the boy. Let the lad stumble through that one if he could. Cherubini took secret pride in the fact that he himself was one of the few musicians who could read it with ease.

Docilely, Jakob drew up the music stand which the maestro had indicated and placed the music upon it. Picking up his bow, he began to play. Herr Offenbach sat stiffly on the edge of his chair. Maître Cherubini relaxed, leaned back, and shut his eyes.

Softly, but sweetly, the first notes pervaded the room, then, as the melody built up, the tone began to soar. Without any apparent hesitation or self-consciousness the young boy read along, lost in the beauty of this hitherto unknown work, manipulating his bow with ease as the complicated arrangement piled motif upon motif.

The old man opened his eyes cautiously and cocked his head to one side. He sat up straighter, his hands grasping the arms of his chair. Suddenly, with an alacrity belying his years, he jumped to his feet, interrupting Jakob.

"*Parbleu!*" he exclaimed, with the first enthusiasm he had shown. "The ruling is wrong! You are a pupil of the Conservatoire! I will go myself to the Ministry, my little friend, and you will be received as a student here—I give you my word!"

For the first time since they had entered the music room Herr Offenbach leaned back in his chair, smiling wanly.

3

When Herr Offenbach left Paris he had the pleasant feeling of having accomplished everything possible that a man in his circumstances could have achieved for his sons. They were decently, if modestly, housed in a garret up in Montmartre which they shared with the sons of another violinist from Cologne. This cut the costs of their lodging to a minimum, and while their rooms were rather bare and sometimes cold, for young, healthy fellows it was all somewhat of a lark. Best of all, they were out of the Marais, the Jewish quarter of Paris, which meant they were on the road to complete emancipation. Not that Herr Offenbach was ashamed of being Jewish, nor had he ever instilled in his children any desire to deny their racial origin, but he was devoted to the idea of complete racial and religious freedom. While he had a simple and devout belief in the God of his fathers he had little interest in the orthodox synagogue; in fact, he cared little for any sort of formalized religion.

Naturally, as the easiest means of earning the money to support his plentiful progeny, he had taken on the temporary job of cantor in one of the Paris synagogues and got his boys places in the choir as well.

Meantime, Jakob—or Jacques, as he was already being called in French—had secured a place as violinist in the orchestra of one of the boulevard theatres. Wouldn't the family be proud when they heard that! It looked also as if Julius—Jules, now—was going to be employed by the theatre as well. Of course, Jacques' efforts had helped bring that about. Even so, Jules was a competent violinist and, the position once secured, would be able to hold his own.

Somehow the trip back in the stagecoach—four days bumping over rough and dusty roads, with tiresomely regular stops to change teams—was not as fatiguing as Herr Offenbach had feared. He enjoyed his conversations with his various traveling companions (always careful to mention that one of his sons was studying at the Conservatoire), but more often he was lost in memories of the past and daydreams of the future.

As the coach jolted out of Paris he had given a last look around at the city he had grown to love. He observed the many details which he had overlooked in his concentration upon an rival three months previously. Still in his mind was the possibility that some day he might be able to move here with his entire family. The idea was tempting, but with the continuing responsibility for growing children he had to admit it would be a hazardous undertaking.

Not like those days thirty years before when, as a young man of twenty, he had first moved to Cologne. Cologne had then seemed a great improvement over Offenbach, the town on the Main from which he had come. It was a big bustling city, with plenty of opportunity for a young musician like himself.

Isaac Eberst, as he was then, had settled down in Deutz, the Cologne suburb and amusement center, where he had found a niche in one of the dance-hall orchestras almost immediately. This was not only more profitable but more to his liking than bookbinding, the craft in which he had been trained. On Saturdays, of course, he had augmented his earnings as cantor in the local synagogue since, thanks to his father, who was also a cantor, he was trained in that field too.

As Isaac Eberst was to some extent a foreigner in Cologne people generally designated him as the fellow from Offenbach "der Offenbacher," and in the course of time it became his proper name. When he was married, about a year after his arrival in Cologne, he signed the marriage certificate "Isaac Offenbach."

Marianne, the daughter of a respectable money-lender and

manager of a lottery office in Deutz, was a quiet, gentle but
warmhearted girl. Isaac had certainly never regretted his marriage, although sometimes he felt he had not brought her the
comfortable life which he had promised her. One after another,
in rapid succession, had come children, until now there were
twelve, so that while his financial situation had improved, the
costs of rearing such a family had always outdistanced his
earnings.

It was a particularly hard struggle when nine out of twelve
children were girls. Well, one of them was already married and
taken care of, and Julie and Isabella no doubt would be married
soon. Jacques and Jules were on their own now and the burden
was lightening. The other boy, little Michael, was barely five,
so perhaps they could move to Paris before he grew up.

At any rate, the situation was by no means as desperate as
when the Offenbachs had moved into Cologne proper. That was
back in 1816, during the so-called Wars of Liberation, when all
the German States were in turmoil and the amusement business
had seen a lot of failures. There were five children even then
and Isaac had been unemployed. There had been only one thing
left for him in Deutz, a return to the bookbinding which he
loathed. But in Cologne itself he could get a little work as a music teacher. After all, he was proficient with several instruments
and he was not uneducated. He had even done a little musical
composition, setting it to verses of his own.

During those years he had managed to give music lessons to
his own children as well, but only with Jacques had he come to
the full realization of his own limitations.

Jacques had not been born until three years after they were
settled on the Street of the Bells, in the Judengasse, June 21, 1819.
By the time the child was six, Isaac had started him on violin
lessons. Never had he seen a child advance so rapidly. Within
a year he could actually play acceptably and when he was eight
he was entertaining himself by writing his own compositions.
The trouble had been to get the boy outdoors to exercise and
play a bit. While a friendly child, he nevertheless loved music
above everything. Besides, in a family that size, there were only

rare moments when he was absolutely alone. But with that youthful ability of concentration, the boy could have lost himself in bedlam.

They worried because he was a puny, weak child. Actually, looking back on it, the boy had never been seriously ill, though he had constantly disobeyed the injunction to "go out and play," sneaking unobserved into an unused room to work at his music instead.

The boy did not, however, fit into the accepted pattern of the infant prodigy. Despite his frail physique he was a normal, playful, even mischievous child, with a consuming curiosity regarding everything that went on about him. He had a considerable talent for prankishness and practical joking.

Isaac Offenbach still had to laugh as he thought of the time he brought home the violoncello. Jacques was about ten then and wildly eager to try the new instrument. It was entirely too big for such a small boy and he was forbidden to touch it. Apparently though, when the grownups were away, Jacques would sneak upstairs into a shuttered room and try it for himself.

It was several months after its acquisition that Isaac took little Jacques along with him one evening to his chamber-music group. They were planning to play a Haydn suite that night and the three men already assembled grew impatient as the cello player failed to make his appearance.

Young Jacques sidled over to his father and whispered: "Please, may I play it?"

Isaac burst out laughing and repeated the request to his host.

"But he has never touched a cello," the man protested.

Quickly, with a shrewd, darting look at his father, Jacques admitted to his secret practicing. Isaac knew perfectly well he should have reprimanded the boy, but he was too amused. He continued to laugh and finally said: "Well, why not let him try it?"

Ruefully, he had to admit that the boy had been expecting him to do just that.

Of course, Jacques was too small and his arms really weren't long enough yet, but he made a quite passable effort.

It was during this period that Isaac realized he must find a teacher more advanced than himself for Jacques. It wasn't easy, with the expenses of such a large family, but he was willing to make sacrifices so that Jacques would receive the best musical education possible.

Herr Alexander, that old skinflint and eccentric, had the reputation nevertheless of being the finest teacher in Cologne. Everybody considered him a terrible miser and referred to him sarcastically as "the Artist" because of his weird attire. He invariably wore a threadbare old coat adorned with tarnished brass buttons and with the tails reaching almost to the ground. At the same time, he carried an ivory-handled cane and sported atop his hideous brown wig a really fashionable broadbrimmed hat. He was disagreeable and sharp, but he was an eminently good teacher.

In spite of his ability, Herr Alexander took no interest in his pupils whatever beyond the monetary value they represented to him. He charged the equivalent of twenty-five cents a lesson, an astoundingly high price in those days, and the fee had to be paid in advance of the lesson; otherwise he bowed his way out. This often was a source of real chagrin to the Offenbachs, who had great difficulty in producing the pfennigs on the spot, but usually they managed to spare Jakob the humiliation, as well as disappointment, of foregoing a lesson.

Within a very short time, certainly less than two years, Isaac had again to do some reckoning. Jacques had learned all that Herr Alexander had to impart; he was manifestly ready for a still more advanced teacher. Even Herr Alexander admitted this, indirectly. The boy's own compositions had been so mature that Herr Alexander found little to suggest by way of improving them.

Isaac Offenbach had learned of a younger man, a fine cellist himself, named Bernard Breuer, who had achieved quite a reputation in Cologne through the songs he had written for the

local carnivals. Arrangements were made for Breuer to give
Jacques lessons in composition.

Again there had been the question of finances. But by this
time both Jules and Jacques were competent to play in public
and so was their sister Isabella. Isaac rehearsed them together
carefully, and then, armed with a repertoire of both operatic
and dance music, they were hired out in the restaurants and
taverns of Cologne. Isaac, with a shrewd sense of publicity
values, advertised Jacques' age as even less than it really was
as he knew there was nothing like being paced by an infant
prodigy to enhance a trio's drawing powers.

For Jules and Isabella, these almost nightly performances
were simply a necessary means of earning money. For Jacques
they were a thrill. He loved the noise and clatter of the crowded
restaurants, the clink of beer glasses, the animation of the habitués. In the very midst of playing he would daydream about
when he would be famous, when everybody would hail him a
"maestro" and he would conduct his own works in taverns twice
as big. His eyes would sparkle as he pictured the scene and on
his face a happy grin would spread. Sometimes patrons would
nudge each other, pointing to the droll-looking little boy, and
they would grin back at him, in friendly fashion, for his smile
was infectious.

It was after Isaac was forced to recognize that Jacques had
also absorbed all young Breuer had to offer that he had to face
up to the decision to send him to Paris. Jacques was not only a
good musician but he had definite leanings toward composing.
In which field the boy would eventually find his place, Isaac
could not foresee, but he was sure of one thing—the boy was a
potential genius. Never had he doubted this since Jacques had
first started to play. Perhaps at times Isaac had not been strict
enough with him—he had undoubtedly spoiled him to a degree
unthinkable with the other children—but what could one do
when one was faced with such obviously exceptional talent?

Poor Marianne, she had wept and protested when Isaac had
broached the Paris idea. They were so young, her boys, even
Jules. Paris was so far away, in a strange land full of pitfalls

It was, she had heard, a wicked place. Besides, the spring be
fore, tales of the terrible cholera epidemic raging in Paris had
reached Cologne. Thousands had died.

Of course, Isaac had retorted sharply, they would not go
while the city remained pestilential. And Paris, she must know,
was the goal of all artists, especially if they happened to be Jewish as well. There the boys would find a real future, free of the
fears and degradations they faced in Germany. Yet it was not
until he had secured the introduction to Cherubini that she
had completely capitulated.

Indeed, Marianne had known all along that she could not
stop their going. In her heart she also knew that Isaac was right.
But it was a horrible wrench for her, whose whole life had been
submerged in her children, saying goodbye to her two sons who
were going so far away that she did not know when she would
see them again.

The girl, Julie, had written that after Frau Offenbach had
returned home from seeing them off on the stagecoach, completely dejected, she had leaned on the stove and burst into
tears. Fortunately, Isabella had come in almost immediately or
Marianne, oblivious of the pain, would have had her arm burnt
off.

Now, though, Herr Offenbach knew that the sharpness of
the pain of parting, aside from the physical injury, must have
worn off and that Marianne would be as happy as he in the
knowledge that both her boys were playing in fine, big theatre
orchestras and that little Jacques was actually a student at the
great Conservatory.

Herr Offenbach found, in fact, that the distance back to
Cologne was much shorter than he had remembered it.

4

While Jacques thought often of his family back in Cologne,
he was only occasionally homesick. He had hated saying goodbye to his father because he was closely and sincerely attached
to him, but on the other hand, in spite of his mere fourteen

years, he had only a slight feeling of insecurity and strange
ness. He had adored Paris from that very first afternoon of arrival By now, he had explored vast stretches of it, picked up
a working knowledge of the language, made a number of friends,
and discovered that life, on the whole, was delightful.

Well, practically—for there was the ever-present reminder
that money was needed to keep one ali/e. In the garret which
he and Jules shared with the Lütgen brothers in the Rue des
Martyrs, on the lower slopes of Montmartre, there was a continual stretching of their meager communal funds. Jacques, being the youngest, had been designated to do the marketing. The
older boys, after a fashion, cooked. Jacques preferred his specific chore because it gave him the opportunity to roam the
streets. Armed with his empty cello case, in lieu of a market
bag, he spent an unconscionable amount of time wandering
among the vegetable stalls. Frequently there was more wandering than purchasing, due to the inevitable fact that there
were insufficient coins jingling in his pocket, and on these lean-
est days the boys stuffed themselves with potatoes and soup
greens exclusively.

Jacques' frail body appeared frailer than ever, but with his
amazing vitality he managed to cover a lot of ground. Fortunately the Rue des Martyrs was near the hub of the city and
it was only a short walk to the big boulevards.

During Carnival time, just prior to Lent, he was scarcely
ever home. People said it was not so gay this year with memories of the previous spring when the awful cholera plague had
struck from across the Channel and left twenty thousand dead
in its train. Too many remembered the masked figures fallen
suddenly in the streets and the carts, like tumbrils, rolling along
the boulevards with their load of dead. But for Jacques, who
had missed all that, even the somewhat subdued pre-Lenten
celebration of this year was wonderful.

During this season masked balls were held in the various
theatres, the Théâtre des Variétés being the most notorious,
where Musard conducted and they danced the cancan.

The cancan, like the *chahut,* was just another variation of the *galop* which, in any of its ramifications, was frowned upon by the authorities. But the cancan was even wilder and more frenzied than either of its parent dances. Couples danced indecently close together, with vulgar gestures and suggestive movements of the body, only to break apart as the female partner, usually with a high kick disclosing her garters, was flung toward a new partner. The beat of the music, rapid to begin with, would grow more hurried until at the finale the dancers would group four in a row and gyrate madly around the floor. This wild dance was said to have been brought back by soldiers from the low haunts of Algiers. In any case, it was the new rage of smart boulevardiers. Though the moral element of the city protested against it, it was in essence a revolt against the formality and dullness of Louis-Philippe's regime.

Unquestionably, Jacques' mother would have considered this Carnival season among the "pitfalls" of Paris. The roistering in the streets was continuous, with Japanese lanterns strung from the trees adding an unaccustomed brightness after dark. The theatre and dance-hall doors stood wide open, spilling the turbulent strains of the cancan as well as the participants in this primitive mad dance into the streets. The loud tooting of paper horns added to the din as open carriages and coaches, laden with costumed merrymakers, pushed through the crowded boulevards. It was the season of the bacchanalia and, protected by masks, the dandies and their mistresses mixed indiscriminately with the lower elements of the populace.

Jacques lacked the money to invest in a ticket to one of the balls, but he found that in the ebb and flow of dancers from the huge halls it was simple enough to gain entrance. Seeing the scrawny, wide-eyed little boy, who looked even younger than his fourteen years, some half-inebriated group was sure to think it a joke and adopt him in their midst. And Jacques, with all the exuberance and innocence of his youth, flung himself into the high kicks and intricacies of the cancan.

Jacques adored the frenzied rhythm of the dance and regretted the closed doors of the dance-halls after the Carnival season was over. Because then he was limited to the outside of some café-concert where, leaning against the picket fence, or higher wall, he would listen to the music in the garden beyond. Unfortunately, the music was confined to the decorous waltzes and round dances, the cancan being too uncouth for such respectable establishments.

Late that summer Jacques found a berth in the orchestra of the famed Opéra-Comique, which he pridefully recounted in a letter to his family. Undoubtedly, the fact that he was a registered student at the Conservatory had been a requisite of consideration. The truth was, however, that he was shirking classes willfully, and shortly after his acceptance at the Opéra-Comique, he quit the Conservatory entirely. He wrote his father that he had not been getting enough out of the classes to warrant the expenditure. His father was inclined to think that this was true, since Jacques had never been dilatory about his music, but he was sorry, and told him so, that he had not waited for a diploma. However, the boy was supporting himself now, so it was up to him.

Soon Jacques was growing equally bored with the rehearsals at the Opéra-Comique. He hated the repetitions, over and over. Being unquenchably mischievous, he was concocting little games and tricks to while away the time.

His neighbor and fellow student in the orchestra, Hippolyte Seligmann, was slightly older—Jacques, having attained the advanced age of fifteen was nevertheless still the baby of the organization—but they were immediate and good friends. It was Jacques, though, who generally thought up the pranks, such as running a cord from one music stand to another and thereby causing weird vibrations during the playing. Another way of showing off was by playing alternate notes of the score with Hippolyte. Monsieur Valentino, the conductor, was a strict disciplinarian and was determined to put an end to this foolery. He fined the boys regularly until Jacques' minuscule salary of eighty-three francs a month became alarmingly near non-existent.

What made it worse was that Jacques had also given up his position in the synagogue choir. Whatever his musical talents, singing was not among them. In fact, it bored him to death.

Face to face with the slavery of money, or rather the lack of it, Jacques would wander disconsolately along the boulevards, looking in at the crowded cafés and imagining the day when *he* would be able to sit at one of the tables. Sometimes in this period he had twinges of homesickness, feeling deserted and that his friends were few, but soon his fertile brain was distracted by some new scheme.

Often he would shut himself in the garret room and set about composing a *galop* which he envisioned taking the boulevards by storm. The problem was where and how to sell it. At other times he would try to figure out how, on his limited funds, he could manage to hear some of the fine music being produced in Paris.

Jacques and Hippolyte shared a mutual ambition and that was to hear the current tragic opera *La Juive*, about which everyone was talking. People were discussing whether its success was due to the intrinsic value of its music or to the magnificent production. Jacques and Hippolyte would debate its merits from the excerpts they had heard, but there could be no final decision until they had heard it in its entirety. On their present earnings, however, it looked as if it would be some time before they could get together enough money for tickets.

One day it was announced that the next rehearsal on the agenda of the Opéra-Comique would be a light opera called *L'Eclair*, by Fromental Halévy, the composer of *La Juive*. Jacques immediately began to concoct schemes for making the great man's acquaintance. This proved less easy than anticipated. Certainly he saw Halévy frequently enough during rehearsals, when the composer sometimes took the baton himself, but there seemed to be no opportunity to speak to him alone. One of the minor members of an orchestra could scarcely pop up and introduce himself, let alone ask for a ticket to *La Juive*, which was Jacques' intention.

Finally he hit upon a solution. Halévy was chorus master at the Opéra and if he were to waylay him before a performance perhaps . . .

Early one evening the boy stationed himself outside the opera-house door. The winds howled down the alley leading to the stage door off the Rue le Peletier and Jacques shivered in his too-light redingote. He shivered also from excitement, but in his mind he knew exactly what he was going to say. In a short while he saw the huge form of Fromental Halévy silhouetted against the evening sky. Jacques took a step forward.

"Excuse me, *Maître*," he said with as much aplomb as he could muster, and the big, bearded man, startled, turned around. "I want very much to hear your opera, which is playing this evening," Jacques went on hurriedly, "but I cannot afford a ticket. Is there any way I could get in otherwise?"

Fromental Halévy stared at the intent, curly-headed youth and thought there was something familiar about him. The boy, talking nervously and rapidly, soon cleared his mind on that point. Yes, he was a cello player at the Opéra-Comique which was closed that evening. Halévy could not help but be impressed by the earnestness of the youth.

"Do you particularly want to see well?" he asked.

"I wish above all to hear well, *Maître*," Jacques responded diplomatically.

"Then come with me and we shall listen to *La Juive* together, in a place from which you see very badly, but which I always use when I want to judge the effect of the music, particularly the choruses."

In a daze, Jacques followed the great man in the door.

"We climbed to the gallery," he recounted afterward, "where he was given a box from which I listened to the performance all ears, without missing a single note of that magnificent score."

In Jacques' mind it was definitely the intrinsic value of the music which was responsible for the success of *La Juive*.

During the intermission Halévy queried the young fellow about himself. He was a fatherly man and the boy's enterprise appealed to him. Moreover, Halévy was a professor at the Conservatory and took more than a passing interest in aspiring young musicians. Candidly, Jacques told him why he was no longer a student there, how he felt that he was not getting enough from his cello class to warrant the expense. What he really wanted to do was to learn more about orchestration, hoping some day he could write operas himself.

Halévy was impressed, even more so as he listened to the boy's intelligent comments on *La Juive*. He asked the young man about his background—Jacques' French was by now quite fluent, but his accent was unmistakably German—and began to feel a special affinity to the lad. For Fromental Halévy, now a Frenchman, originated from a similar background. He also had been born a German Jew and he felt an admiration for the boy's father, who had not only sent him to a country where there was little racial discrimination, but to a land which led the world in the arts.

At the end of the performance, as Jacques vociferously thanked him for his kindness, Halévy interrupted him.

"Look," he said, "outside of the Conservatory, you know, I also conduct composition classes of my own. It seems to me, from what you have told me, that they might interest you—particularly the advanced orchestration. In any case, if you would like to, come around when you can. . . ."

Jacques walked home in a trance. It was the greatest thing which had ever happened to him. Now he could really visualize himself as a boulevard composer. Some day, like Halévy, he would be able to take some other young man up into the gallery of the Opéra to hear *his* works.

He hurried to tell Jules and the Lütgen boys about his wonderful luck and was pleased to see them react with the proper awe. The next day at rehearsal he related his good fortune to Hippolyte Seligmann and was rewarded by the latter's open envy. Even greater tribute came when Halévy himself remembered to say a word after rehearsal.

Having achieved this triumph for himself Jacques was, actually, anxious to share it. Never petty or jealous, he knew that Seligmann too was a talented cellist. And then there was Jules. Whereas he never felt any special closeness to his brother he was, after all, one of the family and he owed it to him to do what he could. Besides, Jules was a good musician and on nis own merits had succeeded in securing a place in the orchestra of the Théâtre du Palais-Royal.

It proved easy to drop a word now and then with the great Halévy. Jacques had already mentioned his brother during that first evening's conversation. In a day or two he found an opportunity to introduce Hippolyte Seligmann to the composer. Without quite knowing how it happened, both Jules and Hippolyte found themselves also in attendance at Halévy's classes.

Perhaps Halévy himself was the least astonished at this augmentation of his group of students. The presence of many of his pupils could only be explained by the natural kindness and sympathy of Maître Halévy.

Certainly he never regretted taking Jacques under his patronage. Nor did Jacques ever complain of boredom in these studies. He idolized Halévy. Not only did the great composer give him the formal training in orchestration so necessary to his success, but he was always accessible for advice when Jacques needed it. He was probably more grateful to Halévy than to any other single person, except his father, for helping him along in his career.

The generous instincts of Halévy were further demonstrated when, during the following summer, he thoughtfully wrote Herr Offenbach himself: "I see your sons quite often; sometimes they come to ask my advice, which I naturally give them with the greatest pleasure. I hope you will be pleased with them; the younger one, particularly, seems to me to be destined for great success as a composer and I will consider it an honor to have been the means of aiding him by encouraging and seconding him in his work and studies."

5

There was a young man named Jullien attending Halévy's classes who, though only twenty-four, was already an orchestra conductor, leading the band at a newly opened café on the fashionable Boulevard du Temple. The Jardin Turc, like many of the café-concerts, was in a tree-shaded garden with a long covered gallery extending around three sides where the patrons could stroll about or sit when it rained. When the weather was good they danced in the clearing beneath the trees. While it was too recently opened to judge its success the very lavish, oriental-style decor marked the Jardin Turc as a future rendez-vous of fashion.

Naturally, Jacques regarded Jullien as an acquaintance of especial significance. He had not yet had any music published, but if he could persuade Jullien to accept one of his waltzes, publication would be automatic. Paris was dance crazy and it was in the café-concerts that the new waltzes were first tried out. Such roisterous dances as the *galop* and cancan were, of course, not acceptable in any respectable café-concert.

Having quickly learned that Jullien was anxious to make a name for himself as a launcher of new dance tunes and might therefore be interested in seeing what Jacques had to offer, the latter gathered together some of his compositions and paid a call upon the young orchestra leader.

Jacques appeared at Jullien's apartment with a massive sheaf of music under his arm. Jullien was startled.

"Is all this yours?" he demanded.

"Of course," said Jacques. "But if you don't find anything you can use here, I've plenty more at home."

Jullien looked at him skeptically, but the truth was that Jacques had been writing music steadily, just waiting for an opportunity like this. Besides, his brain seethed with melodies. In fact, his principal difficulty had been that of getting one tune down on paper before another one crowded it out of his mind. The lightly scrawled little notes testified to the hurry with which they had been put down.

As Jullien fingered through the music, it was only too apparent that much of it suffered from overhasty writing. Nevertheless several pieces showed possibilities and he laid them aside to try out later.

For the next day or two Jacques was in a feverish state waiting for the verdict. He was sure some of the waltzes were quite presentable—but suppose Jullien didn't feel that way? When

Jullien informed him that he had decided to accept three, Jacques grinned with relief.

"One, however," said Jullien, "will have to be revised."

Jacques assented cheerfully, listening patiently to Jullien's suggestions, then hurried back to his garret to make the recommended changes.

The following day he was back again and when he handed the music to Jullien the latter, without further ado, sat down at the piano to try it out. He spread the music on the rack.

"But this," he exclaimed, "is something else!"

"Oh, yes," agreed Jacques, "I thought of that on the way home and decided it was better than the other waltz."

Jullien stared at him, dumbfounded.

"What are you going to do with the other?"

Jacques shrugged. "Perhaps use it . . . some day."

The summer of 1836 Jacques really began to feel like a man of the world, a boulevardier, as he strolled around the covered gallery or under the trees of the Jardin Turc. At last he was on the inside of a café, not outside looking in. Moreover, he had scored a modest success with his several waltzes, one in particular called "Fleurs d'Hiver" gaining quite a bit of attention. The large publishing firm of Le Ménestrel printed it and, even better, in their trade journal of the same name they had referred to him as "a talented young man."

It was even more gratifying when "Fleurs d'Hiver" gained sufficient popularity to be included in the repertoire at the stylish Opéra and Opéra-Comique balls the following winter.

Aside from the *éclat* attending these encomiums, the pecuniary rewards were gratifying. Jacques actually found himself several hundred francs ahead instead of the twenty or thirty that usually constituted his entire capital. Where other young men in his circumstances might have husbanded this windfall prudently, he was gaily improvident. Perhaps it was a natural reaction to his background, to the years of necessary penny-pinching. Besides, he was sick and tired of shabbiness, of the hand-me-down garments of his brother's that accounted for most of his wardrobe. Also, he felt that his bettered position in the music world made it imperative that he look the part and not stalk the boulevards like some tattered café musician. Whatever the reason, he dissipated his new affluence as quickly as he had acquired it.

Jacques bought himself a long, dark, high-buttoned jacket with a smart velvet collar, and several pairs of gaudy nankeen trousers. These latter were his particular joy, in contrast to the sobriety of the rest of his costume. He had already slicked down his wavy hair, which fell long over his ears in the fashion of the period. Now he let his sideburns grow to mutton-chops, giving him an air, so he felt, of greater dignity and maturity. Then he topped off this sartorial splendor with the requisite of every dandy—a monocle. This was a necessity, he insisted naively, since his eyes bothered him occasionally.

Looking at his reflection in the glass of the shop windows he passed, Jacques was very satisfied. For the first time in his life he considered himself properly dressed for the career on which he was launched. Unfortunately, the Jardin Turc closed with the first autumn frost and he had to wait until the following May before again taking up his position as composer for that orchestra. Ruefully, he had to admit that not only were his pockets empty but that his sartorial acquisitions had run him into debt.

He continued, not too happily, as cellist with the Opéra-Comique orchestra. More than ever he hated the vexations and irritations of the constant rehearsals, the humiliating treatment meted out by arrogant composers and conductors. As soon as he could get a footing as a popular composer, he intended to leave the Opéra-Comique.

Early the following spring, Jullien approached him with a special assignment. Putting classical music to dance rhythms had become quite a vogue and Jullien, not to be outdone by other conductors, had conceived the idea of taking much of the music of Meyerbeer's popular opera *Les Huguenots,* which had received such acclaim the year before, and setting it to waltz time. Delighted, Jacques went to work on the project.

When the Jardin Turc reopened, gaslight had been installed

with the hoped-for effect of making it a really fashionable gath
ering place. On the opening evening, Jacques' arrangement o
the music from *Les Huguenots* was played to a crowded caf
and, in the applause that followed, he was called to take a bow
In his pleasure over this attention he also felt the satisfactio
of knowing that he was correctly garbed for the occasion.

This vogue of converting serious music into dance piece
fascinated Jacques, and one day when fragments of some Jewisl
spiritual music which his father, as cantor in Cologne, used t
sing came into his head, Jacques thought he had hit on a ne
idea. Putting them together, with some interpolations of his owr
he made a charming waltz which he named "Rebecca." Jullie
was equally pleased with it and put it immediately into re
hearsal.

But Jacques had not foreseen the repercussions. The patron
of the Jardin Turc, most of them completely unaware of its ori
gins, seemed to like the new waltz, but *Le Ménestrel*, which th
year before had called him "a talented young man," now pro
fessed to be shocked.

"Was it absolutely necessary," demanded *Le Ménestrel*, "t
burlesque melodies sanctified by religious observance, in a wan
ton waltz?" And the paper added sarcastically, "But nowaday
it is necessary at all costs to be original."

The tirade went on for several paragraphs. Jacques was puz
zled. He failed to see any great difference between transformin
Les Huguenots into light music and doing the same with an
cient Hebrew chants. By nature he was not deeply religious an
his father, notwithstanding his official position in the synagogue
had instilled no orthodox religious views in his children, bring
ing them up with a broad and simple conception of God.

In any case, Jacques was unable to comprehend the attitud
of reverence common to most people, in which something wa
set apart from daily life, shut up in a compartment as it wer
He was constitutionally incapable of religious awe or of an
reverence for so many things men ordinarily held sacrosanc
Never during his entire life could he understand why other

were shocked by his casual attitude toward conventional religion.

Jacques did not have to worry overly about *Le Ménestrel*'s diatribe. Jullien continued to introduce his music and *Le Ménestrel*—the publishing end—usually brought it out. Also, he had made a new connection, so that when the Jardin Turc again closed its gates at the end of the summer he was not nearly so depressed. Monsieur Valentino, under whose direction at the Opéra-Comique Jacques had been working for the past four years, had found a new position at the Concerts Saint-Honoré, an institution on an entirely different plane from the Jardin Turc. While one could sip tea, coffee, or a brandy here also, the dance music was interspersed with serious and classical selections.

Although Valentino's relationship with Jacques was that of the stern teacher to a mischievous pupil, he nevertheless had a high regard for the young man's ability and was more than willing to consider his compositions. Jacques produced a waltz for him and then, by way of variety, wrote a ballad. When this latter was accepted by Valentino, he tried writing a nocturne.

At last Jacques felt as if he were getting somewhere. He was beginning to be recognized in musical circles and the number of his acquaintances had vastly widened. He had also acquired a pupil of his own, an aspiring young cellist. With this additional good fortune, Jacques hesitated no longer. He resigned from the orchestra of the Opéra-Comique. It seemed to him the first time since he had come to Paris that he was able to breathe freely.

Shrewdly—though it was no hardship—he kept himself in evidence about town, appearing frequently at the numerous cafés where it was worth while being seen. He moved from the garret to a small apartment nearby, as befitting his new circumstances. There was an air of importance to be observed in his manner also.

"Young Monsieur Offenbach seems to believe he is about to dethrone Strauss," observed *Le Ménestrel* pointedly. Evidently some member of the editorial staff had no fondness for Jacques.

Momentarily, Jacques was upset. The great Johann was play
ing that winter season in Paris and Jacques well knew that the
Gemütlichkeit waltzes of the famous Viennese ranked far above
his efforts. He was afraid people were laughing at him. Then
he decided to laugh too. He had already learned that a man in
the public eye must not take criticism too much to heart.

Besides, he knew he *was* a talented young man. Hadn't the
great Paganini made a point of coming over and shaking hands
with him just the other evening?

6

Jacques possessed the gift of making friends easily, but with
it came the corollary of almost as easily—if unintentionally—pro
voking enmities. Jacques regretted these antagonisms because
he himself hated no one. Occasionally, since he was quick-tem
pered, he would utter some cutting remark, but as his anger was
always fleeting he was amazed when he realized that he had
hurt someone and was anxious to make amends.

Jacques was not only essentially good-natured and gay, but
he had a sharp sense of the ridiculous, even when it concerned
himself. Having no illusions about his own physical appearance,
knowing full well what a comic, ugly figure he was, he capi
talized on it and made fun of himself. At least he got attention
and that was what he wanted.

He wanted attention principally, of course, to further his am
bitions. But just as fundamentally he needed attention because
he could not bear to be alone. Sometimes he took a *lorette*—
streetwalker—back to his room with him as much because he
wanted company as because of the exigencies of the flesh. He
couldn't afford the luxury of any permanent attachment. Often
he wandered the boulevards, or nursed a half-empty glass in a
café until late in the night, putting off the necessity of return
ing to his lonely room. People were essential to him and he could
conceive of no greater misery than living without them.

While young Offenbach was not only a good—and frequently
witty—conversationalist, he usually displayed a reciprocal inter

est in any companion. He was such a friendly and entertaining young man that most people liked him instantly. There were quite a few, however, who found his complete self-confidence galling and who just as quickly and definitely detested him. His conceit infuriated them. Certainly shyness had never been one of Offenbach's major characteristics, nor had he ever shown any doubt about his musical talents.

"Have you heard my new nocturne, the one Valentino is playing?" he would ask, and add, "It's really lovely."

Or he would blandly announce: "Next year I expect to do a short opera."

No wonder *Le Ménestrel* jibed at him. Yet, to those who liked him, his conceit was so preposterously naive as not to be taken seriously. Obviously, Jacques considered his remarks simple statements of fact and did not exclude the possibility that others were equally talented. He was always quick to admire the ability of another man and jealousy seemed not to be in his make-up.

Jacques had formed a close friendship with another young composer and fellow-countryman, Friedrich von Flotow, who was one day to gain fame with his opera *Martha* in which the haunting, if saccharine, melody, "The Last Rose of Summer," would win popular acclamation. In 1838, when he and Offenbach first met, Flotow had just scored his initial success at the Théâtre de la Renaissance with an opera, *The Shipwreck of the Medusa.*

They were an incongruous pair, these two, the successful twenty-six-year-old composer and the aspiring nineteen-year-old boy. Except for his nationality, Flotow's background was the antithesis of Jacques'. He was an aristocrat, well-to-do, and somewhat of a dilettante. He was handsome, charming and exceedingly popular with the ladies. He had been living in Paris for about ten years and generally moved in the most exclusive social circles, an unknown world to the little Jewish boy from Cologne.

Nevertheless, the two of them got on excellently from the start. Flotow was easygoing and unpretentious and he found Jacques good company. Also, they had in common their mutual

love of music but, whereas Flotow composed simply for the en
joyment of it, Offenbach had the added necessity of earning hi
livelihood.

"Why don't you play in the salons?" Flotow asked one day.

"That would be just splendid," Jacques laughed. "The only
trouble is, not a single one of my acquaintances has a salon."

Flotow thought for a moment. Suddenly he exclaimed: "I
have it! Suppose I ask my friend, the Countess de Vaux—you
know, she really has an appreciation of music and they say many
reputations have been made in her salons. . . ."

"That would be very kind of you," said Jacques in an uncertain voice.

"Not at all. She is a good friend of mine—and a very fine
woman," added Flotow.

Though Jacques was deeply appreciative of Flotow's good
intentions, he was inclined to consider his offer a little impetuou
and was surprised when Flotow called upon him a few days
later.

"It's all arranged," Flotow announced cheerfully. "The Count
ess says she will put us down for a short number at her nex
salon—that's next week. I suggested—I thought it might be bet
ter for a start—that we play a duet. Is that all right with you
old man?"

"*Mon dieu!* Yes—nobody wants to listen to a cello alone any
way. But do you really mean it?"

"Of course I mean it—why else would I be here? Now we've
got to pick out some appropriate composition that's not too long
—you know, a ballad or some other song. Have you anything?

Excited, Jacques dashed over to an untidy stack of his music
on the floor in the corner. This was a wonderful opportunity
He knew it and was grateful for Flotow's thoughtfulness. Hi
quick brain registered the fact that it would be a great advan
tage if they played one of his own pieces.

Flotow joined him, crouched on the floor, and together they
went through the pile of papers.

"No, no, this won't do—none of your dance music for the
Countess' salon. Something with a little more body to it."

Jacques got up and went to his wardrobe. From the floor of it he extracted several additional sheets of music.

"Here is an étude I've been working on—or maybe something could be done with this. . . ."

Flotow looked at these pieces critically.

"No," he said at last, "they're *too* heavy. I'll tell you, suppose you and I, together, write something specially for the occasion?"

Jacques had a momentary twinge of disappointment. Then, as he reflected that he would at least be co-author with his name appearing along with that of the composer of *The Shipwreck of the Medusa*, he considered himself a reasonably lucky fellow.

"Fine!" he responded, brightening up, and he quickly brought out the ink and quills.

7

On the evening of the Countess de Vaux's salon Jacques was very nervous. He was somewhat reassured when Flotow remarked on the smart cut of the new evening clothes which Jacques had bought for the occasion. But his hands, constricted in his tightly buttoned white gloves, were perspiring.

Jacques envied the assurance of Flotow as they entered the Countess' apartment. Suddenly he felt unaccustomedly shy. His cello seemed overly large and unwieldy and the elegance of his surroundings reduced him to the natural timidity of a nineteen-year-old. Nevertheless, as the Countess came forward to greet them he waited quietly by Flotow's side for the introduction and then, with impressive dignity, made a low bow and kissed her hand. The Countess, an attractive middle-aged woman, smiled and Jacques smiled back.

The young men were ushered into a small room off the salon to await their turn. Jacques remained abnormally quiet and Flotow gave him a sharp look, wondering if his young friend was going to spoil everything with stage fright. At that moment, the strains of a violin floated into the anteroom. The first number on the evening's program had begun. Jacques cocked his

head and sat up straighter. Involuntarily, his fingers made the
motions of touching the stops on an imaginary violin. Soon he
had entirely forgotten his surroundings in his interest in the
music.

When time came for their turn Jacques was greatly relaxed
but he was still unprepared for the brilliance of the salon. The
light of a hundred candles gleamed down from the crystal can-
delabras on the elegant gowns of the ladies and the white shirt-
fronts of the immaculately garbed gentlemen. The big room
was packed and the low murmur of conversation indicated the
temporary lack of interest in the newcomers.

The young men seated themselves and, as Flotow struck the
chords on the piano, Jacques set about tuning his instrument.
Finally he nodded to Flotow and they began their composition.

Slowly the room quieted and then, suddenly, Jacques was no
longer aware of anyone. He and Flotow were not only well
rehearsed, but in addition they were playing something *they*
had composed and for which they had more than a casual fondness.

The audience sat completely silent. At the beginning there
had been a side glance or two, a raised eyebrow, a half-smile.
Most of the guests were familiar with Flotow, but the appearance of young Offenbach was such as to cause a momentary
elevation of eyebrows. In the first place, the cello looked so
large in front of the slight figure as to seem menacing and as
he began to play he appeared to wrap himself around it in the
weirdest contortions. The effect was that of an attack. As his
bow stroked over the first notes this gave way to the illusion of
subjugation. He and the cello began to merge into one curiously
distorted figure.

When the number was finished there was a moment's pause,
then loud applause. From a far corner came cries of "Bravo!"
"*Bis!*" "Encore!"

By degrees Jacques returned to reality. He looked around
him and slowly began to smile, his mouth spreading into an
infectious grin.

"Encore!" again rang out.

Jacques glanced at Flotow and at his signal they started their carefully prepared encore. Again, when it was ended, came the cries of "More, more!" as well as gratifying applause. But they were prepared to go no further and besides, the Countess had specified only a "short number."

That evening ended in a pleasant haze for Jacques. The Countess was more than gracious in her compliments and the guests, many of them, went out of their way to make flattering remarks. Jacques had the sensation of intoxication although, as he was naturally abstemious, he had accepted no more than a glass or two of champagne. But he had found that this new world of society was not as strange and foreign as he had anticipated. Before the evening was over he was quite as loquacious as usual, exchanging pleasantries, and feeling very much at home.

That night he slept soundly. It was late the next day when he was routed out of bed by the arrival of Flotow who reported that he had seen the Countess de Vaux, that she was very pleased, and that she would like them to play again at her salon next month.

Throughout that winter, Jacques and Flotow repeated their duets innumerable times, not only at the Countess de Vaux's but elsewhere. It was through her, indeed, that they received many of their engagements. Jacques became the Countess' special protégé and, as time went on, he was a frequent visitor to her home. She took a motherly interest in him and he found that he had someone upon whom he could rely for advice and assistance. Many times since coming to Paris he had been lonely and felt the need of his family, but now the warm friendship of the Countess greatly alleviated this condition.

Jacques and Flotow were constantly writing new pieces for their salon engagements—it was generally understood that the music be composed especially for the occasion. Sometimes Jacques alone composed a ballad, sometimes Flotow; often they worked out something together. They collaborated ideally, neither of them jealous, but full of mutual admiration. There was every reason, of course, for Jacques to look up to the older,

more successful man who had also been his benefactor, bu
Flotow had an honest respect for Jacques' facility for producin
agreeable airs.

Ballads were the specialty of the times, but also romanti
waltzes, nocturnes, and fantasies. It was the era of Romanticis
—of de Vigny, de Musset, and Hugo in literature, of Chopin i
music. It was inevitable that they try to imitate the incomparabl
Chopin.

A patroness, of course, was a requisite for success in th
salons and this function the Countess de Vaux carried out ge
erously. Under Louis-Philippe a new society had sprung u
made up of the newly rich industrialists. As always with th
nouveaux riches, they took their cues from established societ
the nobility. *Le Ménestrel,* which had already given Jacqu
passing attention, was the bible of those aspiring to hold salon
Each week it published one new composition introduced in a
established salon, to which words were usually added. Durin
that year Jacques had the gratification of finding himself in th
select group with words to his ballad written by no less a perso
than the Countess de Vaux herself, under the patently tran
parent pseudonym of the "Baroness de V. . . ." With this hel
ful push, Jacques discovered that he was quite in demand.

After he was well established he and Flotow played togethe
less often. Flotow was too rich to be much more than a highl
successful amateur. For young Offenbach, as always, it was
livelihood. Later he teamed up frequently with his old frien
of Opéra-Comique days, Hippolyte Seligmann, and occasionall
with his brother Jules.

He turned out quantities of music—waltzes, concertos, fa
tasies, ballads—and by the end of 1838 he felt he had sufficie
material to give a complete concert of his own. The Countes
de Vaux had been urging him to take this step for several month
and promised her full support. As Jacques' goal of a career wa
that of a composer, a concert was essential to secure attentio
in the proper quarters. Also, while he now had several pupi
it would consolidate his position as a teacher during the interi

At the end of January, 1839, the concert was held in the aud torium of Papé's music store, a proper place for a newcomer. Not too large a hall, it had good standing in music circles.

As usual, Jacques looked out for his brother's interests and included him on the program, hiring a piano accompanist (and piano) as well. This, plus the rental of the hall, was a considerable drain for him but, as Flotow pointed out, it was not as great as might be expected. Concerts of this sort were generally held in the daytime, so that there was no worry about lighting costs, and as people therefore attended in daytime dress, the heat question, which would have increased the expense, did not have to be reckoned with. In warm winter clothes the audience was not likely to be aware of cold feet.

Due to the kind interest of the Countess de Vaux, the auditorium was full. More to the point, the audience was enthusiastic and several critics wrote complimentary reviews, the most important being that of *Le Ménestrel*, which freely praised Jacques' polished style of execution as well as the charm of his compositions.

8

Young Jacques Offenbach had made friends in many quarters. He had, in a modest sort of way, become a man-about-town. Through his salon playing he had gained social entree in the most exclusive circles. As a fine cellist, as well as a striving composer, he was known in theatrical and musical groups. It had not turned his head at all. While he liked his society friends, he had not dropped any of his old cronies. He simply, as always, liked people. In fact, he naively thought most people were nice.

And people, in general, liked Jacques. They liked him for his unpretentiousness (except, perhaps his conceit as a musician), for the fact that he did not pose or try to hide his background. They liked his simplicity, his general good nature and high spirits.

They were even impressed by his appearance, because Jacques by careful grooming had achieved an air of distinction. His clothes fitted him trimly and were chosen to give him added

height. They were also planned to give him individuality. In
variably, he wore a small, flat, black bow tie, a severely tailored
shirt and a jacket of dark broadcloth or other somber material
Only one item of his attire stood out and that was the flam
boyant trousers. While gay patterned trousers were *de rigueur*
Jacques' were inevitably gaudier than most. On anyone else they
would have been *too* gaudy.

His monocle also gave him a note of distinction, for again
though monocles were the hallmark of the dandy, Jacques' small
birdlike, but penetrating eyes—one of which gleamed startlingly
through glass—frequently had a disconcerting effect upon the
person he addressed. To many, there was something even un
canny in his direct gaze. As for Jacques, he had grown quite
accustomed to this bit of dandyism and he wore his monocle
nonchalantly and almost constantly.

Men liked him and, better yet for his enjoyment, so did
women. Jacques had a decided eye for pretty women but unti
recently his contacts with the opposite sex had perforce been
confined to an occasional formal introduction at a café or to an
encounter with a *lorette*. Now, since he frequented salons, he
had met a different type of women, the well-bred *mondaines* of
society and, to his joy, discovered that they found him attrac
tive. Always delightfully well-mannered, having a gift for gra
cious compliments and a natural aptitude of attentiveness, he
had, besides, the good taste of discretion. Perhaps he partially
appealed to these women because he represented something so
totally different from their own backgrounds, by birth and edu
cation and appearance; but also he was always careful to pro
tect their reputations and not banter their names in public as
so many gay blades were inclined to do. Jacques made no seriou
attachments, but he had many passing affairs and the gift of
retaining a friendship after the affair had cooled off.

Young Offenbach was only twenty but he was already a ma
ture man. Having had to live on his own and, except for an
occasional tiny money order from home, having supported him
self since he was fourteen, Jacques had practically skipped ado
lescence. Most of his acquaintances were older than he—some

far older—but he was quite capable of holding his own in any company.

Fascinated by the theatre, Jacques spent a great deal of time in the company of actors, playwrights, and entrepreneurs. Also, he considered his salon compositions as mere apprenticeship for his goal as a composer of theatre music. At that time Paris, certainly regarded as the musical center of Europe, seemed scarcely to produce any plays without some musical accompaniment. There was a great vogue for one-act plays, two or three of them comprising a program, and invariably one or two musical compositions—perhaps a love song for the hero or heroine or a background for the entire act—were interpolated.

Anicet Bourgeois, a new acquaintance of Jacques', was co-author of one of these short plays which was to be produced at the renowned Théâtre du Palais-Royal. It was called *Pascal et Chambord,* and Bourgeois, impressed with Jacques' ability, asked him to do several songs for it. One of these, at least, was to be sung by the hero, whose role was taken by no less a personage than Achard, the principal basso at the Opéra-Comique.

As usual Jacques' facility enabled him to turn out the required number of songs in the course of a few days. However, in view of the circumstances, he gave an equal amount of time to polishing them. Considering one of them, on second reading, not quite up to standard, he calmly tore it up and composed its successor. When he appeared with his music for rehearsal, he was quite well satisfied.

Jacques was more than pleased to be at last a real part of the theatre. As a nominal director, he took himself very seriously and in his mind's eye he saw himself from now on as a definite part of the theatrical scene. The time for rehearsal was short, as these one-act plays succeeded each other with incredible frequency. They were not expected to play longer than a month or so, but on the success of one depended future assignments.

Jacques had very little idea of the merits of Bourgeois' play but he was confident of himself. That is, until near the end of rehearsal when Achard, the basso, started the finale. Suddenly Jacques realized that he had not allowed for the limited range of

Achard's voice—in fact, he had written the music without thought as to who was to interpret it—and that most of the song was now impossible. He immediately volunteered to write something else but was quickly squelched by the reminder that they were already in rehearsal, that the play was to be put on in a few days and that there was no time. There was only one thing to do and that was to cut out the measures unsuitable to Achard's voice, which reduced the song almost by half. There and then he doctored what phrases were possible, but he felt like a surgeon as he slashed the rest.

His chagrin was complete when his father, who had been apprised of the great event, decided to come to Paris for the opening. Instead of being present at his son's triumph, he witnessed a fiasco. In all fairness, the failure was not entirely Jacques'. *Pascal et Chambord* was, in any case, a second-rate playlet. Actually Jacques' music, if not of the highest calibre, was nothing to be ashamed of.

Herr Offenbach comforted him.

"You have to expect failures, my son. And it is better to have them first. You are young—and you have plenty of time for success."

He asked to look at some of his other compositions and studied them carefully. Even better, he gave some considered criticism. "Here," he would say, "you have something—it's a delightful idea, but you hurry the theme too much. Now, you're inclined to be too hasty. Take more time on things. Build them up."

His father's visit was a joy for Jacques. He loved taking him about with him, introducing him to his musical friends, the type of company his father found most congenial.

Herr Offenbach had come to Paris again with the notion that he might live here with his family. But after a month, he grew fearful of the idea. It was all very well for his sons; they were young and Jacques, anyway, was bound to be successful. But Herr Offenbach was growing old. He was tired, and the difficulty of establishing himself in this big impersonal metropolis discouraged him. Better to stay in Cologne, where he was known and was assured of a modest living.

It had been nearly six years since the boys had left Cologne and before returning Herr Offenbach impressed on them that it was their duty to make a visit soon. Both Jacques and Jules were anxious enough to do just that. Jacques had been thinking of it for a long while but in trying to establish his reputation as a cellist he had been continually postponing the trip. Then he had thought with the play . . . well, he had planned to give up the cello in favor of composing and if *Pascal et Chambord* had been a hit . . .

"Jacques," his father admonished him, "it upsets me that you are thinking of giving up the cello. You are a fine cellist. As a composer . . . some day you'll succeed, no doubt, but meanwhile you *have* the cello. To me it is terrible at any time for a good musician to renounce his instrument."

And when Herr Offenbach was informed that a farewell dinner was being given for him by one of Jacques' friends, he made one request—that Jacques would play something for him that night.

With touching filial devotion, Jacques finished and polished a concerto upon which he had been working and carried it, along with his cello, to his friend's apartment. It seemed as if he had never played with more tenderness than that evening. His touch was superb, and the long pianissimo passage particularly lovely.

It was almost the only occasion on which Jacques had played during his father's visit and the latter, knowing what a special tribute it was, surreptitiously wiped the moisture from his eyes.

"Promise me," he said later that evening, "that you won't give up your playing."

"I promise," answered Jacques simply.

He also promised to come home in a couple of months. He and Jules could perhaps give some concerts in and about Cologne which would help defray costs.

As Herr Offenbach again took the stagecoach back home he

was smiling. The parting was only temporary. He would be
seeing his sons soon. He knew he could count on it.

6

The Street of the Bells in Cologne was a street only by courtesy. Actually it was a twisting dead-end alley of old-clothes
shops and second-hand furniture dealers, so narrow that a handcart could just squeeze through. And a handcart, just as in their
penetration of the Jewish quarter of Paris six years before, was
the feature of the first home visit of the Offenbach boys.

The alley was roughly cobbled and always musty-smelling.
On this occasion however, the schoolboy Albert Wolff, who lived
just a few doors from the Offenbachs, sniffed appreciatively as
he approached their door. Cakes were baking, he knew, and
not even his mother's cakes were as wonderful as those of Frau
Offenbach. And as he hesitated the door opened suddenly and
Frau Offenbach appeared and looked eagerly toward the open
end of the street. Then she noticed the little Wolff boy and said
"Yes, Albert, I'm baking special cakes. I haven't spared sugar,
butter, or eggs. This is a special day for us all. My boys are
coming back from Paris today. You run along to school now—
my Michael is already there—but you be sure to come in later."

Albert could scarcely contain himself. It was not only the
promise of Frau Offenbach's marvelous cakes, but he was eager
to see the heroes of the neighborhood, the two big Offenbach
boys who had been off all by themselves and making a great
success in the far-off city of Paris.

As for Herr Offenbach, meantime, he was putting on an almost convincing show of calmness. He had learned by courier
that Julius and Jakob (the *Jules* and *Jacques* they were known
as in Paris, he was afraid, would sound too pretentious here)
were due some time during the day, but from his own extensive
traveling he knew that the coaches were likely to be anywhere
from hours to days off schedule. Besides, the boys were young
men of experience now and they'd arrive eventually. Let Mother
jump in and out of her kitchen and back again to fret over the

tempting dishes being prepared in her gleaming copper pots. So he relaxed, at least outwardly, in his big worn armchair in the tiny living room just off the spotless kitchen. But even his stoically maintained casualness cracked when he heard a clatter outside the door and his wife screaming:

"Julius! Jakob! *Meine Liebchen, meine Kinder!*"

For little Albert Wolff, just the age—twelve—of his schoolmate Michael, the youngest Offenbach boy, that was an evening to be remembered through the years. He was pleased to recall it long later when he, too, had become established in Paris, a man of standing in the world of letters. He would always laugh uproariously when he recalled how he had suffered from indigestion for several days after the Offenbach boys had returned to Cologne.

In the best tradition of mothers, Frau Offenbach wept copiously as she greeted her two adventurous sons. She just could not bring herself to realize that they were self-reliant young men, particularly the little Jakob, who had been only fourteen when he had left home.

Herr Offenbach, with his usual understanding and appreciation of the uses of publicity, had already made calls on such friends as he had on the staffs of the local newspapers. His missionary work had quickly borne fruit, for that very morning the important *Kölnische Zeitung* had run a front-page story on the home-coming of Cologne's famous young musicians.

That evening the cramped Offenbach dining room was ablaze with the special candles in the big chandelier, usually lighted only for religious festivals. The table was loaded with all sorts of delicacies and bottles of Rhine wine. Relatives, neighbors and friends filled the little house almost to suffocation. They all believed, thanks to Herr Offenbach's glowing reports, that the boys were a huge success in Paris, giving recitals and concerts all the time.

After the cramming of food and wine and the drinking of Frau Offenbach's excellent coffee, the evening naturally took on a musical turn. Herr Offenbach worked out various instrumental combinations, besides the cello solo by Jacques. Even little

Michael had to perform. But the returned boys got the most fun out of their old trio with their sister. And the volatile Jacques amused them all with his descriptions of the café-concerts of Paris, not to mention the glittering world of the salons he had managed to become a part of.

Out of the Street of the Bells, beyond the Jewish quarter tales of the Offenbach boys spread about the town. Their minor achievements in Paris naturally were magnified in the various retellings—and obviously helped by their publicity-wise father. There were many notices in the papers and their evenings were filled with request performances.

Despite all this acclamation, everybody agreed that the Offenbach sons were just the same, not spoiled at all. Jakob, of course, had been merely a mischievous lad when he had gone to Paris. Now he was a mature man. And so well dressed. They were impressed with his monocle and his carefully tailored clothes. But most of all, they were pleased to see that success had not gone to his head.

As for Jakob—Jacques—he was truly happy, surrounded by the affection and warmth of old friends and family. He did notice though, as he never had before, the shabbiness and poverty of his home and the drabness of provincial Cologne. Six years of Paris, of beautiful tree-lined boulevards, of bright cafés, of gorgeous salons—all this made the comparison inevitable. Nevertheless, the house on the Street of the Bells was his home and even its worn furniture was glossed over by sentimental attachment.

During the three months Jacques and Jules remained in Cologne they went out often, visiting old friends, joining their father's chamber-music group. Everywhere they played willingly for their friends. And they gave one big professional concert in Cologne, which was gratifyingly well attended. In fact it paid the entire costs of their trip.

Because in such a short while it was time to go back to Paris the goodbyes proved as difficult as at their first departure—for who could tell when they would be able to make the journey again?

As for Jacques, encouraged and cheered by his father, he was returning to Paris determined to achieve the success which these nice but gullible Cologne friends believed had already been his. Parting from his mother was the hardest task, she whom he loved so tenderly, who could always soothe and calm his ruffled spirits. He promised her, as soon as he made enough money, that she was to make a trip to Paris. She shook her head, smiling, although there were tears in her eyes.

"No, you come home again."

But Jacques still played with his pleasant notion. On the tiring journey back to Paris he daydreamed, seeing in his reveries his mother's astonished and delighted face as he drove her in a carriage along his beloved boulevards.

10

The Offenbach boys returned to Cologne much sooner than they had anticipated, only this time it was not a happy homecoming. There were no celebrations. Twelve-year-old Michael had contracted typhoid and his frail body lacked the strength to pull him through. A hurried letter from their father told them the sudden tragedy. And there was an even greater sorrow. Frau Offenbach, prostrate with grief over the death of her baby son, was seriously ill herself. It was advisable that the other boys return at once. So, just ten months after they had left, Jacques and Jules slipped quietly back into the sorrowing house on the Street of the Bells.

The doctor greeted them.

"You are the best medicine she can have. Now your mother will get well," he said.

Frau Offenbach did rouse herself at the sight of her other two sons. But it was evident that something had gone from her spirit. Too many years of toil and struggle, too much childbearing, too much concentration on her family perhaps, were defeating her.

Both boys spent a good deal of time by her bedside, but it was Jacques mainly who made her smile. He would tell jokes,

tease her and try to distract her. Sometimes one of his sister
would join them and Jacques would banter with her as wel.
His irrepressible high spirits were having their effect. Finally
one day, the doctor made the pronouncement they had bee
hoping for.

"I think she is on the road to recovery."

"You see," said Jacques, laughing, to his mother, "you wer
just playing tricks to get us home!"

As she grew better, the boys played for her. Sometimes the
had little family concerts, with their father and one or other o
the girls joining in to form a small orchestra.

Mostly they played the classics: the three B's—Brahms, Bee
thoven, Bach—or Haydn, or Mozart.

Mozart was always Jacques' favorite. He and his father ofte
discussed the respective merits of the different great composer
Herr Offenbach liked Mozart's music well enough, but he wa
always amused at the untrameled enthusiasm Jacques indulge
in at any mention of that music-master's name. With all the as
surance of his twenty years he would flatly state: "No othe
composer can even approach the lyric beauty of Mozart. Listen!
he would say excitedly. "Just listen to this passage!"

He would hum part of a melody from *Don Giovanni*. "Isn'
that divine? It's like the music of angels!"

Jacques' speaking voice was deep and pleasant, but he ha
no gift for singing. However, so happy was he these days ove
his mother's improvement that he was constantly humming o
whistling throughout the house. One day as he was absent
mindedly whistling, his father exclaimed: "Heavens! Do yo
still remember Zimmer's waltz?"

"Who is Zimmer?"

"I have no idea," answered Herr Offenbach, "but his was
popular waltz when you were a child."

Jacques remembered. His mother used to sing it to him an
it always delighted him. Now the tune came back to haunt him
Unfortunately, all he could remember was eight bars, and n
one could supply the rest. He asked his mother once, but sh
shook her head.

"I've forgotten now, though it is true it used to be a favorite of mine."

As Frau Offenbach improved, Jacques and Jules planned once again to go back to Paris. Again they were without funds and, as usual, they planned another recital to finance their return. This time Jacques felt it was a more uncertain venture, for it hadn't been so long since their last concert in Cologne. He knew it was not a good idea to overdo it. So, in order to highlight the program, he set to work on a fairly ambitious composition. It was called *Grande Scène Espagnole* and included a spirited bolero. Spain was the popular setting of the day for the Romantics and the *Grande Scène Espagnole* was in the best current romantic style.

It was a great success. The *Kölnische Zeitung* praised the whole concert highly, but it went into paeans over the lovely romantic work of Herr Jakob Offenbach.

When Frau Offenbach heard all this, she really smiled with pleasure and the house on the Street of the Bells once more became a joyful household.

Then, suddenly, with no warning whatsoever, a week later Frau Offenbach died. Her heart had remained weak and no one could help her.

Jacques was overwhelmed with grief. He was dazed. No longer could his gay spirits rally the others of the family. It was he who most required consolation now. He, who had been the closest of all to his mother, felt an ache beyond anything he had ever suffered. In his misery he would retire alone to his room, to remain there for hours. His cello stayed in its case, untouched. For the time being, it roused too many memories of music played for his mother's benefit, of association with his loss.

He tried to assuage his sorrow by scribbling verses, in the tradition of the Romantics of his time. They were bad verses, but they eased his misery somewhat. In his heart he questioned the unswerving faith of the true believer. He himself could find no solace in religion. Nevertheless, one of his poems ended with the conventional and banal line: "God's will be done."

11

Had it not been for the Countess de Vaux, it might have been even harder for Jacques. When he returned to Paris he was literally penniless and in need of immediate employment, but it is always difficult after an absence from such a competitive scene to reinstate oneself promptly. He had already sensed this following his earlier visit to Cologne. Now, again, several months had passed. And to make things even more difficult, this time he lacked the drive and strength to re-establish himself. He was still suffering from the shock of his mother's death and he was physically and spiritually depleted. Most of all, he needed sympathy.

When the Countess saw him she understood completely. She invited him to dinner and tried to console him. As Jacques poured out his misery, he felt greatly eased. The Countess, a devout Catholic, urged him to turn to the Church, but at this Jacques shook his head and she was too wise to pursue it.

Intelligently, the Countess tried to revive Jacques' interest in Parisian life. She told him the latest gossip, the scandals of the boulevards, which salons were now most important, all sorts of amusing trivia and, as Jacques had done with his mother, cheered him by jokes and teasing. And before he left, she arranged to have him play for her guests the next week.

In a short time Jacques was once more in demand but, while his mental state improved, his physical condition did not. He was overworked and undernourished. He had little appetite at any time and in his uncertain financial state the easiest thing to do was to forego a meal. However, one evening he suddenly fainted while playing and this really frightened him.

One of his troubles was that he was supporting his brother as well as himself, for Jules was unemployed. Never more than a competent violinist, Jules completely lacked initiative and seemed to feel that someone would take care of him. Nervous and irritable as he was these days anyway, Jacques finally turned on Jules in fury and told him he was through supporting a useless brother. To his astonishment—for he grew ashamed when he thought of this scene afterward—this had a salutary effect. In a very short time, Jules had landed a place in a boulevard orchestra.

Jacques' engagements were generally solo ones these days. (His friend Hippolyte Seligmann had become a rival, albeit a friendly one. Von Flotow, working on another light opera, had given up the salons.) This meant more money for him but also demanded greater ingenuity. Ordinarily, there was little to distinguish one cello player from another. Sometimes he introduced a *mirliton*—a reed-pipe—at his recitals by way of variety. He had taught himself to play it and composed several pieces especially for it, among them a polka and a march.

Jacques knew that much of his success depended upon his being somewhat of a musical clown and he had the good sense of showmanship to capitalize on it. His first appearance was still greeted with a gasp of astonishment and when he was playing he continued to startle his audiences. As one boulevardier described young Offenbach: "He and his cello fuse into one like a centaur and appear to be galloping into space."

One evening, while playing, Jacques suddenly plucked a string in a curious sort of way and then slapped his instrument with the flat of his hand. The effect was an excellent imitation of a dog barking and his audience was convulsed. A few minutes later, as he was rendering a pastoral, he used his bow to mimic the trill of a bird. Again his audience was delighted.

Jacques thereupon expanded his tricks. He was such an expert technician that he could reproduce an apparently limitless variety of sounds, not only dogs barking, but geese hissing, ducks quacking, women chattering, the sounds of a bagpipe, or even a waterfall. He was not simply playing the fool either, as he had a very definite conception of the value of these tricks. He wanted to evoke moods and by such clever manipulations of his instrument he created visions of a peaceful countryside, the bustle of a city, etc. At the same time, he had converted himself into a sort of one-man orchestra.

He continued to write his own music and, as he gained rec-

ognition of his specialty, he launched on an ambitious progran
He decided to set some of La Fontaine's fables to music. In al
he did six of them.

While the papers and musical periodicals in general ha
been giving him fine notices, the *Gazette Musicale* did refer t
him as an "eccentric," a designation with which he could no
quarrel. La Fontaine's fables, however, brought a furor of abus«
on a wider scale somewhat like *Le Ménestrel's* denunciation
few years back of his use of ritual Hebrew chants in a ligh
waltz. La Fontaine belonged to the classics and was as sacro
sanct, the critics felt, as religion. One of them remarked sar
donically that Offenbach seemed to have forgotten the most im
portant fable of all, that of the mountain laboring and givin
forth a mouse. Even so, it was generally admitted that the fabl
of the cricket and the ant was a delightful waltz.

Jacques could no more comprehend the critics' attitude nov
than he had *Le Ménestrel's* in regard to "Rebecca." Indeed, h
openly and volubly disagreed with them. He considered that h
had hit upon a *genre* which was both amusing and successfu
and he had the temerity to say so. Unquestionably he did hav
an original approach, whether worthy or not, which set hir
apart from the run of salon performers.

It was paying him, moreover, a decent, if sometimes unce:
tain living. One could never make a substantial living as a sma
concert player, but Jacques had by no means given up his ir
tention of eventually becoming part of the theatre world. Mear
while, he was gaining more and more attention and, whethe
notices were good or bad, his performances were given cor
sideration.

He had even been approached by a concert manager and, i
1842, two years after his return to Paris, he was offered a tou
in Germany. Jacques accepted with alacrity. It meant a ver
definite rise in the concert field. It meant, also, sometime du
ing the trip, a visit with his family. But most of all, it seeme
like a well-earned vacation. Though the profits after deductin
the expense of the tour were not comparably greater than thos
produced by the continuing round in Paris, his program wa

by no means as strenuous. While he ate more regularly and no longer feared a fainting spell, Jacques was still not in good shape. The rounds of the salons seemed incessant, plus the additional work of grinding out new compositions between engagements. Besides, artists were expected to contribute their services to occasional charity benefits, and these affairs seemed to occur with annoying frequency. All this had made terrific demands on his limited physical strength.

The German tour filled several months, and when he returned his health was much improved. He had found the change of scene and new acquaintances invigorating. For the first time he had traveled by train, as railroads by now had spread pretty well over Europe. Such luxury was wonderful and much less tiring than the bumpy, slow old diligences. At the same time, Jacques loved the excitement of travel, of strange places, and so was doubly pleased to find when he got back to Paris that new engagements had been contracted for in Belgium. His concert manager, John Mitchell, was an Englishman and he also promised Offenbach a later tour in England.

First, however, Jacques insisted on giving another recital in Paris. Mitchell agreed that it was an excellent idea, so that Jacques would not lose contact with his home ground.

This time the Salle Herz, a larger hall than Papé's music store provided, was decided upon. The program was to be entirely of Offenbach's own compositions and, undeterred by the critics' reception of La Fontaine's fables, he planned a burlesque of one of the best known Romantics of the era. This new project, the high light of the program, was especially ambitious. With one eye slanted toward the theatre, it was to be a capsule-size operetta.

It was called *Le Moine Bourru* (*The Hunchbacked Monk*), and in essence was simply a long duet. Two figures, each of whom thinks the other is a ghost—and the ghost of a monk, moreover—begin to sing cheerful songs to give themselves courage. Eventually they recognize each other as neighbors and finally go home together, happy in the non-existence of any ghostly monk.

To the audience, the burlesque was immediately clear. There was no question about its resemblance to Victor Hugo's *Hunchback of Notre-Dame* and it was also plain that Offenbach was making good-natured fun of grand opera in general. To enact the duet, Jacques had secured the services of two fine singers, one of whom was a friend of his from the Opéra-Comique.

The reaction of the audience was unequivocal. So insistent was their applause that the entire duet finally had to be repeated. And the critics, perhaps realizing that their previous dicta were outmoded, joined in the popular reception.

Jacques had guessed right. He had originality, and his sense of burlesque, the very lack of respect for which he had been taken to task, was now building him a modest reputation.

In the wake of this new triumph, he set off for his tour of Belgium.

12

The party seemed to be going quite well, but Mme Mitchell like any good hostess, paused to look about. It was a warm early spring, that year of 1843, and the sound of fans clicking open and shut vied with the rustle of taffeta and stiffened silk skirts. The passementerie and beading of the evening gown sparkled in the light and Mme Mitchell, who had been looking forward to the day when gas would be installed in the house reflected that it would never equal the charm of candlelight.

It shone down with beautiful effect on the shapely shoulder of her young daughter, Herminie, who was wearing her first evening gown. The soft pink of her dress, overlaid with lace contrasted well with her black hair, stylishly hanging in ringlets over her ears, and with her dark eyes, while the low-cut gown showed her full bosom to advantage. As a matter of fact, she had the same Spanish beauty as her mother, for Mme Mitchell came from Madrid. Mr. Mitchell, her second husband, was English but her two eldest children—Herminie and the boy Pepito—were entirely of Spanish blood.

Again Mme Mitchell glanced at the clock on the mantel and

wondered why her husband was so late. He had said he'd be detained, but by now . . .

There was a burst of laughter from the group surrounding the General. Well, at least, the guest of honor was a success. The General, a Spaniard like herself, was a newly exiled Carlist. He was a dashing figure and the ladies were obviously attracted to him for Mme Mitchell could just glimpse his resplendent, bemedalled uniform in the center of the room.

She moved to join the group, but at that moment the doorbell rang and she stopped short. Undoubtedly her husband had come at last. As the entrance hall was just off the drawing room she now walked instead toward the door. The bell sounded again, a long violent ring. Mme Mitchell was startled, remarking that her husband might at least give the servant time to arrive.

She was more startled when a moment later the door was opened and, instead of her husband, an apparition burst into the hall. At the same time she was vaguely conscious that all conversation had stopped in the salon.

The newcomer looked like some fantastic character out of one of E. T. A. Hoffmann's *Tales.* He was extraordinarily thin, with a pointed face and a long, hawk nose and in his right eye was a monocle attached to a wide black ribbon. It was his eyes which were the most curious feature—bright, dark eyes which gleamed in an odd way. There was something birdlike in them too. This curious person also resembled a bird in the quick way he had darted through the door.

Now he was stopped on the threshold of the drawing room, smiling, his eyes wrinkled to slits. Meanwhile Mme Mitchell, oddly discomfited, was simply standing still, staring. The unexpected guest moved toward her and bowing, said: "Mme Mitchell? My name is Jacques Offenbach. Your husband asked me to come in this evening."

Mme Mitchell's husband was none other than Jacques' concert manager.

Quickly regaining her poise, Mme Mitchell smiled affably and presented the strange young man to her guests. They all regarded him with intense curiosity. Finally, someone asked: "You are a musician, I believe, Monsieur Offenbach?"

Jacques turned, beaming: "Yes. I have just returned from a concert tour in Belgium. A wonderful success! In Brussels I actually had to play six encores! So much better than the old days in the Opéra-Comique orchestra——"

And then he launched into a description of the time when he and Seligmann attached a string to the music stands.

"Just what effect would that have?" someone else asked.

Jacques looked quickly about the room. Over in the corner stood a piano.

"Come," said Jacques, "I will show you," and abruptly moved toward it.

Several people followed him curiously. Jacques ran his right hand over the keys. Still standing, his foot reached for the pedal.

"It's like this . . ." he began.

By the time Mr. Mitchell put in his appearance, Jacques was the absolute focus of attention, while the guest of honor, the Carlist General, had been reduced to a mere onlooker. Jacques, seated at the piano, was holding forth, playing and singing snatches of tunes. He had no voice whatsoever but the over-all effect of the singing and playing was pleasant and entertaining. Shy Herminie, Mr. Mitchell's stepdaughter, was actually leaning on the piano.

She was fascinated. Never in her sheltered life had she encountered such an unusual person and she also sensed that he was just as extraordinary to this worldly group of friends her mother had invited this evening. There were no longer little groups here and there about the room, just one large collection of people gathered around the piano where Jacques, interspersing his playing with conversation, talked about anything and everything that came into his head—his student days at the Conservatory, about his father in Cologne, about personalities in the salons. His genial manner, his amusing stories and his funny accent all combined to captivate his audience.

Jacques Offenbach was a natural extrovert and quite unabashed by the attention he had attracted. Yet he was by no

means of that insufferable breed known nowadays as the Life
of the Party. He liked people so much that he was able to project
his feeling for them with no effort. Naturally, the audience immediately responded with their quite evident liking for him.
In reality, he was not even fully aware of the extent to which
he had taken over the evening. Only once, looking up suddenly
and encountering Herminie's earnest gaze, did he momentarily
lose aplomb. His fingers struck a sour note on the piano. Grimac-
ing, he turned to the company and remarked: "Seeing this
charming young lady made me forget everything for the moment!"

Herminie flushed and turned aside. But when she looked
back, young Monsieur Offenbach was smiling gently and, tim-
idly, she smiled back.

It was her first party and Herminie had fallen in love.

13

Jacques, as was customary, made his formal call on Mme
Mitchell a few days later, bringing her a bunch of flowers. He
had considered bringing the young daughter a bouquet as well,
but was afraid this might be presumptuous. After all, she
was scarcely a grownup.

Mme Mitchell greeted him cordially and invited him to have
tea. She had, after getting over her initial astonishment, taken
quite a liking to this extraordinary young man and found him
even more enjoyable on second acquaintance. As a matter of
fact, the whole household had been discussing him ever since
the party and the consensus had been that he was quite a remarkable and entertaining fellow.

Nevertheless, Mme Mitchell was a trifle surprised when Herminie joined them. Herminie was only fifteen and while Mme
Mitchell had been at pains to instill in her the social amenities,
the girl was inclined to rely upon the excuse of youth and evade
such boring formalities as receiving duty callers.

Herminie looked radiant today. Her eyes were sparkling and
her cheeks were rosy. As she moved gracefully across the floor

Mme Mitchell noted approvingly that the girl was going to b
a beauty.

To Jacques, Herminie was simply the loveliest creature h
had ever seen. Ever since the party he had been haunted by he
It was ridiculous. She was little more than a child, but for som
reason he kept seeing those huge, liquid black eyes gazing a
him earnestly across the piano.

Before long Mme Mitchell became aware that young Mon
sieur Offenbach was directing his conversation mainly towar
her daughter. She was vaguely annoyed. But Herminie, thoug
she said little, dimpled prettily.

From that day on, Jacques was a frequent visitor at th
Mitchells'. They were a hospitable household and Jacques, a
ready on excellent terms with the elder Mitchells, also mad
friends with the boy Pepito and the younger Mitchell childre
But it was always dark-eyed Herminie—whose full name wa
Herminie d'Alcain—whom he wanted to see. He too had falle
in love, for the first time in his life.

Jacques had known many women and he considered himse
experienced in the ways of sex. He was very susceptible t
feminine charms, but hitherto his affairs at most had been i
fatuations. There could be no question of an "affair" with He
minie. The innocence of her youth would have made such a
idea monstrous. He, who had often been accused of disrespec
at last understood what it meant to be in awe of an ideal. He
minie was not like others.

He continually discovered new traits in her. Her sweetne
and gentleness were apparent from the beginning, but as he sa
more of her she revealed an animation he had not at first ob
served. She would ask him questions about his concerts and h
would play his new compositions for her. Herminie displayed
real appreciation of music and he began to depend on her r
actions.

She was never permitted to be alone with him, of cours
Like any properly-brought-up young girl of the era, Hermin
was closely chaperoned by her family. However, it was easy t
say a few words, to give an indication of his sentiments whi

ostensibly playing the piano. Naturally, some of his new ballads were undisguisedly love songs ("Words by Jacques Offenbach," he would say with mock seriousness) which only added zest to the game they were playing. Because Herminie grew so bold as to sing the songs occasionally too. They were two conspirators against the family.

This pleasant idyll was broken early in the summer when Jacques was obliged to go on tour. He had been invited to take part in a musical festival at Douai. Later he went to Cologne for two recitals, where his father as usual took care of the advance publicity.

This absence only confirmed to Jacques his earlier conviction that he was deeply and seriously in love. He missed Herminie terribly, just those stolen *entretiens* by the piano, and he knew that somehow he must convince Mme Mitchell of the sincerity of his love.

Upon his return from Cologne he formally asked for Herminie in marriage and was shocked to find he was not taken seriously. Mme Mitchell simply refused to entertain the notion. Monsieur Offenbach was a likable enough young man, she admitted, but to marry her daughter—it was absurd. She was far too young. How could she know her own mind? Besides, what financial guarantees did he have?

Jacques had to admit the justice of this last question. He had been playing constantly, better, he felt, than he ever had before. Indeed, he had become the rage of the salons. But his financial position remained unstable and he tried desperately to increase his earnings.

As for Herminie, she had very much made up her mind. She intended to marry Jacques and displayed a surprising stubbornness at her mother's importunings. However, she was under age and Mme Mitchell refused to give her consent.

The two young lovers hit upon an expedient which would force Mme Mitchell to take them seriously. It was a bold gesture on their part and might bring retribution tumbling on their heads, but they considered it well worth the gamble.

One of Jacques' love ballads—one which he used to sing

surreptitiously to Herminie—was published. It was called "A Toi"—"To Thee"—and was dedicated to "Mlle Herminie d'Alcain." To make it more pointed, a picture of Herminie adorned the cover.

At this impertinence Mme Mitchell was righteously angered. Such familiarity was only excusable in a fiancé. The impropriety otherwise was obvious and, as anticipated, it placed Mme Mitchell in a dilemma. Either she must close her door to Monsieur Offenbach in the future, which would make for a rather scandalous situation, or accept the inevitable. And it was becoming increasingly apparent to Mme Mitchell that the forces of youth were eventually going to win.

Jacques had gone off on a prolonged provincial tour and immediately upon his return to Paris gave another recital of his own compositions, including a well-received "Bohemian Dance." The polka, newly imported from Bohemia, was the latest dance fad in Paris. He also did a couple of bravura pieces, previously tried out in Cologne, one a fantasy on themes from Rossini's operas and the other a ballet called *Musette. L'Artiste,* one of Paris' leading periodicals, spoke of him as "one of the most successful virtuosi of the season."

Fortunately for Jacques also, "A Toi" had achieved an unprecedented popularity, being sung and played everywhere that autumn.

All this combined to give Jacques renewed confidence when he returned for Mme Mitchell's answer. She still withheld her approval but finally went so far as to promise her consent if Jacques agreed to two conditions.

First and most important was that Jacques become a Catholic.

Jacques' father, to whom he had previously confided his situation, had suggested that perhaps the fact that he was Jewish was an obstacle. From a racial point of view, it appeared that this had never been the case, but from a religious angle, Mme Mitchell could not countenance a non-Catholic son-in-law. She herself was devout and Herminie had been brought up strictly within the tenets of the church.

For Jacques no sacrifice whatsoever was involved. Creeds simply did not concern him and he had no feeling for any given church. Fundamentally he had a sense of piety, despite charges to the contrary. Whether this should be manifested by membership in the Catholic or any other church made no real difference to him.

His long-time patroness, the Countess de Vaux, was pleased when she learned of the decision and unhesitatingly consented to be his godmother. Her loyalty and friendship for Jacques had all along been a helpful influence in his suit for Herminie's hand.

The second of Mme Mitchell's conditions was that Jacques test his abilities by a season in London. While Paris was the artistic center, London was the greatest city in the world, and on his success or failure there one could approximate his future. Mr. Mitchell had for some time been anxious to try out Offenbach in London and the suggestion no doubt originated with him. Again, Jacques was willing and under Mr. Mitchell's management he set off in May.

Word of his triumphs was not long in reaching Paris. He played in public concert halls; he played in numerous homes of the aristocracy. He was far removed from the shy boy who had first entered Countess de Vaux' salon. At twenty-five he was well versed in the ways of society. His comedy was in good taste and highly amusing. At the same time his very obvious ability as a sound musician was appreciated. People found Jacques most engaging and invitations were heaped on him.

Yet all the while Jacques was homesick for Paris. Paris was his home. It would always be the city he loved most in the world. More important at present, it was the city where Herminie lived. He longed to see her and was impatient for that day, not far off, when she would be his wife. Mme Mitchell's two conditions had been fulfilled and she could no longer withhold her consent.

Mature man of the world though he had become, Jacques nevertheless retained a boyish gleefulness over his achievements. It was an engaging quality which took the sting from his natural conceit and a quality he was never to lose. He had a lot of

fun recounting his triumphs to his friend, the young playwright
Emile Chevalet.

I know you have already heard talk about my success in the wonderful city of London. Last Thursday I
played before the Queen, Prince Albert, the Emperor
of Russia, the King of Bavaria, etc., etc. In other words,
before the best court circles. I had an enormous success. However, in spite of all the honors that are heaped
upon me here, I still prefer my beautiful Paris and
spending my time among my real friends. Here everything is imposing, but cold. There, on the contrary,
everything is gracious, charming and . . . warm, particularly if one has a few real friends. So, my dear
Emile, I am longing to shake hands with you again, I
am impatient to return to Paris which contains everything I hold dear, all whom I love. You understand,
don't you, dear Emile? If you are able to push my appearance at Court, I feel in advance that you will do
it. Speak to our friends Gonzales and the Essarts about
it. Next week I have two marvelous concerts, better
than any yet. Last week I was invited to dinner by the
Society of Melodists, whose President is the Duke of
Cambridge. Well, my dear fellow, as you might guess,
there was music after dinner. I played my *musette* and
they all made a terrific amount of noise, banging on the
table for fully five minutes, shouting at the top of their
lungs: "Encore! bis! encore!" I had to play the same
piece over again. As you can see by all this, I had no
less success here than in Paris. And I am beginning to
be a bit proud. When I return to Paris I won't be able
to see you any more, I who am only used to associating with Lords, Dukes, Queens, Kings, Princes, Emperors! Emperors, my friend! I can no longer lower
myself by talking to a mere commoner, though I can
write him as you see, my friend, and I am taking advantage of it. . . .

It was late in July before Offenbach got back to Paris. He had made quite a bit of money and could honestly maintain that he was able to support a wife. Mme Mitchell's two conditions had been fulfilled and there was no further obstacle to his marriage with Herminie.

On August 14, 1844, they were solemnly wed in the Catholic Church. She was sixteen and he was twenty-five.

CHAPTER TWO

The Curse of the "Evil Eye"

1

The doorbell rang once again and Jacques hastened to answer it. The small living room was already packed with people and the guests were overflowing into the hall. This time it was Friedrich von Flotow, and as Jacques directed him where to put his opera cape and hat, the doorbell sounded once more. Beaming, Offenbach rushed back to greet the latest newcomer.

In the drawing room Herminie wondered how they were going to take care of all the guests. Each week there were more than the time before. It was Friday evening and the Offenbachs were "at home." There was nothing formal about their *soirées*—this would have been impossible in view of the smallness of their apartment as well as their limited finances—but neither Jacques nor Herminie had any use for conventional entertaining. These weekly gatherings were confined to their intimates. But, as Herminie quickly discovered, Jacques' "intimates" were legion. Either you were an "intimate" of Jacques or you weren't his friend at all.

There was really no need to worry about the comfort of the guests. One had only to look around to see that they were thoroughly at home and enjoying themselves. Even the women, in their full skirts which took up so much room, seemed not to mind when the stiffening was occasionally crushed against the furniture. Already the Offenbach "at homes" were being talked about on the boulevards and Jacques' acquaintances waited hopefully for invitations.

What made these parties notable was their very informality. There were no servants and the guests themselves followed the hostess into the kitchen to partake of the cold meat, hard-boiled eggs and salad. The men put up card tables wherever they could find space and brought out the wine bottles. There was perhaps no other home in Paris where casualness was carried to such a delightful degree.

Usually Jacques plotted some sort of buffoonery for the evening's entertainment. Sometimes it was a skit, lampooning some current theatre hit such as *Le Desert*. (This was a romantic poet's eulogy of the feeling of infinity in the desert and his pity for the townsman, imprisoned behind walls. In the Offenbach version, the hero complained in reverse about the climate and the lack of sidewalk cafés in the desert.) At other times, the guests entered into some such childish game as "Follow the Leader."

Jacques had never been so happy in his life. He loved entertaining and he was excessively proud of their wonderful, if small, apartment on the Passage Saulnier. Nowadays he had a feeling of stability such as he had never known. Rarely now did he suffer those fits of despondency which used to overcome him when he was alone. Herminie was always near at hand. She would sit and embroider while he worked on his compositions; she was there to greet him when he returned from a recital or a tour of the boulevards, ready to soothe his ruffled spirits when he was irritable.

Everybody liked and admired Herminie. She was gracious, tolerant and unobtrusively intelligent. Not even Jacques' enemies had anything to say against Herminie, though there were

many who considered it an odd marriage. A foul rumor had bee
making the rounds to the effect that Offenbach had the "ev
eye." It had been started as a joke, presumably by the journali
Théophile Gautier, who couldn't abide Offenbach, but ther
were those who, uncannily affected by his curious glitterin
eyes, took it seriously. The most vicious example of this gossi
was in a newspaper comment at the time of his wedding to th
effect that Jacques, catching sight of his reflection in a sho
window was frightened of himself and hastened to get marrie
immediately.

Herminie was amazingly unperturbed by such slanders. Sh
knew Jacques was an unusual person—that was why she love
him—and quickly concluded that such attentions were compli
ments in reverse. She worshipped Jacques and her devotion neve
wavered in all her years with him.

She also had the knowledge that she knew a Jacques wit
whom no one else was acquainted. She was close to that Jacque
who grew despondent and weak and frightened, that Jacque
who could not bear to be alone. It was she to whom he turne
for comfort and encouragement. It was she who remained un
changing when he switched from irrepressible high spirits t
irritable nervousness.

She had a mannerism of stretching out her right arm in
broad, sweeping gesture.

"Jacques," she would say, "it makes no difference."

Sometimes his utter disregard of money *did* make a differ
ence. Young though she was, Herminie was an efficient and eco
nomical housekeeper and she was continually bedeviled by th
fact that Jacques refused to co-operate with any budgetin
scheme. It was a reaction to his incessant poverty. Those wh
have suffered penury inevitably react to money in one of tw
ways—either they become parsimonious from fright, or the
delight in the ability to spend it. Jacques belonged to this latte
school. The only times when Herminie made him uncomfortabl
were when she asked for an accounting. He would have pre
ferred—and told her so—that she abstract the necessary fund
from his pockets.

Jacques was frequently depressed because he had made no headway with his theatre ambitions. Only then would he be free of the specter of poverty. He worked hard enough, but the financial future of a concert performer was circumscribed. Now Herminie was pregnant and his responsibilities would soon be increased.

For a long while Jacques had been trying to get consideration from the Opéra-Comique. He felt that his career lay in the writing of comic opera or musical satires; on a larger scale the sort of thing on which he had built his reputation in the salons. But in recent years the Opéra-Comique, instead of confining itself to light operas as its name warranted, had been trying to rival the regular Opéra in the production of serious and tragic music dramas. Not only were light operas becoming rare in its repertoire but even these few were old-fashioned and outmoded in treatment.

Offenbach, frustrated in his attempts to gain attention from the Opéra-Comique, attacked it bitterly. He was sincerely convinced that it was not only overlooking the very field which it should represent, but that it needed enlivening by an infusion of new blood. Unfortunately, Offenbach's propensity for expounding his theories to anyone who would listen did as much to hinder as assist him toward his goal. Many shared his views, but Monsieur Basset, Director of the Opéra-Comique, was conceivably outraged when Offenbach's comments were relayed to him and he resolved to have no traffic whatsoever with that impudent young man.

Jacques had, however, cultivated acquaintance with numerous journalists to some avail. From time to time a friendly critic would support him in print with pointed remarks, for the benefit of Monsieur Basset, such as "I have just come away from a superb concert by Offenbach with full confidence that this talented composer will soon be given a libretto by the Comique." That sort of sally was received in silence by Basset.

Over a period of months a succession of these manoeuvres nevertheless apparently took effect. Monsieur Basset agreed to see Offenbach and commissioned him to adapt an old one-act vaudeville piece, *L'Alcove*, which had been a success back in 1833, for production at the Opéra-Comique.

L'Alcove was a frothy bit of nonsense about bygone revolutionary days, but Jacques knew that he must subdue his tendency of burlesque to the Comique's classical style. He confined himself to occasional, but well-planted, humorous touches. Extremely excited about his long-sought assignment he was painstaking in his efforts and was determined in this important enterprise not to make the error of too hasty writing. He worked over his score, ruthlessly destroying and rewriting, for several weeks. Finally, satisfied, he carried it to Monsieur Basset.

Monsieur Basset, said his secretary, was not in. So Jacques returned the next day. Still Monsieur Basset was not in. He kept on coming back. But Monsieur Basset was either not in or occupied. In any case, he did not receive Offenbach. Jacques exhibited a humbleness, a patience, which were not normal to him, but he was desperately anxious to break down the resistance against him. For several months he hounded Monsieur Basset's office—to no avail. And Jacques' contract was only verbal, a so-called gentleman's agreement.

Whether Monsieur Basset simply took this cruel means of vengeance for Offenbach's oft-repeated criticism of the direction of the Opéra-Comique or whether upon meeting Offenbach he had reacted to the "evil eye," Jacques never knew. All he did know was the torment of disappointment.

When it became obvious that Monsieur Basset would never see him, Offenbach produced *L'Alcove* at a concert of his own. This was a more ambitious project than any heretofore, being held in a leading theatre with the assistance of actors and singers from the boulevards. His journalist friends staunchly supported his efforts. One, the critic of *La France Musicale*, wrote: "On leaving the hall everyone was humming the prettiest tunes from the operetta and wondering why on earth Offenbach should be left to wait in vain upon the threshold of a temple that has been opened to so many mediocrities."

One of the leading composers of light opera of the period, Adolphe Adam, was also in the audience. He too wrote music reviews and was unstinting in his praise but, better than any review, he commissioned Offenbach on the spot to do a comic operetta for the Théâtre Lyrique, which he was planning to open to fill in the gap for which Jacques had so much criticized the Opéra-Comique.

Here at last was something on which Offenbach could pin his hopes. The Théâtre Lyrique opened in November, 1847. By that time Herminie had given birth to a daughter, whom they named Berthe. Offenbach was the traditionally proud father, although he had secretly—and equally traditionally— longed for a son. Well, that would come later. They would have a large family. Meanwhile, the Théâtre Lyrique reassured Offenbach of the future. With the chance presented him by Adam he visualized himself winning over the boulevards, with success following success.

They had decided to postpone production of Offenbach's play until early spring but by January they were working on plans for its presentation and Jacques bustled about in a state of bliss.

Then in February, 1848, the Revolution broke out, the Revolution which dethroned Louis-Philippe and which, once again, changed the whole course of French history.

2

On the night of February twenty-third the streets were thronged with celebrants, due to the fall of the Guizot Cabinet. For many months there had been ominous rumblings from the exploited working classes who clamored for liberal reforms and even demanded the abdication of the King himself. The newly rich industrialists and bankers, with the guilty conscience of the exploiter, viewed the still orderly manifestations with alarm. And the Man in the Tuileries grew panicky. About ten o'clock that night a fusillade suddenly rang out from the Ministry of Foreign Affairs (where Guizot had held office), firing into the throng gathered about the building and killing several.

Instantly the mood of the crowd became menacing. The

ordinary citizen sped home in fright, street lights went out, and in the houses shutters were drawn and lights turned off. Offenbach, sitting over a coffee with a group of journalists at the Restaurant Divan, heard the news early and hurried back to Herminie and the baby.

It was quiet on the Passage Saulnier but down the street on the boulevard and in many other parts of town rioting had started. Lamp posts, benches, *vespasiennes*, pavements and even trees were being torn up. The rioting continued throughout the night and in the morning the mobs moved closer to the Tuileries.

Off the Champs-Elysées a municipal guardpost fired on the revolutionaries trying to take over and its men were massacred by the infuriated crowd. At another guards' barracks at Château d'Eau, the same performance was repeated. In this case, the building was set afire and all the soldiers within roasted alive.

The Municipal Guard had remained loyal to the King but the larger and better equipped National Guard joined the people and Louis-Philippe was lost. The Citizen-King abdicated and fled with his family.

Meanwhile, what had begun as a workingmen's orderly protest had become a lawless bacchanalia. The rabble went through the deserted Tuileries and, enraged by the regal splendor in which their "citizen" monarch had lived, ripped the tapestries and draperies, broke up the furniture and priceless bric-à-brac. Hooligans, shouting obscenities, jumped on the Queen's bed, and a prostitute, parading in the Phrygian bonnet of revolution, seated herself on the throne. Men and women went out from the Palace wearing scarves and sashes of damask and velvet torn from the furnishings.

As the days of rioting continued, hunger began to be felt in the city, the delivery of foodstuffs being held up by the revolutionaries. The big industrialists, with their families, fled the city first. The small businessmen followed.

On the Passage Saulnier, Offenbach was in despair. Politically speaking, he was untouched. He had no particular political beliefs. Voting in most of Europe was confined to the propertied classes, if permitted at all. The people who patronized his con-

certs were the nobility or the rich industrialists—the voting elite,
if you wished—against whom the rioting had started, but Jacques,
who was never a snob, counted friends in all classes. His political creed, if any, was humanitarian. But violence he could not
abide and what was happening in his beloved Paris was a
tragedy.

Moreover, he was a foreigner and in times of revolution there
is no place for foreigners. As the food shortage made itself felt
he grew additionally anxious for the welfare of his family.

One by one the theatres had closed down and he knew that
his play was doomed. The Revolution had, in fact, eliminated
all means of his earning money, for naturally there were now
no salons either.

The only sensible thing was to return to Cologne. He could
not go to the Street of the Bells, as his father had moved in with
a married sister, but at least they would be near his family and
the people he knew.

One bleak day they set off with their small daughter in a
diligence. There was no question of a train, for their financial
status was again precarious. In fact, it was only because Herminie had secretly saved a little money that they were able to
travel at all. When they stopped at Homburg en route, Jacques
recklessly decided to gamble a few of their remaining florins
at the Casino. The idea was born of desperation and fortunately
he won, easing their condition temporarily.

On their arrival in Cologne they found that it was only relatively more peaceful than Paris. Revolution had broken out like
a rash all over the face of Europe and the German States too
were in the throes of upheaval. The Wars of Liberation, begun
in desultory fashion after the defeat of Napoleon, had received
new impetus with this second French Revolution. In Frankfort
a call went out for deputies to a German Federal Parliament to
unite the various principalities. Republican sentiments were pro-
claimed but, when assembled, the Parliament seemed to contain
more monarchists than democrats. They were mainly concerned
with *which* monarchy should head the new confederation.

Offenbach discovered that his father was optimistic about

the future. He believed that one outcome of the present unrest would be a democratic state which would bring complete emancipation to the German Jew. Jacques, who had once more been made conscious of the anti-Semitic sentiments pervading Cologne, could not go along with his father's optimism.

He himself suffered no outright insults or inconveniences, but the casual generalities expressed here and there by the man in the street made the atmosphere of Cologne abhorrent. He had grown to loathe his native city and despised what he considered only a pretense of republicanism. In Cologne, unlike other parts of the German States, there were no physical excesses, but there was a great show of patriotic fervor. Herminie and little Berthe seemed safe from violence but the atmosphere was both depressing and degrading.

They had been forced to take a cheap furnished room, in which they all three lived and where Jacques, with the aid of an old piano, did his composing. The only livelihood he had been able to find was in carrying out commissions to do patriotic songs for the new "republicans." He deliberately wrote sentimental bathos like "Song of the German Boys" and "German Fatherland." The *Kölnische Zeitung* referred to him as "our very own" but Jacques felt absurd and miscast. His father told him that he must not be too upset about the trash he was composing and that really, in their small way, these songs were helping democracy through its birth pangs.

Strangely undemocratic was the celebration in August of the 600th anniversary of the laying of the Cologne Cathedral's cornerstone, attended by the King of Prussia and an Austrian Archduke, as well as a deputation from the new Parliament. Offenbach was asked to make a musical arrangement befitting the occasion and to play his cello. He compiled a medley of Rossini's music, which was neither patriotic nor Germanic, but which gave him satisfaction.

The slight political disturbances in Cologne seeming to have passed, Offenbach made plans for a concert. He arranged a German version of *L'Alcove*, the act originally destined for the

Opéra-Comique, but it was received apathetically. Not a single notice appeared in the papers.

Both Jacques and Herminie were terribly homesick for Paris, although Jacques as usual was more vociferous. The failure of his concert only added to his unhappiness and the constant realization that because he was born a Jew he was merely a "second-class" citizen furthered his misery. When word reached them that Louis-Napoleon had been elected President and that France had returned to law and order they immediately made plans to return.

On December 20, 1848, the new President took the oath to "regard as enemies all those who may attempt by illegal means to change the form of the established government" and a month later the Offenbach family was again installed on the Passage Saulnier.

3

Back in Paris, Offenbach made the rounds of the cafés, drinking nothing more expensive than a coffee or taking an occasional ice, renewing contacts. Adam had lost his lease on the Théâtre Lyrique, so that possibility was out. There was a new director at the Opéra-Comique and Offenbach tried to interest him in a commission, but to no avail. He returned to the boring round of concerts and salon recitals. One of his many acquaintances was the Count de Morny, half-brother to Louis-Napoleon, who arranged an invitation performance at the Elysée Palace, home of the new President. This was a signal honor and afforded Offenbach his first meeting with that lesser Napoleon who was soon to make himself Emperor.

Notwithstanding this minor accolade, Jacques had lost enthusiasm for concerts. He was neglecting his practice and confining his compositions to the lightest and most frivolous pieces, which suited the mood of his listeners, but the papers criticized him for descending to such trivialities. Yet anything more ambitious no longer seemed worth the effort. Jacques suffered with the frustration due to interminable disappointments and had lost confidence in ever achieving real recognition.

In April, 1850, his father died, adding to his depression. His father had never doubted that he would eventually succeed, bolstering Jacques' morale even during the miserable months in Cologne.

Nor did Herminie vacillate in her belief in him. She was his only comfort these days. He had never been particularly close to his sisters and he had long been more or less estranged from Jules. Though his professional career caused him considerable worry, his home life was close to being ideal. But Herminie was pregnant again and, while Jacques looked forward to a son, he was gravely concerned by the additional financial burden this would entail.

He was tormenting himself with his problems as he sat lunching alone at the Café Cardinal one day. This was the famous theatrical café and restaurant on the corner of the Boulevard des Italiens and the Rue de Richelieu. It was an extravagance for Jacques to eat there, but it was a place in which aspiring actors, playwrights and composers considered it politic to put in an appearance. Offenbach saw no one of any importance on this occasion and he began to doubt his good sense in coming but, he reflected, as he never had much appetite anyway, he could keep the cost to a minimum. It had got so, he mused, that the aspirants had crowded out the very producers and directors whom they were seeking.

Nothing he did seemed worth while any more. Here he was already thirty-one years old, he'd been struggling in Paris for sixteen years—and what had he to show for all those years of effort? Oh, yes, he was a successful concert performer, wrote unimportant little songs, but one of these days they'd be dropping him for new talent. And then where would he be? Anyway, it could never be a real career. But just how was he ever going to break into the theatre? *Mon dieu,* it was ten years since that one attempt with Anicet Bourgeois!

He'd been pestering people for so long now that they hated the sight of him. He had talent, plenty of it. He was still sure of that. But apparently that wasn't enough. Maybe those who said he had the evil eye were right. There was that business with the Opéra-Comique. And the Revolution had wrecked his chances with Adam. There must be a curse on him.

Lost in these dismal thoughts, Jacques was no longer conscious of anyone in the restaurant when, suddenly, he became aware that someone was standing in front of his table. He glanced up to see an impressive-looking man with a fan-shaped beard, but a total stranger to him.

The man, without preamble, asked: "Would you like to revolutionize the Comédie-Française?"

Though Offenbach was taken aback, he managed to dissemble it. "Certainly," he replied airily. "I'm a man who likes to be in the midst of things."

He hadn't the faintest notion what the man was talking about and whether it was a joke or not. But when the man introduced himself as Arsène Houssaye, Offenbach recognized his name to be that of the recent editor of *L'Artiste*. As a matter of fact, he knew a good deal about him by reputation. Houssaye had not only been a first-rate editor, but he was a well-known boulevardier, a *bon vivant*, and quite a bit of a rake, and he was the present lover of the great tragedienne Rachel.

As he drew up a chair, Houssaye indicated that it was through Rachel that, just the day previous, he had been made director of the great state theatre. The Comédie-Française was primarily the theatre of the classics—Molière, Racine, Corneille —but in recent years, while it clung to its reputation and presented in monotonous succession the familiar dramas, it had sunk in popular esteem. Nowadays its seats were only half-filled and the new director had been appointed to make renovations which would bring it back to its old glory.

Houssaye had been thinking over the reforms he intended to institute when he had spotted Offenbach sitting across from him in the dining room. He had recognized him since he had heard him play on numerous occasions and had been greatly impressed with his exquisite musical sense. It occurred to him that one of the first reforms to be made at the Théâtre Français was in the orchestra, at the moment a decidedly second-rate out-fit. The orchestra was an integral part of the theatre as, in the fashion of the period, songs were usually interpolated in the production. Yet at the present moment there wasn't even a real orchestra leader, the first violinist filling that role, using his bow as a baton and counting time loudly enough to be heard throughout the audience.

All this Houssaye expanded upon to Offenbach, winding up by offering him the new post of conductor with a budget of eighteen thousand francs—six thousand for himself, twelve for his musicians.

Jacques trusted that his voice did not betray him. He tried to observe the proper detachment in accepting the offer. But six thousand francs a year was more than he had ever earned in his life.

When he parted from Houssaye after lunch his first instinct was to rush home and tell Herminie the extraordinary news. Then, on second thought, he decided to make a few early business calls. Before the afternoon was over, Offenbach had already recruited half his orchestra.

He was still full of excitement when he burst in on Herminie. It was wonderful to watch her face light up and her sweet smile spread as he told her the good fortune. In her characteristic gesture, she extended her arm out toward him.

"You see, Jacques!" she exclaimed. "I told you not to despair."

4

The theatre was only half-filled when the musicians filed into their pit. It was not an impressive audience from any point of view. Practically no one was in evening clothes and they lacked the festive air associated with theatres. Many slumped deliberately in their seats, while others wandered aimlessly up and down the aisles. None seemed aware that the orchestra was about to commence. Herminie, seated with a friend in a box, watched apprehensively. It was the night of Jacques' debut and she was extremely nervous.

But as Offenbach made his appearance from the wings and marched briskly to the podium he had an electrifying effect upon the audience. People sat up straighter in their seats and those in the aisles paused in astonishment. For the first time in the memory of most of the regular clientele, an orchestra leader stood before them in evening dress. Jacques' sure theatrical sense was manifest in his careful grooming and, as the lights dimmed, everyone was aware of the flash of his white gloves as he wielded the baton.

The orchestra began with the tender aria from Flotow's recent opera, *Martha*. It progressed to a delightful intepretation of the minuet from Mozart's *Don Giovanni*. From that time on, it made no difference what the selection happened to be—the audience of the Théâtre Français knew it was listening to an orchestra such as had not been heard in that old playhouse in many years, if ever.

It was a wonderful night of triumph for Jacques, and Herminie shared it with him, receiving the congratulations backstage and going later to the Café Cardinal to celebrate.

The news of Offenbach's success as a conductor was quickly noised about Paris. Several music critics had been on hand for his opening performance, others flocked there later, and excellent notices began to appear in the papers. Even the renowned, though cantankerous, Berlioz paused to give him favorable attention.

As for Offenbach, he felt that he had just climbed the first rung of the ladder and he gave himself wholeheartedly to his new job. He had proven himself a fine conductor and now he wrote music of his own to intersperse between the acts. Unlike many conductors, he was meticulous in his courtesy toward the members of his orchestra, always treating them with tact and respect ("The unhappy memories of my own days in the Opéra-Comique orchestra are too well seared on my mind") and the result was that the men outdid themselves in efforts to perfect their performances. They even laughed good-humoredly when Offenbach occasionally, in a burst of enthusiasm, would take a violin from one of the men and play it himself.

Houssaye reported with amusement: "He takes Lully's violin to accompany Molière and Hoffman's to accompany Musset." It was Offenbach's theatrical sense coming to the surface once again. He was, as always, a good showman.

Offenbach wrote incidental music for several new plays, as well as for the classic repertory of the theatre, among them *Le Bonhomme Jadis* of Henry Mürger and *Romulus*, a one-act play by Dumas *père*. Under Houssaye's direction the old theatre had been reinvigorated and Houssaye, in turn, was grateful for Offenbach's fine contribution toward it.

Nevertheless, troubles began to arise. In spite of Houssaye's support, opposition to Offenbach was apparent. The Théâtre Français, which received a state subsidy, was actually run by its stockholders—and its stockholders were none other than the actors themselves. Their salaries were on a percentage basis and their first outcry came when Offenbach ordered a few orchestra seats removed, not only to make room for the increased number of musicians, but to improve the acoustics. In vain he pointed out that these seats had for the most part remained unoccupied. To the actor-stockholders they represented potential profit.

Next came the inevitable professional jealousy. Not only did the excellence of the orchestra vie with the stage production, but Offenbach's own compositions were receiving too much attention. His music for Mürger's *Bonhomme Jadis* brought this to a climax. While it was customary at this period to have musical accompaniment with practically every type of play, the actor-stockholders contended that only songs that were indispensable to the action of the play should be permitted. Houssaye, of course, did what he could for Offenbach, but there was some justice in this latest criticism and it was finally decided to defer to their wishes and concentrate on the between-the-acts concerts.

Still unsatisfied by this capitulation, several of the actors resorted to additional petty vexations. It was understood that the curtain would not rise until the bell rang, which in turn was when the orchestra had finished its selection. But the actors already on stage declared they were ready and demanded that the curtain go up immediately. Nightly, the stage-manager replied that Monsieur Houssaye had particularly instructed him to wait. Nightly, there was bickering and these dissensions went on endlessly.

Offenbach felt himself thwarted at every turn. Yet his greatest discouragement was to discover that even a first-rate orchestra could not overcome the apathy of the typical Comédie-Française audience. Intermission to an audience usually meant a time to stroll in the lobby and converse with acquaintances. Many of Offenbach's cherished efforts were therefore played to empty seats. Adolphe Adam, attending one evening, spoke glowingly of one of Jacques' songs as a *petit chef-d'oeuvre* of color, grace and originality. But he added the caustic comment: "It proves that one must not cast musical pearls before . . . the audience of the Théâtre Français."

Apparently no one else had even heard the song.

It was not surprising that Jacques, again affected by the virus of discouragement, soon confined himself to rehearsals, leaving the actual conducting to the first violinist except "where a real conductor is indispensable, such as for Gounod's score for *Ulysses.*"

Young Charles Gounod—he was a year older than Offenbach—had won recognition, if not monetary success, with his opera *Sappho* the previous season. Houssaye had now commissioned him to do music for the new play *Ulysses* which the Théâtre Français was producing. Jacques had the greatest admiration for Gounod's manifest genius and collaborated with him to the best of his own ability. That the play lived up to the highest expectations was in no small way due to Offenbach's fine interpretation of Gounod's score.

It was during the early discussion stage that Houssaye first asked Offenbach to come to his office, in order to go over the music with Gounod. A piano, as a matter of fact, had been installed there. When Offenbach arrived he found quite an impressive assemblage of well-known figures already present, including Victor Hugo, Alfred de Vigny, Alfred de Musset and

Count de Morny. The last named, as usual, was sporting a hydrangea in his buttonhole, a subtle way (except for the incredible size of the boutonnière) of proclaiming that he, like the Prince-President, was Queen Hortense's son, since the French name for hydrangea is *hortensia*.

Jacques was already acquainted with the Count but the others were personally unknown to him. He considered it a great honor to meet these outstanding literary figures and—for once—respectfully kept himself out of the limelight. Indeed, he remained unobtrusively on the edge of the gathering, listening to the beautiful flow of language of the great Hugo. De Vigny was rather quiet, interrupting only with an occasional trenchant remark.

But it was on the somberly silent Musset that Jacques eventually fixed his gaze. The brilliant, half-mad poet was patently nearing the end of his short life. His handsome face was distorted by the ravages of his absinthe drinking and other excesses, an occasional nervous twitch accenting his bad physical condition. Offenbach found himself staring at him with horrible fascination. De Musset suddenly seemed aware that he was being watched and, turning abruptly, glared in his direction. Jacques felt uncomfortable and was relieved when Houssaye suggested he go over the music with Gounod.

As usual, the moment he turned aside to music he forgot his immediate surroundings. He was entranced with Gounod's score and played it magnificently. Everyone was impressed, and as he finished, Gounod leaned over and grasped his hand in a gesture of appreciation.

The others in the office crowded to the piano to extend their congratulations, not only to Gounod but to Offenbach as well. As Jacques looked around he saw de Musset's eyes still fixed on him. There was something so eerie in his stare that it gave Jacques a creepy feeling. In order to regain his aplomb he returned the look with his own steady gaze, his funny birdlike eyes sparkling as usual through his glasses. (He had substituted a full pair of glasses, on a broad black ribbon, for the monocle of earlier days.)

To his astonishment, Musset addressed him. Would Monsieur Offenbach, he enquired, write a love song for his own one-act play which the theatre was producing?

Jacques relaxed in a grin. He was delighted, of course. De Musset might be a madman, but he was also a man of unquestioned talent and it would be splendid to have his name billed with him.

De Musset's play, *Le Chandelier*, was a pleasant, light thing whose success depended mainly on a song. It was the story of a young lawyer, named Fortunio, who was in love with a client's wife. Thinking his love reciprocated, and not knowing she is having an affair with another young man and using Fortunio simply to throw the husband off the scent, he sings her a love song. There is such magic in the song that the wife is caught in her own trap and succumbs to Fortunio's charm.

The actor who was to play the role was not a professional singer, but he had a soft, tenor speaking-voice and Jacques considered it perfect for what he had in mind. He took a special joy in writing this song for which he felt sure he had created a particularly appealing melody.

"Listen, Herminie," he called, as he was working in the apartment one day, "isn't it beautiful?"

Herminie came into the room and listened attentively as he played it through on the piano.

"It is lovely, Jacques," she answered when he had finished, "truly lovely."

Indeed it was. There was more than a hint of pathos in it, as there should be with all love songs, and a deceptive simplicity that made it exquisite.

"I like it better than anything I've ever written," said Jacques simply.

This was a surprising statement, as few of his compositions ever seemed to give him more than momentary joy. In a month they were usually forgotten. But his affection for this new song apparently went deeper as, in spite of all the fine music he later wrote, "The Song of Fortunio" remained his favorite.

He carried the new piece proudly to Houssaye's office for

the tryout. De Musset was already there and bowed formally
as Jacques entered. Jacques beamed back at him, though again
he had that unaccountable feeling of discomfort at the sight of
the poet.

Delaunay, the actor in question, came over to the piano to
go through the song. Jacques played the opening bars and then
Delaunay started to sing. A look of real horror crossed Offenbach's face. Abruptly he stopped and folded the music.

Delaunay's speaking-voice was a tenor, but the voice which
had just boomed through the office was a heavy bass. The whole
charm of "The Song of Fortunio" depended on the lightness and
delicacy of touch. What the unwitting Delaunay had just com-
mitted was a massacre. "The Song of Fortunio" was dead. For
a terrible moment Offenbach thought he was going to cry.

His mind flashed back to that other contretemps when he
had composed the wrong type of song for Achard. This time it
seemed even stupider to him, for he knew Delaunay very well.

Another song was eventually substituted but it was impossible to reproduce the ethereal grace of the original "Song of
Fortunio," particularly since the new song had to be composed
with the singer's bass voice in mind.

Jacques sadly laid aside the original "Song of Fortunio," positive nevertheless that at some future date it would receive its
just acclaim.

There was a curious aftermath to this whole unhappy affair.
Jacques' uncanny feeling about Musset had substantial founda-
tion. The poet was mentally ill and subject to hallucinations.
Probably he had heard the absurd rumor of Offenbach's "evil
eye." At any rate, the ill luck over the "Fortunio" song convinced
him that Offenbach was an evil man and he ostentatiously
avoided any further contact with him, giving renewed impetus
to the ridiculous allegation.

5

On the night of December 1, 1851, the Count de Morny attended the Opéra-Comique. He was always a notable figure in

his own right, well known to boulevardiers long before the advent of Louis-Napoleon. Unlike his half-brother, he had passed most of his forty years in Paris. He was an extremely handsome man, with a great deal of wit and charm, and was much sought after by his boulevard acquaintances. He was, too, exceedingly cynical and unscrupulous, but his polished manners made him the object of female as well as male attention. He himself had a great liking for pretty women, and this evening, in his usual debonair mood, he spent more time ogling an attractive brunette through his opera glasses than he did in attention to the stage.

No one watching Morny imagined that, on his specific instructions, proclamations were at that very moment being printed announcing the dissolution of Parliament and the holding of a plebiscite, while the police were equally busy arresting a number of people designated by the Elysée clique as "potentially dangerous."

In the morning Paris awoke to find these selfsame posters plastering the city and to the realization that the Prince-President had become dictator. Mainly through the clever conniving of his half-brother, Louis-Napoleon, blandly ignoring an oath taken just three years before to "regard as enemies all those who may attempt by illegal means to change the form of the established government," had taken over absolute power. The date was an auspicious one—it was both the anniversary of the Battle of Austerlitz and of the coronation of the First Napoleon.

Strangely, the First, the Great Napoleon, had once displayed the same hesitancy at grasping the reins of power. He, too, had had to be pushed into his Brumaire *coup d'état* by a brother, Lucien. And now the Third, the Little Napoleon, had to be almost kicked into taking decisive action by a brother, the strong-willed Morny.

A half-hearted attempt was made to rouse the proletariat against this new usurpation of their rights as citizens, but too many of them remembered the blood bath of 1848 to offer anything beyond token manifestations. The nearest thing to armed revolt came on December 4, but this was quickly suppressed. Several hundred people were shot on the streets that day, including a number of innocent bystanders, but from that date onward Paris seemed as unchanged as if the *coup d'état* had never taken place.

Offenbach sent a note to his sister Netta, in Cologne, whose daughter was attending boarding school on the outskirts of Paris: "Everything is quiet here, so we have just sent Julius to see little Isabelle. She is quite well and very pleased at having been present at a Revolution, although at a safe distance. We, too, are all as well as could be. I hope that Paris will live again in joy and glamour as it did before."

Jules—naturally Jacques called him "Julius" to his sister, particularly as he wrote her in German—was handy for just such errands. While Jules again was playing with one of the boulevard orchestras he continued to importune his brother for pecuniary help and dropped in frequently at the Passage Saulnier exactly at mealtime. He had no compunction about making demands on Jacques.

Herminie was confined to the apartment most of the time these days. She had given birth to their second child, another girl, whom they named "Mimi." While Offenbach had again hoped for a son he was, of course, devoted to his children. Little Berthe, the firstborn, was now a conspicuous and active member of the household and Offenbach expended a good deal of energy riding her piggy-back, playing hide-and-seek and other childish games with her.

Their home life was tranquil. Yet Offenbach did not confine himself to the strict path of rectitude. He was continually getting himself involved, sub rosa, in a succession of mild love affairs. In a country little ridden by puritanical inhibitions it would have been strange indeed if he had not. Even Herminie, had she been aware and had she then expressed herself, would have considered constancy too great a demand upon any man and particularly upon Offenbach, in view of their extremely youthful marriage and his continual association with people of the artistic world. She knew that fundamentally she possessed Jacques' unswerving devotion, and that was all, she felt, that any wife could ask. Offenbach had too much respect for her to be anything but discreet in his extramarital relationships and Herminie, engrossed in her household and children, evinced no symptoms of the jealous wife, if, indeed, she had any notion of Jacques' divagations.

Arsène Houssaye, years later in his memoirs, observed that although Offenbach was naturally cheerful he became morose with increasing frequency due to troubles attendant upon his love affairs. He suggests that Offenbach was a very active Lothario but, as Houssaye himself was continually involved with women, he perhaps could not have conceived that any man could be less so. In any case, whatever the number of inamoratas, none counted with Offenbach for more than passing fancy. He genuinely loved Herminie and any other woman was fundamentally unimportant.

Jacques' moroseness was more likely due to other causes. His position as conductor at the Théâtre Français held out little more hope for the future than the old round of playing in the salons. True, it paid him much better but, since Jacques was always susceptible to another's tale of woe, the Offenbach financial state showed little improvement.

One evening at the end of the month he returned home, looking sheepish, with a hundred and fifty francs in his pocket instead of the five hundred francs salary which he presumably drew.

"Well . . . " he stammered, and launched into a complicated story about a member of his orchestra who had a large family and illness and—well, the man really needed the money.

Herminie laughed. She would have done the same thing in the circumstances. She was equally tenderhearted. Why, just that day she had encountered a poor woman on the street and—well, she gave her a little silver piece too.

"There is only one thing to do," observed Jacques, astutely, "and that is to earn more money."

He might have added, far easier said than done. He had never let up in his efforts to sell a play to some boulevard theatre. One act was all he aspired to as yet, but it was to be an operetta, not just a play with a song or two interpolated. He had a good friend, Léon Battu, a struggling young playwright, and the two of them joined forces to work on a pastoral they called *Le Trésor de Mathurin.*

Jacques shrewdly decided to give a concert of his own once again in order to draw attention to his talent as a composer, which had certainly been submerged at the Théâtre Français. *Le Trésor de Mathurin* would be presented then for inspection—offered for sale, as it were. He secured the services of singers from the Opéra-Comique, having in mind that through them he could gain the attention of that august theatre itself. Once more it had changed directors and, he hoped, its earlier attitude concerning him.

Berlioz, if condescendingly patronizing, was still friendly to Offenbach and actually went so far as to introduce him to the influential critic, Jules Janin, whose salons Jacques began to frequent. In spite of this support, however, *Le Trésor de Mathurin* did not make the stage of the Opéra-Comique or any other playhouse.

In a gesture of bravado, Offenbach and Battu burlesqued their piece one evening at the Offenbach "at home." Jacques himself sang the leading role, which was comedy enough with his off-key bass voice. The "Fridays" were more popular than ever, with the small apartment always uncomfortably overcrowded.

The next day, when Offenbach saw Henry Mürger, at that time a widely read columnist with his gossip of the theatre world, he burbled: "My dear Mürger, I had a wonderful success last night! Everybody was enthusiastic! We had two hundred people!"

Mürger was amused at Offenbach's enthusiasm and exaggeration, but as he liked Jacques and as he always welcomed copy, he duly chronicled this "great success."

Battu and Offenbach decided that they would continue their teamwork and turn out playlets and more playlets until someone would be forced to notice them. They buoyed each other up instead of sinking into despair. Fortunately Jacques' energy was boundless. Although he remained incredibly thin, he was in good health and far removed from the peaked, weak young man of a decade back.

Meanwhile, on December 2, 1852, a year to the day after the *coup d'état*, Napoleon III was crowned Emperor. In the plebiscite of a few weeks before, seven and a half million out of the eight million voters had indicated their preference for a Second Empire. And on January 3, 1853, the new Emperor of the French was wed, with due pomp, to the beautiful Spanish Countess Eugénie de Montijo. It was universally accepted as a genuine love match, as she herself was not of royal or imperial blood.

Offenbach and Battu, discussing plans for their latest essay, agreed that Spain would make a timely setting. The plot was simply a collection of interwoven love affairs with a happy ending (all confined to one act) and they called it *Pepito*, a slight compliment to Offenbach's young brother-in-law. It also happened to be a name he liked.

This time the collaborators found reward for their perseverance. It was accepted and produced, on October 28, 1853, by the Théâtre des Variétés. In its modest manner it was successful and Jules Janin went out of his way to give it a review, at the same time taking a dig at the Opéra-Comique for its long-time coyness toward Jacques Offenbach.

Offenbach was thirty-four years old and this was his first theatre success, small though it was.

It proved a very ephemeral success. Offenbach had counted on some commissions following its appearance, but nothing came of it. A few months later he was writing his sister Julie, pitifully: "The golden future of which I have dreamed is not approaching."

This was in May, 1854, and the primary purpose of the letter was to deter Julie from paying a visit to Paris. Much as he would have liked to see her, he dared not take on the responsibility of her visit. In order to make her understand, he had to admit that he could no longer even pay for his wife's clothes, saying also that the cost of living had become very high and that he intended to emigrate to America in the autumn in the hope of making money there. The main cause of the present misery, he remarked, was "this cursed war," meaning the Crimean conflict, which was under way.

Jacques was writing music criticism for Arsène Houssaye's old paper, *L'Artiste,* in order to augment his earnings. It was also work which brought him a certain prestige and which he enjoyed, and he wrote in a lively and entertaining style. His special target was invariably anything which smacked of the pompous—music or people—as in an article appearing in January, 1855.

"The success of many of our composers," he wrote, "resembles the most fashionable ladies on the boulevards in that their crinolines are excessively luxuriant. In suitable light they look substantial enough and show pretty colors, but looked at closely, *en déshabillé* or at the piano, as the case may be, they are phantoms—phantoms inflated with wind and noise."

Perhaps there was also a bit of personal rancor against these composers who were less talented but so much more successful than himself.

The daily grind of his unrewarding conducting job at the Théâtre Français was making him bitter. He felt lost in its obscurity. Only once in recent years had he received any noteworthy attention and that was when young Prince Jerome, cousin of the Emperor and son of the onetime King of Westphalia, so much enjoyed a schottische played during an intermission that he not only insisted upon an encore but the next day sent Offenbach a magnificent diamond tie-pin, accompanied by a pleasant note, as a gesture of recognition. Jacques was quite overwhelmed with this dazzling tribute.

But he would have been happier if he could have pawned the expensive pin. Such was the mental and financial condition of Jacques Offenbach at the moment.

CHAPTER THREE

"Mozart of the Champs-Elysées"

1

In 1855 Paris was enjoying a prosperity such as it had not known in many years. There was a tremendous boom on the Bourse and money seemed plentiful everywhere. Arsène Houssaye made the enormous sum of 825,000 francs in one day's operations and advised Offenbach to better his own finances in the same fashion. Offenbach made a face. Not having the capital to gamble and being entirely at the receiving end of high prices, he continued naively to blame his fate on "this accursed war."

Actually the war in the Crimea had no noticeable effect on Paris. Even the workingman rejoiced in the good times, for Napoleon III—or his advisers—had been shrewd enough to give the first sop to the proletariat. His was a government of cheap bread, workers' holidays, and new homes for the poor. All over the city new houses were going up.

Nor was this building confined to workers' quarters. Under the direction of the brilliant Baron Haussmann, Prefect of the Seine, plans were well under way for the further beautifying of

the already beautiful city. Avenues were being widened and
buildings were being demolished, opening vistas of hitherto un-
dreamed-of grandeur. What was not obvious to the populace
was that these changes also made military operations against
any possible uprisings more feasible both through and within
the city.

The people, watching the daily improvements, viewing the
handsome new monuments being erected, gave their unstinted
allegiance to the new Emperor. Napoleon III was enjoying a
tremendous popularity. There was a festive air throughout Paris.
At Court, where the lovely Empress was setting the fashion for
the newer, fuller crinolines, there were brilliant balls and receptions. On the boulevards the cafés were jammed and the
theatres filled to standing room.

Everyone, it seemed, was enjoying prosperity except Offenbach.

Early in the year another aspiring young composer named
Hervé, tiring of the lack of encouragement he too found on all
sides, opened a small theatre of his own, Les Folies Nouvelles,
for the express purpose of assuring himself production. Jacques,
learning early about his plans, hurried to submit something of
his own to Hervé. With Jules Moinaux, who had assisted Battu
with the libretto of *Pepito*, a gorgeously nonsensical act about
a double-bass player who falls among cannibals was concocted.
It was called *Oyayaie, or the Queen of the Isles*, and Hervé,
glad to give a hand to a fellow-composer, accepted it promptly.

Jacques immediately foresaw the potentialities of Hervé's
playhouse. Also, he asked himself why he didn't do the same
thing, start a theatre of his own. As a matter of fact, the idea
was not new. He too had been considering just such a move for
a long time, but because of his incessant daily worries he had
lacked the necessary impetus. Besides, granted he could raise
the capital, it was not an easy matter to procure a theatre. All
of the established ones—and these were mostly too large for his
purpose—were leased under long-term contracts. There was, too,
the problem of getting a license to operate. Hervé, until recently orchestra conductor of the Palais-Royal, was also music

teacher of the young Empress and it was through her good offices that he had finally been granted a license.

While Offenbach was still vaguely wondering how he could achieve the same goal he learned of an ideal little theatre to rent. During that spring Baron Haussmann's plans had been pushed at an accelerated pace because the Universal Exposition was scheduled for Paris in the summer. It was being built along the Right Bank of the Seine, off the rustic Champs-Elysées. The magnificent Palace of Industry was already nearing completion. And in the very shadow of it, on the Square Marigny, stood a tiny ramshackle playhouse. It was very dilapidated but it *was* a theatre. Once it had belonged to a magician who had given shows in the wooded park, but for a long time now it had not been used. Previously its location had been too far out from the main stream of the city to be a practical choice. Now, next to the entrance of the Exposition and in proximity to a collection of smart dance pavilions and cafés under the trees, it was ideal.

Jacques rushed to make inquiries. Yes, the theatre was to be rented and there were already several applicants for it. Just two weeks before the opening date of the Exposition, on the first of May, Jacques entered his name along with twenty others.

On the same evening, when he left the Théâtre Français, he began the rounds of the cafés. First he went to the Café Cardinal, in search of backers for his enterprise; he looked in at the Café Anglais, where the well-to-do and influential were generally to be found; he dropped in later at the Brasserie des Martyrs and the Riche, where the journalists usually held forth. During the next week with his customary energy he visited most of the cafés along the boulevards in search of support for his hoped-for project.

He appealed to Prince Jerome, who had made him such a lavish gesture previously, and to the puissant Count de Morny. He even appealed to Henri de Villemessant, editor of the important daily *Figaro*, whom he actually knew only slightly. But so convincingly did he plead his case that the shrewd, hard Villemessant surprised him by not only promising to put in a word at the proper source but also, if Offenbach succeeded in getting his theatre, to give him financial backing and free publicity in his widely read paper.

Offenbach, in his enthusiasm, was proving himself an excellent salesman. Although he may have appeared to act on sudden impulse, his ideas on the type of showhouse he wanted had long been crystalized, as his intimates well knew. When he used to storm against the Opéra-Comique he would say: "The idea of gay, cheerful, witty music—music with life in it—is being forgotten! The Opéra-Comique no longer knows its own name—it isn't the home of *comic* opera. Its composers only write *grand* opera."

But his idea was not simply to take over the functions of the Opéra-Comique. He saw a modern type of comic opera—satirical music, burlesques that laughed lightly but never viciously at the idiosyncrasies of life. In short, Offenbach pointed out, the true *opéra-bouffe*—on a large scale the sort of thing on which he had founded his salon prestige. The name of his theatre would indicate that. "Les Bouffes-Parisiens" he said he would call it.

Immediately, as with anything Offenbach attempted, the lines were drawn. His friends showed an intense loyalty toward him; his enemies were savage. His onetime patron Berlioz, irritated by what he considered Offenbach's presumptuous articles in *L'Artiste*, sneered at him. Those who had connections with the Opéra-Comique automatically disparaged him. But Count de Morny, who was well disposed, put in a valuable word for him and so did Prince Jerome.

Meanwhile, on May 15, a dreary, wet day, the Universal Exposition was officially opened. Blandly ignoring the Crimean War still in progress, the Emperor dedicated the Palace of Industry as a Temple of Peace.

Yet the days passed and still no decision on the theatre was announced. Offenbach was frantic with worry. Unless the license came through soon it would be too late for the Exposition season. And nightly, after work at the Théâtre Français, he would make the rounds of the cafés again, hoping to find someone who could force the issue. Finally, on June 15, the word came. The license had been granted and Offenbach had triumphed over his twenty rivals.

Immediately he announced that the Bouffes-Parisiens would open on July 5, seeming to many an incorrigible optimist, considering the fact that the theatre had to be redecorated, really almost rebuilt, a cast and orchestra hired, authors recruited, and music composed, to say nothing of rehearsals. All that Jacques had to go on were a few notations he had made on what to do and whom to see in the wild event that he was granted the license.

But he went to work with an astounding vigor. During those next twenty days Herminie saw him only fleetingly as he interviewed someone at the apartment or came in late at night for a few hours' exhausted sleep.

From the beginning, he exhibited his innate sense of theatre. He hired a fairly extensive troupe, some of whom at least were outstanding boulevard players. For the others, he haunted the little out-of-the-way café-concerts in search of potential talent. Shrewdly, he intended to build up his reputation in part through the creation of his own stars. Such a choice was Berthelier, a tenor from a café-concert, to whom Offenbach entrusted a leading role in his first production.

Many of Offenbach's friends warned him that he was hiring too large a company for his purpose, as his license permitted him only three actors on the stage at a time. This bizarre practice of issuing theatre licenses which at the same time limited the number of players on the stage antedated the Empire by many years. The original reasons for it were lost in obscurity but the ruling remained unchanged. Offenbach, as a matter of fact, had been luckier than Hervé whose permit allowed only *two* actors on the stage at a time. Jacques' response to his friends' criticism was that he intended a frequent change of bill of three or four one-act operettas and that he did not propose to have his players double throughout the evening. He remarked that an audience liked variety in its actors as well as in its plays.

One of the people on whom Jacques relied greatly for advice was his old mentor and teacher, Fromental Halévy. Busy man that Halévy was, he always had time to encourage his protégés of whom Offenbach was only one of many. One day, not long before the scheduled opening, Jacques burst into his study. Fromental Halévy looked up smiling from his desk and indicated a seat but Jacques, as was often the case, was too fidgety to sit down.

"Something terrible has happened, *cher maître*," he said, walking about agitatedly. "The whole show is ruined! But I don't know what to do about it."

Jacques was so excited that it took a few minutes before Halévy understood the situation. Jacques, it seemed, had enlisted the services of a rather prominent playwright, Lambert Thiboust, to write a prologue for the opening. Now, at this late hour, he had discovered that Thiboust had reneged on the assignment.

"It's too late to find anyone else. Besides, whom could I get? Battu and Moinaux are already busy on other acts. You know Méry? He let me down first. Maybe they all want me to fail."

Halévy, sympathetic, pondered for a moment. "Why don't you get my nephew?" he said at last.

"Who?" asked Offenbach, nervously playing a tattoo with his fingers on the chair arm.

"Ludovic Halévy." And noting Jacques' puzzled look, he explained further. "He is actually a clerk in a Government office, but he wants to do plays. He has talent too—I've seen some of his work. None of it's been produced. He's only twenty-two and you know as well as anyone how hard it is to make headway in today's theatre."

Jacques nodded, doubtfully.

"But the boy knows the technique of playwriting. He was brought up on it. His father, my brother, is Léon Halévy."

At this last remark, Jacques perceptibly brightened. Léon Halévy was known on the boulevards.

"What is more," continued the older man, "Ludovic inclines toward the kind of thing you want—comedy, satire."

"When could I see him?" demanded Offenbach, jumping to his feet.

Fromental Halévy glanced at his clock.

"Go to his home from here. He is likely to be there. Incidentally," he added with a twinkle in his eyes, "Ludovic has a special distinction. He was actually born in the Institut de France! His mother's father, you see, was its architect and was allowed to have his own apartment in the building. At least that guarantees his artistic background."

Jacques laughed, but his mind was already concentrating on the interview with young Halévy. Thanking the older man, he hurried off and down the stairs.

2

Offenbach's first impression of Ludovic Halévy was that he appeared more mature than his twenty-two years indicated. He was a tall, nice-looking young man with chiseled features, dark eyes and a fledgling beard. His manner was quiet and courteous, but it was obvious that he was flattered when he learned the reason for Offenbach's call. Offenbach himself took an instant liking to him.

Quickly Jacques explained the urgency of his need, and when young Halévy assured him that he could be relied upon, he wasted no time.

"Fine," he said briskly. "Then please start right away. Just a little one-act play with songs, about anything you like. Only —there's just one little thing. You must put in a hundred lines I've got here. They should go right in the middle in the place of honor."

Offenbach fished in his pocket for a piece of paper.

Young Halévy, although this was going to constrict him somewhat, agreed amiably.

Handing him the sheet of paper, Jacques explained that the lines had been written by a friend of his and that they were to be spoken by a character representing Fantasy.

"One of your characters must be called Fantasy. You don't mind, do you?"

"Not at all, not at all," young Halévy assured him.

"You see," Jacques explained in his usual candid manner, "when Méry had the job his courage failed him, so I asked Lambert Thiboust, and then he failed me. Now you will replace Thiboust."

"With pleasure," answered Halévy, still with equanimity.

Beaming, Jacques reached for his hat. Everything seemed settled. Then suddenly he remembered something else.

"There's just one more thing," he said, and explained that Thiboust, even though he had failed him, had written one song for which he, Offenbach, had already done the music. "The song was written with Bilboquet in mind." (Bilboquet was a semiclassic character from an old play, *Les Saltimbanques.*)

"Very well," said Halevy. "I like Bilboquet very much."

"As for the third character . . ." Jacques went on. "Oh, yes, I forgot to tell you, I'm allowed to put on plays with only three characters. . . ."

"So there'll be one character I'll have to create myself," finished young Halévy cheerfully.

Jacques smiled disarmingly.

"Create . . . well, alas, I must explain the situation. The part of Fantasy will be played by Mlle Mace and Bilboquet will be played by a first-class provincial actor whom I have just engaged. . . . Well, the third character will be played by Derudder, who is also a member of my troupe. . . . Derudder, the famous mime! So of course his role must be completely silent. By the way, Derudder is the best Polichinelle that can possibly be imagined! You won't mind making him Polichinelle, will you?"

By this time any high hopes young Halévy might have entertained were definitely doused but, if less enthusiastically, he once more agreed. And the one-acter, when he produced it and in spite of the constraints put upon him, revealed an originality which delighted Offenbach.

Thus began a collaboration which was to endure to the end of Offenbach's life.

3

Notwithstanding the various difficulties, Offenbach opened the Bouffes-Parisiens on July 5, 1855, exactly the date he had said he would. The opening night was in reality the dress rehearsal for stockholders, authors and friends. Jacques' father-in-law, Mr. Mitchell, was there, several journalists, and, of course, Henri de Villemessant. Villemessant had kept his word and *Figaro* had not only carried little notes on the impending opening but that very day had burst forth with a huge, extravagant display advertisement.

Ludovic Halévy's prologue, *Come In, Ladies and Gentlemen,* set the mood excellently. It was light and clever and amusing and exactly right as an "opener." The next act, *A Sleepless Night,* was equally well received. Following this came a pantomime. Pantomimes were all the vogue in Paris and this one, to Offenbach's inimitable music, received an ovation. It was a burlesque of Rossini's *The Barber of Seville,* entitled *Harlequin the Barber.*

If Offenbach ever had any serious misgivings about his show —which was doubtful—he was soon reassured. He was hopping about all over the place—backstage giving final instructions and later speeding to the front of the theatre to watch—but wherever he was, he could hear the applause and laughter of the audience.

It was the last act, in which Berthelier was starred, which was his own favorite, however. It was called *The Two Blind Men* and poked lighthearted fun at two professional mendicants who shammed blindness for sympathy. He had done a lively bolero and waltz for them to sing as they encountered each other on a bridge.

When the curtain rose, however, he noted an alarming change in the audience's reactions. There was silence instead of the

laughter he had counted on and an uneasy coughing and rest-
lessness. While he considered *The Two Blind Men* a good-
humored satire on professional beggars infesting the Paris streets,
he realized that the audience was shocked.

After the curtain went down his friends lost no time in telling him how they felt. They were seriously worried that Jacques
would ruin himself at the start with such an act. Henri de Villemessant urged him strongly to drop it. So did Mr. Mitchell.
Even young Halévy protested that the subject was dangerous.

But Offenbach refused to withdraw the act. Stubbornly he
insisted that as it was simply burlesquing sham, there was nothing to be shocked about. His instinct told him his friends were
unduly alarmed and he always trusted his intuition. In the face
of an avalanche of appeals, he stoutly insisted that the show
must go on as it stood.

Nevertheless, the following night he was uneasy. And he
knew the members of his company were exceptionally nervous,
wondering too about the reception of *The Two Blind Men*
by a more public audience. The Prologue and the first act were
greeted as gratifyingly as on the previous evening. The Pantomime also had an enthusiastic reception. But *The Two Blind
Men* was the last on the program and Jacques waited tensely.

As the curtain went up on the two beggars there was a momentary silence. Then, at the first exchange of dialogue, someone began to laugh. The laugh was contagious and quickly
spread and before the act was half over the hilarity of the audience almost drowned out the lines.

Jacques, in the wings, breathed a sigh of relief and his face
puckered in a grin. His intuition had been right!

The Bouffes-Parisiens was a hit from the beginning and of
all the acts perhaps *The Two Blind Men* was the most outstanding. While the repertoire was changed frequently that
particular act seemed destined to remain on the bill forever.
People returned again and again, anxious to see the hilarious
little satire once more. Before it was finally taken off the program it had been performed over four hundred times.

It attested to Offenbach's theatrical genius that, in spite of the discomfort at the little theatre on the Square Marigny, the house was always sold out. The theatre foyer, for instance, was simply an outdoor terrace open to the rain. Inside, the rows of seats were graded so steeply to the boxes in back that a cartoon of the period, showing a scaffolding of heads and squeezed bodies, was captioned: "Strategy of young Offenbach, who makes a theatre from a ladder." As at Offenbach's "at homes," the crinolines of the ladies, grown fashionably wider, only aggravated the crowding. Herminie, coming to see the show one evening, found that there was not even a seat for her and had to be content with a place on the steps.

At last Jacques had attained the success of which he had so long dreamed. His theatre was the talk of Paris and his music was the rage of the café-concerts and music-halls. But he himself was in such a dizzy whirl that he still only vaguely comprehended the enviable position he was achieving for himself. He did not dare give up his job at the Théâtre-Français until his financial situation was resolved and so, throughout that hectic summer, he continued to rehearse the old State Theatre's orchestra, as well as carry out his manifold duties at the Bouffes-Parisiens. He busied himself with every aspect of his playhouse, being his own business manager and stage director, as well as supervising the writing of his plays and composing the music.

As young Halévy learned early, no act was written in which Offenbach's ideas were not injected. Halévy, obviously of an easy-going disposition, far from harboring resentment at Offenbach's constant demands concerning his librettos, respected his shrewd judgment. Offenbach, on his part, had become exceedingly attached to the young man, calling him "Ludo" and "tutoying" him in the intimate fashion of the French language.

Certainly the entire success of the Bouffes-Parisiens was due to Jacques' amazing flair for everything concerning the stage. It was he, for instance, who suggested the timeliness of the comedy burlesquing Englishmen, for the English tourists overran Paris that summer of the Exposition. So the two principal characters in *A Summer Night's Dream* were visiting Englishmen who kept saying "Very good!" and "Quite!" and who sang a

panegyric about Parisian life. He saw to it that the Bouffes-
Parisiens remained completely Parisian, but its appeal was international rather than local.

Yet for all the clever ideas and dialogues the phenomenal
success of the Bouffes-Parisiens would not have been possible
without Offenbach's delightful original music. He facilely poured
out song hit after song hit. Nowadays, he often hired a carriage,
instead of walking, to save time on his numerous pilgrimages
about town. And he would dash off a little song, later to be
played all over Paris, while being driven to or from the theatre.

Very shortly after the opening, Offenbach, peering through
the curtain before the performance one night, saw an enormous
and somewhat familiar figure seated in the audience. It was
none other than the famed composer Giaccomo Meyerbeer. Offenbach was extremely excited and from time to time during
the performance he glanced out from the wings to see the great
man's reactions. To his joy he saw the huge, elderly Meyerbeer
shaking with laughter. As a matter of courtesy Offenbach went
out to visit the distinguished composer during an intermission
and was further reassured.

"It is delightful! Delightful!" Meyerbeer exclaimed. "And
your music—it has all the simplicity and charm of the eighteenth
century!"

At the next change of bill Offenbach again noted Meyerbeer
in the audience. Soon it was evident that Meyerbeer had become a regular "first nighter" and Offenbach thereupon ordered
the box office always to reserve him the best loge directly opposite the stage on opening nights. He also unfailingly visited
him sometime during the evening. He and Meyerbeer became
good, if not intimate, friends.

But it was Rossini who gave him his greatest thrill. The
composer of *William Tell* and *The Barber of Seville* was a shyer,
a far more retiring person than his contemporary Meyerbeer.
Nor was he as ardent a theatregoer, but he came to the Bouffes-
Parisiens regularly and found it quite as delightful as did
Meyerbeer. He too perceived in the gay, lilting tunes the potential genius of Offenbach and, noting the inspirational source of

their pure melodies, he christened Offenbach the "Mozart of the Champs-Elysées."

For once Offenbach was overwhelmed.

"Did you hear?" he asked his friends. "Rossini called me the Mozart of the Champs-Elysées!"

The appellation stuck. It was extravagant flattery but at the same time curiously apt. There was, even in the most ordinary, unpretentious tunes of Offenbach, the classic simplicity of harmony, the felicity of melody leading into melody, so characteristic of his eighteenth-century idol.

No compliment that Offenbach ever received brought him such pleasure as this comparison of Rossini's with the "Divine Mozart." It was only then that he began to appreciate the esteem in which he was now held.

4

Offenbach was used to people breaking in on him when he was at work. In fact, he was so stimulated by people, by excitement, by the general hurly-burly attendant upon theatre production, that he could actually think up new melodies or stage situations while at the same time arguing with a librettist or even granting an audition to a new singer. Yet the manifold demands imposed upon him by the Bouffes-Parisiens were beginning to jangle his nerves.

One August afternoon he was in a rather ungracious mood when a note was brought in to him while he was working in his apartment. It was from the singer, Berthelier, and asked Offenbach to give an audition to a young woman named Hortense Schneider. When he was told that the girl had brought the letter herself and was waiting in the foyer, he made no attempt to hide his annoyance. He didn't see why he should be pestered at home, why she shouldn't apply at the theatre like any other aspirant.

But, as so often was the case with him, just giving vent volubly to his irritation soon dispelled it. Besides, he remembered his own first plea for an audition, that time far back when Maître

Cherubini had finally given him a hearing. Grudgingly, he agreed to see the young woman.

A slim girl in her early twenties, with red-gold hair, was ushered in. She looked frail, even ill, although Offenbach did register that she had the fine full bosom of a vocalist. Just as Cherubini had behaved so long ago, Offenbach motioned the aspirant to a music-stand and handed her a sheet of music from a forthcoming act, *The Violinist*. While the actual music was not so difficult, it demanded clever manipulation to establish the innuendoes in its words. Offenbach struck a few notes on the piano and bluntly said: "Well, go ahead, sing."

The girl was unintimidated. After all, she had long been fighting an uphill battle for recognition. Grossly underpaid in a provincial troupe in her native town of Bordeaux, forced to augment her meager earnings by taking a lover, saddled with a child to support, the mere gruffness of a composer-producer was just another hurdle to be taken. As calmly and confidently as Offenbach himself had performed at the bored command of Cherubini, the young woman tackled the tricky nuances of the song.

Her voice was light but had a soft girlish quality plus a curiously metallic tone. Chiefly, she had the gift, which the theatre-wise mind of Offenbach quickly grasped, of knowing how to put over a song. He saw that she could handle the most daring and risqué piece while giving an audience the impression of an angelic, an ethereal presence.

After a few bars, Offenbach shut the piano with a violent bang and shouted: "Enough! Do you intend to go on with vocal studies?"

Somewhat taken aback, the girl nervously replied that she had hoped to, but that the lack of funds was holding her up.

"Miserable wretch!" Offenbach yelled in his execrable French. "If you dare to take it into your head to do anything so monstrous, I shall tear up your contract! Because you have a contract. Yes, I'm engaging you at two hundred francs a month. Understand?"

The young woman looked at him wide-eyed and, as her expression changed from astonishment to a full comprehension of her good fortune, two roguish dimples appeared in her cheeks. In response, Offenbach's sharp, disconcerting gaze softened to a mischievous twinkle and he began to chuckle. Hortense Schneider really was a most enchanting young lady. Motioning her to a seat beside his desk, he forgot the exigencies which had faced him before her arrival in the pleasant flirtatiousness of the moment.

On that afternoon a friendship, not altogether platonic in its inception, was cemented. Their affair, as such, was short-lived but from it grew an attachment which, despite emotional storm and stress, was to last until Offenbach's death.

5

Offenbach had already given evidence that he was a maker of theatre stars. Young Berthelier, hitherto unknown, had come to fame in *The Two Blind Men,* and in the years to come was to be one of the most sought-after actors on the boulevards. There were others in the Bouffes company who were to win top billing, but Hortense Schneider was Offenbach's first, and greatest, feminine star.

Jacques was enchanted with her. She was difficult and pouted when she couldn't get her way, but she seemed like a little girl who innocently hadn't yet learned better. Only twenty-two, she was already hardened by life and every move she made was carefully calculated.

Hortense Schneider was not in the least in love with Offenbach, in the strict sense of the term, but she had the greatest respect and admiration for him which grew to an honest, deep affection. She confided to him that she disliked her name of Hortense and that her middle name was Catherine. He told her, flatly, that Hortense would look much better in the billing, but from that time on he himself called her "Cath." She was strangely affected by this little thoughtfulness on Jacques' part and, in a curiously sentimental way, allowed no one else ever to call her "Cath," reserving that as Jacques' special privilege.

Also, Hortense Schneider had the good sense, in this case, to understand that their affair had to be strictly sub rosa and that in no circumstances was it ever to reach the ears of Herminie, to whom she knew Jacques was really devoted. There is no record that Herminie was ever aware of this extramarital relationship on her husband's part. For that matter, it was such a well-guarded secret that even Jacques' enemies and the ubiquitous café gossips had little to go on. Jacques and "Cath" took pains to see that there was not even evidence enough to satisfy a boulevard columnist.

Jacques never did allow any personal attachment to conflict with his professional judgment. He felt that Hortense Schneider was a gifted actress and singer; he groomed her carefully for her debut and was convinced that she would bring new laurels to the Bouffes. When, on August 31, *The Violinist* was presented, he knew he had again been right. Hortense Schneider, with her ethereal beauty and the indefinable charm of her singing, was made. As one critic summed it up afterward: "Her singing is in the best of taste. She launches phrases with a subtle, artful smile. . . . She is pretty as an angel."

Hortense Schneider was scarcely the sort of person to remain unaffected by fame. Seeing her name illumined in the gaslight of the theatre entrance, receiving mash notes and flowers in her dressing room, bit by bit she began to display a little more temperament, growing more obstinate and pouting when she couldn't have her way. Nevertheless, she was fully aware of how much she owed to Offenbach and, though they frequently quarreled, she was invariably the first to make up. Their affair, such as it was, was built on shaky foundations, but the honest depths of their friendship proved able to withstand the test of time.

6

In September Offenbach was faced with a new problem. Now that the success of the Bouffes was indisputable he had to find permanent housing for his revue. The playhouse on the Square Marigny was amusing and quaint but it was not equipped for winter weather. Besides, the wooded Champs-Elysées was only popular in the summer. Offenbach simply had to have quarters near the boulevards.

It was a tribute to the drawing power of the Bouffes that crowds still thronged there nightly, in spite of the autumn chill. The box-office receipts frequently topped twelve hundred francs in one evening and, although the costs had not yet been fully met, there was every expectation that the company would be completely solvent in a short while. Offenbach felt so sanguine that at last he was able to abandon his job with the Théâtre-Français and devote his entire energies to the Bouffes. He had long wanted to take this step, but he was cannily careful not to make the break irrevocable. If anything, at the moment unforeseen, did happen to the Bouffes, he wanted some sort of decent living in the background to return to.

In his letter of resignation, Offenbach managed to impart some of the engaging charm he usually displayed in his personal contacts. He assured the Directors of the Théâtre-Français that if they ever needed his services, he would be most happy to assist them again as conductor, composer, or in any capacity commensurate with his capabilities.

In his search for winter quarters Offenbach was assisted by his whole entourage—actors, friends, librettists, journalists. Yet October came and went, November arrived and the Exposition was over, and still no theatre had been found. People braved the now almost frigid weather, but patently the little playhouse on the Square Marigny would soon be forced to close. Jacques made appeals everywhere, *Figaro* and other papers carried notices; all to no avail. A contemporary cartoon showed Offenbach, with a cello under one arm (he was still widely known as a cellist and performed several times on the Bouffes stage) and the Square Marigny theatre under the other, bustling off in search of winter quarters.

Finally one day in November his perseverance was rewarded. Not only did he learn of an empty playhouse, but it was just the type of theatre he desired. It was on the Passage Choiseul, an excellent location not far from the Boulevard des Italiens, and it was owned and run by a man named Charles Comte. Comte's father, a onetime King's Physician, had oddly also been a ventriloquist and had founded the small theatre for children and left it as an inheritance for his son. The son was anxious to rent it. Like the Square Marigny playhouse, it needed a complete renovation but Comte, who was of course acquainted with the Bouffes-Parisiens, was willing to put his own money in as a partner in Jacques' venture.

During the next month Jacques worked with almost the same intensity he had put into the original opening of the Bouffes the past June. The winter quarters on the Passage Choiseul somehow assured him of the permanency of his enterprise. In contrast to the original opening he now had quite a repertoire of acts from which to draw and thus could confine most of his attention to the actual rehabilitation of his new theatre. Halévy, however, wrote one new act, *Ba-ta-clan*, for the inauguration of the winter quarters.

When it opened its doors on December 29, Giaccomo Meyerbeer was seated as usual in one of the best boxes and laughed as uproariously and delightedly as ever. This was especially gratifying to Offenbach, as *Ba-ta-clan* poked amiable fun at grand opera, one parody in particular being on Meyerbeer's own work *Les Huguenots*. Whole passages from *Les Huguenots* were interwoven in Jacques' music. The writing of it had been made particularly easy for him as, by going through his old files, he had unearthed the popularization of that opera which he had done years before for Jullien at the Jardin Turc. Jacques was finding many of his old scores useful for the Bouffes, such as the comic music burlesquing gossips, barnyard noises, etc., which he had performed during his salon days. In *Ba-ta-clan* he had songs bearing such entertaining titles as *La puce qui pense (The Flea Who Thinks)* and *Le navet partagé (The Divided Turnip)*.

Meyerbeer was not alone in his enjoyment of "Ba-ta-clan." Jules Janin, generally very olympian in his attitude, wrote to Jacques that people "laughed, clapped and shouted as at a miracle." Night after night people packed the playhouse on the

Passage Choiseul, just as they had crowded into the summer theatre on the Square Marigny. When, early in the new year, a new café was opened on the nearby boulevard, it was fittingly called "Ba-ta-clan." Offenbach felt that he had reached the very pinnacle of boulevard fame.

But in January, during the Peace Conference in Paris terminating the Crimean War, Offenbach received attention from a different source. Word of the Bouffes-Parisiens' popularity had filtered through the portals of the Tuileries and Their Majesties, curious as any ordinary subjects to see Offenbach's revue, decided on a command performance for the entertainment of the delegates. They requested particularly that *The Two Blind Men* be presented.

This caused the two principal actors—Berthelier and a veteran of the stage named Pradeau—a bad case of nerves. They envisaged Their Majesties shocked as the first audience had been seven months ago and they grew more and more terrified as the hour of the performance drew near.

Coming on the stage that evening they immediately noted the Emperor and Empress solemnly seated in the front row, with the Grand Chamberlain hovering close by. Fortunately, as they began their act they automatically forgot their audience and by the time they sang their first song both Berthelier and Pradeau had completely regained their aplomb. But as they ended the song they both became aware that the Grand Chamberlain had his arm raised and was signaling them energetically. They stared at him in horror. Plainly their worst fears were realized. Their nightmare had come true.

The two unhappy actors stared at each other. Then Pradeau, the more seasoned of the two, was seized with uncontrollable panic. As the Grand Chamberlain continued to make signs, Pradeau turned and ran off stage. Berthelier, overcome at being left alone, fled after him.

Backstage, the Grand Chamberlain hastily joined them.

"What in the world happened?" he demanded.

Berthelier and Pradeau explained. The Grand Chamberlain looked at them with astonishment. "Oh no!" he cried. "I was signaling for you to *repeat* the song. The Empress adores it!"

Abashed, the two actors returned to the stage and repeated their performance from the beginning. This time they dared glance at the audience and the Empress' smile along with the Emperor's audible chuckles assured them their fears had been groundless. A few days later Jacques, who had not been present at the performance, received a testimonial of Their Majesties' enjoyment in the form of a bronze plaque.

Both the Emperor and the Empress became ardent Offenbach fans. While Offenbach neither aspired to, nor ever became a part of, Court circles, to many of the Tuileries' illustrious visitors his music was synonymous with the gaiety of the regime. Many times members of the Bouffes gave command performances and no ball was ever complete without an irresistible Offenbach waltz or polka.

7

June had come again, balmy ethereal June when Paris, like a flower itself, seems to burst into bloom. The gentlemen, their topcoats doffed and light-colored *melons* or *cylindres* replacing the black stovepipe hats of winter, and the ladies, substituting light shawls for their fur-trimmed mantles and donning dresses of bright summer hues, again strolled through the parks and along the newly widened tree-lined boulevards. On the Champs-Elysées the horse chestnuts replaced their early bloom with the full foliage of summer and beneath them the café tables were laid out and the strains of violins playing the latest dances could be heard. And on the Square Marigny the Bouffes-Parisiens had returned to its summer quarters. It was June 12 and *Les Dragées de Baptême,* in honor of the recent birth of the Prince Imperial, and *Watteau's Shepherds* inaugurated the new season. The music credits were signed "Lange" but to the habitués of the Bouffes this was merely a nom de plume for Offenbach.

It was also lacking only a few days of the first anniversary of the Bouffes-Parisiens itself. Jacques totaled up the year's receipts. His venture had taken in exactly 334,189 francs and 35 centimes. In the France of the Second Empire this was an astonishing sum, although naturally the expenses of the first year were not yet cleared. But any businessman would have seen an optimistic gamble for the future. Jacques felt that to continue his prosperous venture he must not stint.

New acts had to be introduced at frequent intervals to give variety to the bill. During the winter season at the Passage Choiseul, outside of *Ba-ta-clan* Jacques had introduced three new acts, one of which, *Tromb-al-Kazar*, again brought Hortense Schneider to prominence. The fourth, and least expensive piece, was a revival of *Pepito*, Jacques' first minor hit of some years back.

Jacques had written the music for every single one of his presentations until, in April, he had produced *Violet's Puppets*. This, another vehicle for Schneider, was by Adolph Adam, the respected and important composer whom Offenbach had wheedled away from the Opéra-Comique. Jacques' pride in this triumph was shattered when, just before the debut of *Violet's Puppets*, Adam suddenly died. Adolph Adam was a much-liked person and Jacques remembered with particular affection when Adam had commissioned him to write for his Théâtre-Lyrique, just before the 1848 Revolution. In spite of these sad auspices, both *Violet's Puppets* and Hortense Schneider enjoyed great popularity.

During the summer of 1856 four more acts were added to the repertoire, interspersed with such outstanding hits of the previous year as *The Two Blind Men* and *The Violinist*.

In July, Offenbach, with his marked flair for publicity, launched a contest. Ludovic Halévy and Léon Battu collaborated on a one-act libretto, *Dr. Miracle,* and a prize was offered of twelve hundred francs, a gold medal and guarantee of production the following winter on the Passage Choiseul for the winning composer of its music. The only restriction on contestants was that none should ever have had anything accepted by the Opéra or Opéra-Comique.

Jacques felt that this would confine the contest to amateurs and, despite his natural interest in the publicity value, he sincerely wanted to help an aspiring young composer and perhaps spare him the years of heart-rending struggle which he, Offenbach, had suffered. He had founded the Bouffes-Parisiens among other reasons because "I felt sure there was something that could be done by the young musicians who, like myself, were kept waiting in idleness outside the portals of the lyric theatre." Nor did he ever forget this noble impulse. He was always receptive to the talents of newcomers, whether musicians, authors or actors.

Fromental Halévy encouraged this contest and he, along with Gounod and Eugène Scribe, the librettist of such fine operas as *La Juive, Les Huguenots,* and *Le Prophète,* acted as the jury. Conservatory students and working musicians took fresh hope from this competition and when the closing date arrived there were seventy-eight entrants.

The decision was a difficult one for the judges. Finally, after slowly eliminating seventy-six out of the seventy-eight, they recommended that the prize be divided between the two final contestants. One of the young men was Charles Lecocq, destined in later years to be Offenbach's rival on the boulevards, and the other an eighteen-year-old boy, Georges Bizet, the future renowned composer of *Carmen* and other operas. Georges Bizet was, as Offenbach once had been, a pupil of Halévy's.

Secretly, Offenbach inclined toward Bizet's score but, true to his word, produced both versions of *Dr. Miracle* the following winter. Neither one received more than passing attention. Lecocq unsportingly blamed his own failure on the division of honors but Bizet was thrilled at even this minor attention. Perhaps Offenbach's personal interest in Bizet also assuaged what disappointment that young man might otherwise have felt. Jacques, whose friends covered every age group, took Bizet into his home where he was soon included among the "intimates."

Offenbach was wont to describe his own music as *le genre gai et primitif.* He considered himself in the eighteenth-century tradition, believing that tunes should be clear-cut and easily remembered. Explaining his theories in regard to the Bouffes-

Parisiens, he wrote in an article in *L'Artiste:* "In an operetta which lasts only three quarters of an hour, in which only three characters are allowed and an orchestra of at most thirty musicians is employed, one must have ideas and melodies that are genuine and easily grasped." And with justifiable conceit, he added: "It is also worthy of note that with a small orchestra—such as incidentally sufficed for Mozart and Cimarosa—it is very difficult to cover up mistakes and ineptitudes which an orchestra of eighty players can gloss over without too much trouble."

It was Offenbach's realization of Bizet's grasp of pure harmony, his understanding of composition, which had first professionally interested him in that youth.

As for Offenbach himself, he was irked by the limitations which his theatre license forced upon him. He had sufficiently proved his musical thesis and longed to throw off the imposed restraints. While the Bouffes-Parisiens continued to play to packed houses, his theatrical sense told him that eventually he would have to expand on the sort of thing he was doing or that interest would fall off.

He felt that it would be stupid to enlarge the orchestra until the actual operettas were permitted a fuller complement of players. Already he had managed to expand to four players. Every act which was produced had first to be passed by the Censor and, by the simple ruse of slipping in an odd character with just a line or two, one act had gone through the Censor's hands unnoticed. This having been achieved once, that functionary apparently decided to ignore this slip in the future as well.

Everyone knew that Offenbach was in good standing with the authorities. Count de Morny's friendship for him, plus the command performances at the Tuileries, served him in good stead. The Minister who was the Censor was also well disposed toward him. So, when back at the Passage Choiseul the following winter, Offenbach decided to put on *Croquefer, or the Last of the Paladins* with a cast of five, no one anticipated any trouble. So sanguine were they that the play was in rehearsal before the script was sent off to the Censor. Then, to their horror, just two days before the scheduled opening, the Censor refused permission.

Everybody was terribly upset and Offenbach's temper was frightful. The actors were used to his sudden bursts of anger during rehearsal, which always passed off quickly, but this time, for a whole day, they considered themselves lucky to escape from him.

The next day, however, Offenbach was smiling again. He had worked out a solution. There was, Jacques recalled, no limitation on supernumeraries. Therefore all one had to do was to find reasonable excuse for the silence of one character. He blandly ordered that "Mousse-à-Mort," the designated character, should have his tongue pulled out by the Saracen, causing him to be mute!

When *Croquefer* opened that night the Censor, Monsieur Fould, was seated in the audience. Just as he strongly suspected that Offenbach was about to defy him, the Saracen made the gesture of cutting off "Mousse-à-Mort's" tongue.

The audience, sensing the trick, shook with laughter. For a brief moment, Monsieur Fould stared. Then, knowing the joke was on him, he guffawed.

Offenbach had won—at least insofar as *Croquefer* was concerned—but he also knew he was as far as ever from attaining his goal of a full-sized production.

8

MY DEAR FRIEND,

You know that every Friday we play the fool at my place, 11 rue Lafitte; it only depends on you to make the cast of characters complete. Friday week, the 20th of the month, no one will be admitted except in carnival costume. You wouldn't have the heart to fail us, so let us count on you.

Always your

JACQUES OFFENBACH

Jacques paused and looked around contentedly. He was quite pleased with the new apartment. Here was space, not like the crowded little flat on the Passage Saulnier. Here he had his study where he could work in peace, alone, instead of in the living room, surrounded by all the family. There was room enough in this apartment for the children—they now had three, all girls, and another child expected in a few months. Maybe, he thought, this one will be a boy. Of course, he'd say nothing to Herminie—she knew, in any case—but how he longed for a son and heir! Still, the girls were sweet. He wouldn't trade them for anybody's children, boys or girls.

Suddenly forgetting his satisfaction of a moment before in his isolated study, he called out: "Why is everything so quiet? You'd think there was a funeral in the house. Where are the children?"

From down the hall came Herminie's voice. "We thought you didn't want to be disturbed."

"I can't imagine where you got that idea," he said shortly.

In answer came a giggle outside the door and six-year-old Mimi poked her head around. Her eyes twinkled mischievously and Offenbach, spying her, began to laugh. He did not admit to favorites but he was always completely taken in by Mimi's liveliness and pranks. People said she was most like him, both temperamentally and physically. He inclined to that summing up himself.

Marching up to her father, Mimi now clambered up on his chair and began to pull his hair. Behind her came the older and more solemn Berthe, followed by gentle little Pepita. Mimi climbed down from her perch and started a tussle with Pepita. Berthe attempted to pull them apart. In no time, the study echoed to squeals and shrieks as the three little girls wrestled with each other. Offenbach, tranquil and no longer lonesome, turned back to his correspondence.

He folded the recently finished note and addressed it to that extraordinary fellow, Nadar. Nadar was one of Henry Mürger's old Bohemian group, a close friend of Baudelaire and of the painter, Gustave Courbet, too. He was an excellent journalist and caricaturist, as well as being skilled in the new craft of photography. Recently he'd become interested in balloons and, so Offenbach had heard, was planning to make an ascent so that he could take the first photograph of Paris from the clouds. One never knew what he'd be delving into next. At any rate, he was a very entertaining fellow and would be an asset at their "at home."

Sealing the envelope, Jacques hurriedly scribbled several other informal invitations—to Gustave Doré, the artist, to Edouard Detaille, also a painter, and reminders to Villemessant and one or two journalist friends. He checked over the list of the invited. He could count on Etienne Trefeu, a young librettist who had become a close associate at the Bouffes. Halévy he would remind at the theatre, also Comte.

Quickly scrawling a few more notes, he again went over the list and decided everyone was accounted for. After all, it was impossible to take care of all his friends at any one party. The following Friday there would be an influx of others. But it was nice to have ample space for a change in which to hold the parties. And Offenbach gazed out the door in the direction of the spacious drawing room.

He was brought back to his immediate surroundings by the noise of the children, who were engrossed in some intricate game understood only by themselves. Jacques looked around his study. Yes, he was beginning to feel at home in this room. At first it had seemed cold and bare, but now the pictures were up and the *bric-à-brac* in place, it was cozy. On the wall over the piano was a picture of his father. Opposite was a recent photograph of himself by Nadar, inscribed with characteristic comedy, "To his own best friend, Jacques Offenbach." Music scores were stacked on top of the piano as well as on the tabouret across the room. These gave him a feeling of being settled too.

Oblivious of the noise of the girls, he pushed aside the finished letters, picked up a half-worked score from the piano and settled down to orchestrate. As his writing table was beside the piano, he occasionally reached out with his left hand to try a chord, his right hand all the while gliding over the page marking down the minuscule and all but indecipherable music notes.

Peace reigned in the Offenbach household.

9

Friday evening, February 20, 1857, was the first meeting of "The Mutual Assistance Society against Boredom" to be held at the new address. This was Offenbach's appellation for the Friday sessions and it had quickly been adopted by his intimates.

The amazing thing about the Offenbach parties was that, although the entertainment to a great extent was planned in advance, there nevertheless remained an air of spontaneity. Each party was dedicated to some "significant" idea and the guests were expected to add their own inspirations to it. Often Offenbach made himself the butt of the comedy, as on the occasion when he announced that the evening would be given over to "Exercises of Strength and Ability in the Offenbach Struggle with the Difficulties of French Pronunciation." He had to support a lot of teasing that night.

The February 20th party was dedicated to "The End of the World." One of those ubiquitous crackbrained religious groups had recently predicted that the world would end shortly and Offenbach had stated his purpose of giving his friends a pleasant memory to take away of their last days on earth.

The costumes were many and varied, but scarcely angelic. Jacques himself was garbed as a *garde champêtre*. Nadar and young Georges Bizet came as babies, Villemessant as a strangely Gallic-looking American Indian, while Gustave Doré scored a triumph, not only in his masquerade as an acrobat, but by entering the apartment walking on his hands.

During the evening a short play, the brainchild of Nadar and a couple of other guests, was given under the title of *The Foundling, or the Taking of Castelnaudary,* after which Offenbach—who rarely played any instrument nowadays—performed his "Polka des Mirlitons," to which Messieurs Léo Delibes, Léon

Battu and Ludovic Halévy gave their own original interpretations of the dance.

Around midnight, just as had been the custom at the Passage Saulnier, the guests, men and women, set up card tables and went out to raid the kitchen.

It was unanimously agreed that the "end of the world" had been joyously celebrated, but it was also decided that a solemn announcement should be made. This was to the effect that, although the end of the universe was "coming," it had been postponed *sine die.*

10

The following morning Jacques was at his desk as usual, going over the list of the previous night's guests. He really had no need to consult the list. He knew. Only one of the invited had failed to put in an appearance. It had really been a gratifying housewarming but, as he never failed to do, he sent the delinquent a short, sharp note registering his disapproval. To Offenbach, the one unforgivable sin was omission.

Herminie looked in to say a young man was waiting to see him. Instantly Offenbach protested that he was busy but, as Herminie imperturbably waited, he added: "Show him in, show him in."

The young man was a journalist come for an interview, and when he reached Offenbach's study, the latter was all smiles. And he couldn't resist a quip when the overly serious newspaperman questioned him on his early musical traits.

"I think my first cry was a trill and my parents always assured me I even cried in rhythm."

The young man laughed and Offenbach, feeling more kindly toward him, opened a desk drawer and offered him a cigar. Then, reaching into his vest pocket, he withdrew a real Havana for himself. This was Offenbach's unique example of stinginess, but when Herminie upbraided him for it he always observed that most people didn't appreciate good cigars. The vest pocket ones were only for exceptional friends.

No sooner had the young journalist departed than brother Jules dropped in. Jacques noted his hangdog expression and waited for the bad news. He was out of work again. Jacques tapped his fingers thoughtfully on the desk top. Jules was a competent musician but somehow . . .

"I think there'll be a vacancy in the Bouffes orchestra next week. Do you want it?"

After Jules had left, Jacques fidgeted for a moment, puffed at his Havana, then turned to the unfinished music score on the piano. He felt as if he had just settled down when an aspiring young singer, sent by a friend, was announced. He scowled, but when told that the visitor was a young girl he immediately brightened.

But this girl proved to be less than pretty. She was, to Offenbach, on the ugly side and he wasted little time. He was courteous but firm. At the moment, no, there was no opportunity at the Bouffes. After she had left, he reached for his writing paper.

"You know," he wrote to the friend who had sent the unfortunate girl, "that in my theatre the public sits very close to the stage and consequently the women have to be even more beautiful than elsewhere."

That done, he returned to his music score. For fifteen or twenty minutes he wrote without faltering then, glancing up at the clock, he abruptly dropped his pen and got up. It was time to go to lunch.

In his bedroom he changed his clothes. He was quite vain about his wardrobe and took some minutes to make his choice. Having decided, he dressed rapidly, carefully brushed his hair and scrutinized himself searchingly in the glass before departing.

At thirty-eight Offenbach was as odd-looking an individual as ever. His hair was beginning to recede and, except for the incredible animation of his face, he had lost all youthfulness of appearance. But he remained quite as dandyish in dress. He still affected a somber frock coat over trousers of violent color and pattern. He combed and waved his sparse hair back with meticulous care. The sideburns had grown to muttonchops and he had added a drooping moustache. Instead of the monocle on a black ribbon there was now a pair of large-paned glasses which had become his especial trade mark. He was incredibly homely but by the very care he exercised in his dress he had attained a sort of distinction.

Offenbach was very proud of his slim figure. Actually, he was painfully thin, weighing a mere hundred and ten pounds but, regarding his reflection in the mirror, he smiled approvingly at the trim fit of his clothes.

On the way out he paused to kiss each of the children as well as Herminie. As soon as he reached the street, he looked up to the apartment balcony for the customary final farewell. Unfailingly Herminie and the three girls came out to wave at him as, beaming affectionately and possessively, he made his way down the street.

If anyone had suggested to Jacques that he was a bit of a tyrant he would have been mortified. He considered himself a respectable, decent, conventional family man. Yet his routine was unvarying and his entire household accommodated itself to him.

At noon he always set off for lunch at the Restaurant Peters. There his now boon companion, Henri de Villemessant, presided over a table made up in the main of *Figaro* correspondents. Offenbach, on his part, was generally joined by one or more associates from the Bouffes. Occasionally it was "Ludo" Halévy, sometimes another young librettist, Hector Cremieux, and most often the devoted disciple, Etienne Tréfeu, who had been associated with him since the opening of the Bouffes. Tréfeu had written the skit *A Summer Night's Dream* and from then on, to a great degree, tied up his fortunes with Offenbach.

Lunch was a pure formality with Offenbach. Never having any appetite he did not share the average boulevardier's delight in food. In fact, his menu never varied—just a soft-boiled egg and a cutlet. Halfway through the latter, he would push his plate away and light up a Havana. Everyone knew Offenbach could be found at Peters' at midday and Jacques, slightly obscured in cigar smoke, usually rounded off his meal happily discussing business. If no one appeared he began to fidget. Then, more likely than not, he would haul a scrap of paper from his pocket and jot down a fragment which had just occurred to him. Hurried little dots, looking more like flyspecks than music notes, were nervously scrawled. In a matter of minutes he would slip the paper back in his pocket and, with a renewed puff at his cigar, relax and beam at the world in general.

Jacques would have had to be ill indeed not to put in his customary luncheon appearance. Restaurants and cafés—and he was almost as abstemious in his drinking as in his eating—were primary ingredients of the Parisian life he loved so much. In the evenings, just as regularly, he was to be seen at one or more of the boulevard cafés. He was, in fact, the boulevardier par excellence.

While the luncheons were purely masculine gatherings, in the evenings Jacques loved nothing more than to escort Herminie to Tortoni's or the Café de Paris for a *glace* or to share a bottle of champagne. Herminie was naturally a homebody and, with three young daughters, she had excuse enough not to go out. Sometimes, though, after the theatre and when the children were in bed, she would accompany Jacques. It happened all too rarely and Jacques would complain, for he was never so proud and happy as when she was at his side. She grew animated in company and her dark eyes would shine brilliantly. Herminie really loved these excursions but, taking her maternal responsibilities heavily, she had to be persuaded.

When Herminie was with Jacques his choice was usually one of the really fashionable cafés. Alone, he was more likely to frequent such literary and artistic rendezvous as Dinochau's or Le Divan le Peletier. In reality, there was scarcely a well-known café on the Right Bank (he rarely traversed the Seine or strayed from the center of town) with which Jacques was not familiar. Sometimes he went to be seen—it was good business for a theatre man—on other occasions, in the tiny café-concerts, he went in search of new talent.

Always it was part of the life he enjoyed. As much as ever, Offenbach required the stimulus of people, movement, excite-

ment. Away from the boulevards, from the gaiety of the ca
and the glamor of Paris theatres, he grew homesick. And wh
in the summer of 1857, it was decided to take the Bouffes-P;
siens to England, his pride in this new triumph was adultera
by twinges of sorrow at leaving his adored Paris.

11

Goethe once observed that only those who completely n
rored the mentality of their epochs were destined for imm
tality.

Offenbach is perhaps a minor immortal, a mere cherub am
the angels, but it is incontrovertible that much of his musi
light, unpretentious music—lives on. Because Offenbach, too, v
the mirror of his times.

His music is bursting with the joy, the effervescence,
carefree disregard of the clouds gathering on the horizon, t
was Paris under the Second Empire. Never profound, but v
an appealing simplicity, his music is of an incontestable o
inality. Whatever its sources of inspiration, it bears the ir
vidual stamp of Offenbach's personality, just as he himself v
a symbol of the period.

Offenbach, the German-Jewish boy from the ghetto of (
logne, was a true Parisian. In spite of his grotesque accent,
the accident of his birthplace, he was completely represei
tive of the Paris scene. Few thought of him otherwise. O
his worst enemies occasionally sneered at him as a foreigne:
German, and rarely, if ever, was the epithet "Jew" hurled at h
The anti-Semitism so prevalent in his native land was little
evidence in France at that time and, although Offenbach ne
repudiated his race or his background, he was mercifully spa
the handicaps of discrimination.

Just as he, personally, was so typical of the boulevardier
the era, so had the Bouffes-Parisiens become an integral part
the Parisian life of that day. His lively musical satires were
pressive of the wit and lightheartedness of the times. Where
Paris danced—from the Tuileries to the lowest *bal muset*

came the inevitable strains of Offenbach's lilting tunes. To think of Paris under the Second Empire one must unfailingly be reminded of Offenbach. Philip Guedalla summed it up by labeling the Second Empire the "Age of Offenbach."

12

Echoes of the popularity of the Bouffes-Parisiens had been heard in London from its very beginnings during the Exposition of 1855. Now, two years later, when Offenbach decided on a season there, the theatre was sold out in advance of his arrival. Even Queen Victoria made known her intention of attending a performance.

Several companies had already started on tours of the French provincial towns when Offenbach, under his father-in-law Mitchell's management, crossed the Channel. Although the success of the Bouffes-Parisiens was undisputed, the theatre was still saddled with a heavy debt and Offenbach felt confident that by increasing his public through road companies this would be entirely wiped out.

The London triumph surpassed his most optimistic expectations and Offenbach sent glowing reports back to his silent partner, Charles Comte. Not only did Queen Victoria honor him with her presence but Louis-Philippe's widow, Queen Amélie, living in exile at Twickenham with her children, requested a special performance there. Such attention, while not remunerative, was flattering, particularly when the exiled Orleanist Queen burst into tears over *Dragonette,* a sentimental playlet about a fife player in the French Army who saves the flag with the cry of *"Vive la France!"*

Later Offenbach had qualms, wondering whether this obeisance to a defunct regime might have repercussions in Paris.

"The idea has come to me," he wrote Comte, "that *my good friends* in Paris might ask nothing better than to misinterpret the simplest thing in the world and would, happily and intentionally, noise about their own malicious point of view."

He remembered, with slight trepidation now, the supper given the troupe at which he had been seated next to Queen Amélie herself. So he suggested that Comte "say a word to our friend, Monsieur Doucet," and added that "God be thanked that the Government under which we live has much too fine perception to find anything ill-intentioned in such a natural affair."

"But after all," he remarked, "I owe the Minister of State a debt of gratitude for the position I now hold and I don't want to displease him in any way. . . ."

Although the Bouffes played a full season in London, Offenbach returned to Paris in a couple of weeks. Like a small boy, he decided not to let Herminie know in advance, but to surprise her. Her very real pleasure in his unexpected return nevertheless was short-lived because within a few days he had departed for Lyon, to oversee the opening of another road company.

"But when I return, Herminie," he said, "*we* are going on vacation."

Herminie smiled, not believing a word. Jacques was only happy when he was active, which meant working, and she couldn't remember a real holiday in their thirteen years of marital life.

To her utter astonishment, he completely fooled her. Returning in short order from Lyon (where, incidentally, he had placed his brother Jules as first violinist) he paused only briefly to write the music and rehearse Hector Crémieux' *The Lottery of the Young Lady* and then announced to Herminie:

"We are going to Etretat." He pronounced it "Eter-Tat."

Herminie was so taken aback that she didn't even demur at the thought of leaving the new baby in the hands of the nurse in Paris. For they had another child now, a *fourth* girl. Apparently God had decided against a boy for the Offenbach family!

Still somewhat surprised, one bright warm early August day Herminie found herself seated in a train compartment with the three older girls and Jacques, steaming out of the Gare St. Lazare. The railway system in France was really remarkable now, one could go almost anywhere, and she and Jacques discussed at some length the tremendous advance in travel in the last ten or fifteen years. Of course, one couldn't go all the way to Etretat, but with one change of trains one could reach the coast in five hours and then there was only a half-hour ride by omnibus. It was really extraordinary.

The whole trip was like a picnic. In fact, they did have a picnic with the fine lunch cook had packed, though as usual Jacques ate precious little of it. But he beamed with pleasure throughout the journey, enjoying the role of paterfamilias. Only once did he speak sharply to the children and that was when they tried to lean out the windows. Later, after the windows were shut, there was no trouble at all. As the clamor of exuberant childish voices mounted in the hot, closed compartment, Offenbach imperturbably pulled one of the inevitable sheets of paper from his pocket and set to work on a new song he had in mind.

It was Henri de Villemessant who had first spoken of Etretat to Jacques, but other friends and acquaintances like Nadar, the younger Dumas and Gustave Doré had been frequenting it for several seasons. It was a simple, unpretentious resort, so Offenbach was told, not fashionable at all but a gathering spot of writers and artists.

From the moment Jacques arrived there he was enchanted with the place. He had never before spent any time at the seashore and, although he was not too fond of dips in the cold Channel water, he loved the sunny mornings on the beach, watching the children play in the sand, and later retiring to the nearby Casino for an *apéritif* before lunch. These gatherings at the Casino, he remarked, were almost like the Restaurant Peters.

It was all a wonderful rest, but in no time Jacques was seeking new outlets for his unused energy. Etretat, except for the small group of visitors, was a fishermen's village in those days, and it occurred to Offenbach that it would be a nice gesture to stage a benefit gala for their families. Why not bring down the Bouffes company? He began to feel sentimental. Why shouldn't those dear souls, as he called his actors, enjoy this wonderful place too?

In short order he was writing reams of instruction to Paris.
The theatre was to be closed for the week end, the company
would take the train Friday at 6:30, he would be waiting for
them in front of the hotel, etc., etc. All seemed arranged when
Offenbach set out to find lodgings for the troupe. This proved
more difficult than he had anticipated and he rushed to Villemessant, who had a villa, for aid.

"Here it is the day before their arrival and I haven't found
a corner for them to lay their dear heads!"

He checked off on his fingers those for whom he had found
beds.

"One of my friends has agreed to go away for two days,
which leaves a room for Mesmacker. Guyot has asylum with the
excellent curate. Désiré can sleep at the town clerk's between
marriage ceremonies. I got on my knees to Mme Blanquet and
she has put out a most upset gentleman so that Mlle Tautin can
lodge there. . . . But what of the others?"

Villemessant chuckled. No one else would have had the
temerity to approach him, but that was what amused him about
Offenbach. Most people considered Villemessant a gruff, un-
compromising and difficult person but Offenbach had never noticed anything of the sort.

"They can stay with me," Villemessant assured Jacques.

"That will be splendid!" exclaimed Offenbach, but there was
no hint of surprise in his voice. He was, in fact, already remembering that he must go over final plans for the show with the
Mayor and, in a moment or two, hurried on his way. But when
the company drew in at the bus terminal Friday, he announced
gleefully: "Monsieur de Villemessant has turned over his villa."

The actors were properly appreciative of the unexpected
good fortune of a week end at the seashore and gave one of the
best performances of the season. The fishermen were equally
delighted with the proceeds of the benefit. But Offenbach ruefully discovered that he was out of pocket by a considerable
sum when the troupe returned to Paris. However, it had been
a great deal of fun.

13

Going over the accounts in September, Offenbach grew worried. The Bouffes-Parisiens, instead of being solvent, was still far from making up its original costs. The trip to Etretat, so much enjoyed by the Paris company, had added to the deficit and Charles Comte took Offenbach to task for that extravagance. Jacques replied, with asperity, that he, Comte, was a skinflint. It was not the first time they had quarreled over finances, although they were good friends.

Their ideas of show business were diametrically opposed. Jacques had no excuse for the Etretat excursion beyond a softhearted whim but he often accused Comte, with reason, of niggardliness. Comte considered himself merely thrifty, but Jacques contended that one could not run a popular theatre parsimoniously. Comte insisted that they should retrench. Jacques believed that the only way to overcome loss was to spend—bigger and better productions, bigger audiences. Comte sarcastically pointed out that this past summer they had expanded with road companies and now were worse off than before. Jacques admitted that the Etretat benefit had been expensive and promised not to repeat it, but he still insisted that now the road companies were inaugurated the costs were bound to decrease.

Offenbach already had several ideas for the new season. His main precept was that one must not grow stale. He also had a secret longing to be taken more seriously.

For the winter of 1858 he planned to produce a light and little known operetta of Mozart's, *The Impresario*. He also approached the great Rossini. Rossini, who had not faltered in his admiration for the "Mozart of the Champs-Elysées," was very receptive. He agreed to give Offenbach a one-act operetta of his early youth, *Bruschino*.

That winter Jacques began to visualize himself as a worthy rival of the Opéra-Comique. Eventually he wanted to do something himself of greater import than the trivial plays of the present Bouffes. The season before he had tried with a serious effort called *The Three Kisses of the Devil* but the public, used to being amused by him, had taken it for one of his routine satires. With a work of Mozart's, plus one of Rossini's, perhaps they would learn to expect something different.

Unfortunately neither of these operettas was spectacularly successful. The opus of Rossini's youth was scarcely representative of the great composer's ability. Rossini, amiable but elderly, cared little. It was even difficult to get him to attend rehearsals and, when he did appear, he refused to take any active part in them. He even declared he would not attend the opening.

"Often a victim but never an accomplice!" he told Offenbach laughingly.

This seriously disturbed Jacques, for the Great Man's presence would add immeasurably to the event. Rossini, of course, realized this perfectly well and, although he kept up his joke to the very end, he was quietly seated in the audience when the curtain finally went up and even rose to join the principals in a curtain call.

Nevertheless, the lukewarm reception of these semiclassical operettas deterred Offenbach from any further efforts in that direction for the time being. Instead, he put on a more ambitious and spectacular work of his own—*The Market Ladies*—in March, which in many respects proved a turning point in his career.

He had unremittingly tried, from the very start of the Bouffes, to have the restrictions of his license removed. As time went on, the limitation to four characters upon the stage had grown more and more irksome but it wasn't until the beginning of 1858 that his influential friends managed to secure him permission for full-scale plays. Now, Offenbach felt, he would truly be able to revolutionize the operetta.

The Market Ladies depended greatly on its crowd scene. Offenbach, with this new opportunity, proved himself again an expert showman. Not only the setting—the market place, les Halles, in the time of Louis XV—but the movement and animation, the colorful costumes and the lighting all showed him to be a fastidious artist. The play itself, with Offenbach's usual delightful music, brought him renewed acclaim—and again he indulged himself in optimistic daydreams.

Not so Charles Comte. The costs of this minor work of art were upsetting and in vain he pointed out that its very legitimate artistic success was not pulling the Bouffes company out of debt. At least not as rapidly as necessary.

In spite of this, Offenbach refused to worry any more. He was now nursing new schemes. *The Market Ladies* was only a beginning. It was merely a one-acter, no matter how elaborate, while he now contemplated a full-scale, spectacular musical. For nearly two years an idea had been milling in his fertile brain but it had been hopeless so long as he was constrained to a tiny cast. Now he could go ahead with it.

During his long enforced sojourn at the Théâtre-Français Jacques had watched performances of many classic tragedies and, with his irrepressible sense of humor, the majority had seemed fit subjects for burlesque. More than one had fallen victim to his irreverence at the Friday evening parties and there seemed every reason to believe that what had amused his intimates would amuse a public audience.

From the days of the Greek theatre onward, the mythological figure of Orpheus had fascinated dramatists. Many plays had been written, almost without exception ponderous and tragic. But Offenbach saw in Orpheus a comic character. Instead of a heartbroken husband whose wife has been carried off to Hades, he visualized a browbeaten husband relieved by the carrying away of his shrewish spouse. In order to burlesque the Greek chorus of ancient days, a character called "Public Opinion" would be introduced to serve as a sort of conscience forcing Orpheus to do the proper thing, reclaim his undesired wife, a character who at the same time would poke fun at the conventions of modern society.

Offenbach had talked this over long ago with Hector Cremieux and Ludovic Halévy. Bit by bit his satire had grown in scope, but until now it had been far from realization.

In the late spring they began to discuss it seriously and Offenbach, traveling constantly that June, supervising openings in

Marseilles, Brussels and Berlin, wrote music at every opportunity on his train trips. He took more care than heretofore had been his habit, tearing up yesterday's composition, writing and rewriting his score.

The Paris company of the Bouffes was back at its summer stand on the Square Marigny but, though the theatre continued to play to capacity, the rumors were now rampant in the city that Offenbach was going bankrupt. It was noised about that he had fled Paris to avoid his creditors. He was, said his enemies, in hiding.

Actually, he was sojourning at Bad Ems, a German spa with a predominantly French clientele. He was decidedly not in hiding, since the papers had already announced the opening of a Bouffes road company at the little Kurpark theatre there.

Jacques had gone to Bad Ems not only to open the theatre but for a much-needed rest as well. He had been suffering slightly with rheumatism the past winter and the waters of Bad Ems had been highly recommended by his doctor. Yet, as he wrote Herminie, the combination of taking the cure and opening a new theatre left him little time for repose. In addition, he continued to work on *Orpheus*.

It was during his stay that he learned that Halévy would be unable to collaborate on *Orpheus*, or *Orpheus in Hades* as they decided it should be called. Jacques was terribly distressed. Not only did he consider Halévy his cleverest librettist but he preferred working with him to any other. Crémieux, while an excellent fellow, worked slowly and tediously and drove him frantic, but Ludo wrote swiftly and easily, making changes and corrections in rehearsal. Besides, he had a special affection for Ludo. This was a bitter pill and, characteristically, Jacques refused to swallow it.

Halévy's reasons were perfectly bona fide. Until recently he had been but a minor Government functionary but, thanks to Offenbach's intercession with the Count de Morny, he had been appointed to the far more imposing position of Minister for Algeria. This meant that he was no longer an obscure departmental clerk and Halévy felt that his new status forbade him to sign his name to a boulevard farce. To Offenbach the solution was simple—he needn't sign his name.

"I have heard talk about your change of position," he wrote Ludo. "Happy creature who hopes no longer to have to work for me! Never fear, I shall force you to. You will take a pseudonym and sign yourself Halevinsky and no one will recognize you."

He followed his joking with a sentimental appeal.

"If I write you today it is because it is just three years since we took up arms together, you as author, I as director. Do you remember? The fifth of July is a date for me; at least, in spite of my daily worries, I only think of it with pleasure. . . ."

His appeal was not lost. Halévy was only too glad to continue their collaboration, but he remained adamant against signing his name.

"In that case," said Jacques, "I will dedicate the play to you."

Which indeed he did. It was the decentest gesture he could think of, to dedicate his best work to Ludo. And never for a moment did he doubt that it would be his best work.

14

"My dear friends," Offenbach announced, "before beginning, I want to ask your pardon for all the disagreeable things I won't fail to say to you shortly."

It was a routine speech, made before the start of any rehearsal, for Offenbach was quite aware of his own impatience and sharp tongue. Too many times he had been called upon to apologize, usually after the soubrette had already burst into tears or the leading man had threatened to stick a dueling sword into him. This way, no one held his recurrent quick temper against him, everyone knew what to expect and it frequently avoided the unpleasantness of tears and wild threats.

Today they were beginning the rehearsal of *Orpheus in Hades.* As Lise Tautin came on stage in the role of Eurydice, Offenbach thought fondly of Hortense Schneider. She would have been wonderful in the part. But she was no longer one of his company. Shrewd little Cath, she had demanded raises until even he, Jacques, realized he could not afford her. Oh, well, she was made for bigger roles and no doubt the Bouffes-Parisiens was too small to hold her. She had been doing remarkably well at the Variétés and he certainly wished her continued good fortune.

Besides, as far as *Orpheus* was concerned, she would not have been available anyway. Hortense Schneider was in temporary retirement following the birth of the Duc de Gramont-Caderousse's son. She had certainly tied herself up with a wastrel. An eccentric and a rake, Gramont-Caderousse, but Cath truly loved him. Probably he was the only person she had loved more than herself and Jacques hoped she would be happy.

As far as Lise Tautin was concerned, this new star had a great deal of ability and charm, and had admirably replaced Hortense Schneider. Professionally Jacques was proud of her, another of his café-concert discoveries.

Suddenly he yelled in his execrable French: *"Une bedide goupure!"*

All action stopped on the stage. *"Une petite coupure,"* "a little cut," were familiar words. They were working, as was customary with Offenbach, from the rough draft of the play. Crémieux and Halévy sat beside him and Offenbach, with his unerring sense of theatre, quickly pointed out the desired changes.

The rehearsal proceeded. In the midst of Tautin's solo Offenbach again called a halt.

"I do not like it—it does not belong there. Further on, further on, Ludo, then there's reason for Eurydice to sing."

He called a rest for the actors and went to his office in the front of the theatre. Fifteen or twenty minutes later he reappeared.

"Here is another song—we will put that in where Eurydice leaves the message for Orpheus."

He laid the newly scrawled song on the piano. The accompanist looked at it, hesitated, seeming to have difficulty deciphering the hastily jotted notes.

"Get up," directed Jacques impatiently, and himself sat down to the piano.

"Yes, that's better," he muttered as he played the new air through, "that's what it needs—you will give me some new verses this evening, eh, Ludo?"

They moved on to the next act and the chorus came out for its opening dance.

"What's the matter?" shouted Offenbach. "Just because you are goddesses must you have feet of clay?"

Obediently the chorus repeated its entrance. Offenbach leaped to his feet and joined them on the stage.

"Like this!" he said, giving an energetic kick and snapping his fingers in rhythm.

There was a laugh, but as Offenbach linked arms with the chorus girl at the end of the line they all went more spiritedly into the dance routine.

Jacques worked hard those early autumn days, shaping and reshaping *Orpheus in Hades*. He was little in evidence about town, and again the word spread that he was hiding from his creditors.

As a matter of fact, the Bouffes' financial condition remained in bad shape and Offenbach was gambling its entire future on *Orpheus*. If it failed, he was utterly ruined. No consideration of failure entered his mind, however. He was positive it would be a prosperous venture and take them out of the red. It would outdo anything he had ever done. Meantime, he must put off— preferably avoid—his most insistent creditors. For that matter, he could be found any day at the theatre.

The endless details and interruptions preceding the opening were enough to unnerve anyone. While all theatre premieres are notoriously nerve-racking an Offenbach opening was, by the very nature of its presiding genius, bound to be grotesquely manic. Just as he worked in his own apartment with people coming and going, so at the theatre his so-called private office had all the seclusion of a railway station.

On the morning of the opening of *Orpheus*, while Offenbach

was making some last minute alterations in the score, a bedraggled workingman burst in and stuttered:

"Maître Offenbach, excuse me, sir. I am from the gas company. The main has burst in the Passage Choiseul and we may not be able to illumine the footlights tonight."

"Well, my poor friend, don't take it to heart. We'll go back to using candles."

This contretemps thus amiably solved, Offenbach saw three strange and furtive-looking figures in the doorway. They were obviously bill-collectors and he lost his aplomb for the moment, yelling for Charles Comte to hold them off. The day went hectically along, punctuated by requests from German tourists who felt themselves entitled to free seats from their fellow-countryman, by Lise Tautin's shrill insistence that she would not go on in the show without a genuine tiger skin to wear in the last scene, by the entrance of a disappointed young librettist whose flimsy contributions had been consistently rejected by the Bouffes, by a message saying that the piccolo player had a fever blister on his lip and, of course, by Comte's repeated entrances with his dismal comments on the poor advance sale.

To cap it all, the Minister of Fine Arts sent word that certain cuts must be made in the text of *Orpheus* before the Censor would allow it to go on. Not to mention Villemessant's sudden appearance with the request that Offenbach act as his second in a duel.

At this last bit of nonsense, Offenbach broke into guffaws. One thing he certainly did not have time for was a duel.

In the afternoon came the final rehearsal with Lise Tautin's new tiger skin, a hurriedly recruited piccolo player, and the Censor's cuts duly made. When Offenbach came home late in the afternoon he was very tired. He sat down in his favorite armchair by the fireplace and fell fast asleep.

He had done all he could and the play, like its plot, was in the hands of the gods.

CHAPTER FOUR

Orpheus on the Boulevards

1

The night of October 21, 1858, a steady stream of carriages drew up to the entrance of the Bouffes-Parisiens. The little knot of spectators gathered on the sidewalk watched with pleasure as the ladies, in their extravagantly tiered and draped crinolines (subtle indication of the affluent times) and their escorts in top hats and silk-lined opera capes stepped under the bright, gas-lit marquee. Overhead the lighted sign announced the opening of *Orphée aux Enfers.*

Inside, the house filled rapidly but even the rustle of silk died down when Offenbach stepped out briskly to lead the orchestra. A spontaneous burst of applause greeted him and no one, seeing his broad smile and twinkling eyes behind the glasses, could have visualized the tired man of a few hours ago.

With a smart rap of the baton on the podium, the lively overture began. One after another the quick rhythms and sparkling melodies poured forth, in such rapid succession they seemed almost to tumble over each other. The orchestra, far larger than heretofore at the Bouffes and therefore of almost overpowering volume, created an intoxicating carnival-like atmosphere.

It was Offenbach, but an Offenbach who had outstripped himself.

As the gas footlights flared up and the curtain rose there was a suppressed murmur of approval. The scene was a pastoral one and the exquisite colors gave it the effect of a Watteau painting. But it was the second act on Mount Olympus and the splendor of the later underworld scene which brought audible gasps. Young Gustave Doré was responsible for the costumes, sets and lighting.

With ingenious new twists to the ancient legend, the plot unfolded. The lines, rampant with wit and satire, ostensibly made merry with the old Greek tale, but in their double-entendre they poked sly fun at contemporary Empire mores and manners. Jupiter bore a suspicious resemblance to Napoleon III and the cabal of the lesser gods suggested Court intrigues. When the somewhat mutinous minor deities of Olympus accused Jupiter of having truck with mere mortals and he nervously defended himself by saying "It's the newspapermen who spread this to injure my reputation!" there was more than a reminder of the recent amorous indiscretions of the Emperor. "Public Opinion," like a Greek chorus, recalled the outward respect for conventions of a not very conventional society, as when Orpheus asked why he must demand his wife back and she responded, "For the edification of posterity!"

It was gorgeous burlesque, but without Offenbach's score it would have been like strawberries without cream. Throughout was his music, always fitting the situation, never forced—sometimes tender, sometimes comic, sometimes frenzied. Such charming songs as the duo in which Orpheus laments "I have lost my Eurydice" and in which a phrase or two from Gluck was impishly interpolated, the "Divertissement of the Hours," the rousing "March of the Gods" (echoing the now seditious strains of the republican "Marseillaise"), the "Hymn to Bacchus," the wonderful tom-tom beat of the "King of Béotie," seemed to captivate the audience. There were *galops*, there were waltzes, there were minuets. But surpassing all was the incredible cancan of the "Bacchanale." It was this marvelous, frenzied dance which brought the audience to its feet. Offenbach had resorted to the rhythm of the once popular, but never respectable, dance of his early days in Paris. In it was packed the excitement and madness of the old pre-Lenten celebrations, as its swift tempo accelerated, ever faster and faster, to the crescendo of the breathless finale.

This was the cancan to outlive all other cancans, an outmoded dance which, revived, became symbolic of the Second Empire rather than of an earlier era. It was the same cancan which, a quarter of a century later, Toulouse-Lautrec immortalized in his Moulin Rouge posters, the cancan of the Bal Tabarin and of the present-day Ballet Russe's *Gaîté Parisienne*.

Had anyone dropped into the theatre just as the finale was being danced, he would have been positive that he was witnessing the greatest hit of Paris in decades. There was no question of the electrifying effect this cancan had upon the audience. Yet backstage, as the curtain was rung down, the players were uneasy.

Offenbach, especially sensitive to audience reaction, knew early that *Orpheus* was not receiving the desired response. Many of the best lines had been greeted with silence and the most hilarious situations seemed to have passed unnoticed. Perhaps his theatrical instinct had failed him. He considered *Orpheus* the perfect *opéra-bouffe* but then—maybe he had guessed wrong.

His doubts appeared to be unhappily realized the next morning as he perused the first reviews. The criticism varied from tepid to hostile. The reviewers, it seemed, were shocked. Not at the subtle satire of the Emperor and his Court (after all, it had been passed by the Censor) but at the irreverent treatment accorded a hallowed classic. What Offenbach had believed was good comedy they piously condemned as bad taste. Just as *Le Ménestrel* had denounced the inspirational source of Offenbach's waltz "Rebecca" long ago, so now they resented the burlesque of both Greek drama and Gluck's fine opera.

None of these reviews, however, touched the virulence of

Jules Janin a few days later in his column in the *Journal des Débats*. Janin was regarded as the sage and dean of Paris columnists. He was also the most pretentious. At an early period he had been friendly to Offenbach and had even praised the beginnings of the Bouffes-Parisiens. His enthusiasm for that institution had been waning of late but nothing had touched the vituperation he poured on *Orpheus*. It was sacrilege, he thundered, it was indecent, to satirize the great Greek legend, not to mention burlesquing Gluck.

Not content with a single review, Janin continued his fulminations in successive columns. The public, at first apathetic, began to evince a curiosity to see this monstrous show and the ticket sales rose perceptibly. Still Janin's diatribes went on.

Then, to everyone's amusement, the omnipotent critic tripped himself up. He had singled out the dialogue of *Orpheus* for special attack, calling it unworthy of the French language. At that, Offenbach and Crémieux began to smile wisely. After a hurried consultation, Cremieux wrote a letter which *Figaro* took pleasure in publishing.

"There is in *Orpheus*," Cremieux pointed out, "a speech which Léonce [the actor who played Pluto] makes every evening on his arrival on Mount Olympus, to the delight of the public. This simple and naive speech, which surpasses all the other comic effects of the play, *is merely a verbatim paragraph from Monsieur Janin's column of May 10, 1858. . . .*"

This revelation of Janin's unwitting collaboration was greeted with hilarity by the boulevard wits. The public now showed an even more lively interest in seeing *Orpheus* and the box office was swamped with orders.

Janin's discomfiture should have been complete. He did desist from further discussion of the authors and the dialogue, but instead he turned his verbal weapons on Offenbach. Finally Jacques accepted this challenge to a duel of words.

"Ah, Janin! My good Janin!" he wrote mockingly. "How much am I indebted to you for criticizing me every Monday the way you do! Did you not attack Rachel? Didn't you criticize Dumas? And Scribe and everyone else who displayed any real talent? I am in honored company. You style my music as abominable half-clad music—the music of carnivals and masked balls! Music in rags and tatters! Still, it never begged a line from you. You insult the composer of *Orpheus,* the librettist of *Orpheus,* the actors who play in *Orpheus,* the public which goes and applauds *Orpheus*—you would, if it were possible, insult the woman in the box office who delivers the tickets for *Orpheus.*"

Offenbach had fun writing that letter. He could afford to. The publicity which Janin had given *Orpheus* was priceless. Thanks to Janin's tirades, *Orpheus* had become the greatest hit the Bouffes had ever known. Everybody wanted to see it and, having seen it once, returned again and again.

True, it was a more finished production than when first presented. All through the week following the opening, Jacques had made *"bedides goupures,"* Crémieux and his silent partner, Halévy, had revised their lyrics, and rehearsals had consumed a large part of every day. Now it moved with a smoothness worthy of the best *opéra-bouffe.* It was satire, it was fantasy, it was caricature, all rolled into one. The innuendoes became more apparent to the audiences and they delighted in the hilarious burlesque of the times.

Offenbach, having passed through the travail of the first weeks of uncertainty, reaped the rewards. His judgment in the selection of *Orpheus* was vindicated. While this bolstered his natural conceit, he was fully aware of the cooperation of his company and gave tangible proof of his gratitude by announcing a raise of salary to all members. The note to Bache, who played the important role of John Styx, was typically Offenbach.

> You have played the role . . . with real talent. Allow me, in view of this success to impose a condition upon you, very difficult it is true, but which out of consideration for your director, you should accept. Beginning the first of the month, I double your salary for the year. In thus acting, believe me, my dear Bache, I have only one objective—that is, to make one ingrate the more.

This extravagance on Jacques' part immediately drew the ire of Charles Comte, but Jacques was in too sentimental a mood to heed him. Besides, *Orpheus* was making money at such a fantastic rate that it was impossible to be coldly practical. The receipts were running well over two thousand francs a day!

Like a child with a new toy, Jacques kept making additions to *Orpheus.* The original chorus of twelve was increased to twenty-four and more instruments were added to the orchestra. At the fiftieth performance the role of Amphitrite was introduced.

Naturally, the phenomenal success was celebrated at a Friday evening gathering at which Janin was toasted with a burlesque entitled "The Impartial Critic, or Once doesn't make it a Custom."

By this time, most of the critics were trying to make amends for their own lack of perspicacity. Offenbach was being showered with praises in print and the music from *Orpheus,* particularly the cancan, was the rage of Paris. As one journalist remarked: "The whirlwind of the famous quadrille is carrying off our entire generation."

The most touching tribute came from the editors of *Le Ménestrel,* who took up a collection in the office and sent a note to Offenbach stating: "The Editors of *Le Ménestrel* owe you a gesture of conciliation. They doubted *Orpheus,* as though one could doubt your music. . . . Please regard as your own property, beginning today, the piano addressed by us to your home. . . ."

Ironically, the publishing house of Ménestrel had secured the complete rights of the music of *Orpheus* for the equivalent of one day's receipts at the Bouffes. Offenbach, frightened, had sold out early, when his intuition had sunk to a low ebb and before Janin's intemperate attacks had insured prosperity to the show.

Temporarily Jacques' financial worries were ended. Both the Bouffes and the Offenbach family were solvent but Herminie, grown cautious, continued to lay aside small sums against the all-too-frequent rainy days.

In his personal habits Jacques was not exceptionally extravagant. He did have a weakness for nice clothes and a love of fine cigars. On the other hand he was a mild bon vivant rather than a roisterous spendthrift. He cared little for drink and less for food. But he did love to entertain his friends and he was an easy touch for any beggar with a moderately plausible story.

Ever since the past summer, however, he had been nurturing a secret ambition and now, with the proceeds from *Orpheus,* he was able to realize it. One day he took a train with Herminie to Etretat and there purchased a villa which had attracted his interest the August before. It was a magnificent gabled affair of white plaster and red brick with a huge porch across the front and a collection of balconies on the upper stories, all with latticed or iron grill railings. It was very modern, contained ten rooms and, even more gratifying, it had a lovely big garden on the cliff overlooking the Channel.

It was the first time Jacques had owned property and it gave him a wonderful feeling of security. Naturally it was baptized "Villa Orphée" and it was here that the piano from *Le Ménestrel* was delivered.

2

In June *Orpheus* ended its first run after a record of two hundred and twenty-eight performances. The Bouffes moved back to its summer quarters on the Square Marigny and three new one-act plays were put on. These, rotated with earlier ones, were in the tradition of the *théâtre intime* on which the Bouffes had been founded.

For the autumn, however, Offenbach again had grandiose plans. This time the tragic adventures of Genevieve of Brabant were selected for his satirical consideration. A term now widely current on the boulevards was *offenbachiade,* meaning that particular genre of *opéra-bouffe* which was exclusively Offenbach's—and the night of the opening of *Geneviève de Brabant* the crowd at the theatre was so dense that special police were ordered out to keep the entrance clear.

Unfortunately, *Geneviève* did not live up to expectations, although the spirit of Schumann would have turned over in any case at the irreverent handling of his chaste "Genovefa." Doré designed the costumes and scenery which even outdid *Orpheus* and Offenbach's music was of his best, but Etienne Tréfeu lacked the delicate touch of Crémieux and Halévy in his libretto. There was a heavyhandedness about it and, after a brief run, Jacques put it aside for some future day.

In its place he put on *The Carnival of Venice* to which Halévy, overcoming his earlier scruples, signed his name along with two other playwrights, Grange and Gille. As usual, though, Jacques had contributed a great part himself. One scene, called "The Musician of the Future," was unmistakably his brainchild. In it he poked fun at the much-discussed Richard Wagner, showing him as the director of a baroque symphony in the presence of Mozart, Gluck and Weber, all of whom plug their ears.

Wagner was living in exile in Paris and, earlier in the season, three concerts devoted to his works had been given at the Opéra Italien. They had caused a great deal of comment in Paris musical circles, most of it unfavorable, so that Jacques' sketch was not only topical but represented the sentiment of the majority.

Wagner, never of an equable temper, was infuriated. Prior to this, oddly enough, he had liked Offenbach's music but, taking this burlesque as a personal insult, he childishly allowed himself to be quoted as saying that "Offenbach's music is a dungheap in which all the swine of Europe wallow."

Much cleverer, if equally malicious, was a bit of doggerel which he wrote and circulated:

> *O wie süss und angenehm,*
> *Und dabei für die Füsse so recht bequem!*
> *Krak! Krak! Krakerakrak!*
> *O herrlicher Jack von Offenback!**

> * Oh, how comfortable and sweet,
>   And how easy on the feet!
>   Krak! Krak! Krakerakrak!
>   Oh, well-born Jack von Offenback!

(Wagner had already begun to show signs of the anti-Semitism which was to play such an important part in his career.)

Jacques, of an easier temperament than Wagner, refused to take affront. He was, instead, amused by the verse. He had never intended any personal insult by his sketch and it was sheer accident that it had been put on the boards at all. After numerous *bedides goupures* to the revue there had been a gap which had to be filled and the scene had been added at the last moment.

As to Wagner's music, Jacques quite honestly found it antipathetical. The musical conceptions of the two men were, obviously, diametrically opposed. Offenbach indirectly stated his own musical philosophy in reviewing the presentation of *Tannhäuser* in Paris the next winter: "To be erudite and boring is not the equivalent of art; *it is more important to be piquant and rich in melodies.*" *

Nevertheless, Offenbach did not confuse professional disagreement with personal enmity. Not so Wagner, whose rancor remained undiminished. Only after Offenbach's death did Wagner, then an old man, partially relent. In 1882 he wrote a friend: "Look at Offenbach. He knew how to compose like the divine Mozart. Offenbach could have been like Mozart."

3

During the run of *Orpheus* a young man from Offenbach's home town put in an appearance at his door. He was none other than Albert Wolff, the schoolmate of Jacques' younger brother Michael; the little Wolff boy who had made himself sick at the first homecoming of Jacques and Jules from Paris so long ago. It made Jacques very sentimental, remembering that reception on the Street of the Bells, when all the neighbors were convinced he was already famous. How many, many years after that it had taken to reach eminence!

Jacques gave the young fellow a pass for *Orpheus* which thrilled Albert but at the same time embarrassed him as his overcoat was so threadbare he was ashamed to check it. More-

* Authors' italics.

over, his funds were so limited he could ill afford to pay the customary tip to the usher, let alone the cloakroom girl. Later, when Albert Wolff laughingly recounted this, Offenbach was distressed, recalling his own early struggles in Paris.

By that time they were good friends. Naturally, Offenbach felt a special attachment for Wolff because the younger man represented a tie with his youth, but he also liked him for himself. Albert Wolff was an agreeable, intelligent and, as Offenbach later found out, loyal friend. Wolff too, no doubt, was subject to the effects of sentimentality but his unswerving devotion went far deeper than that. Offenbach had presented Wolff to Villemessant and thanks to the latter's kindness, Wolff in a short time was working for *Figaro*. Soon he had risen to the post of music critic and columnist, in which position he became Jacques' greatest eulogist and apologist.

During this same period Jacques, quite accidentally, picked up another and very tenuous thread of his youth. At *Le Ménestrel* one day, while correcting proof of the *Orpheus* score, he overheard the publisher giving instructions to return some copy to "that poor old German man."

Offenbach, always curious and sympathetic, looked up: "What poor old German?"

"His name is Zimmer," answered the publisher.

At this Jacques became very excited. Back into his mind rushed the fragmentary tune his mother used to sing to him and he again heard his father exclaiming, "Heavens! Do you still remember Zimmer's waltz?" Oddly, he had never completely forgotten it and from time to time it still came back to haunt him, but his memory always faded after the eight opening bars. It had been such a lovely waltz and Jacques was horrified now at the picture of the broken old composer—if he was the same— no longer able to peddle his songs.

"Where does he live?" he demanded.

No one knew. He had said that he would call at the publisher's in person.

"Please, then," said Offenbach rapidly, "buy his music—pay him ten times what it is worth—and bill me. Only don't tell him

I did it. But when he calls—will you ask him to come and see me?"

The publisher, somewhat mystified, promised to carry out the commission.

As for Jacques, he was impatient to meet Herr Zimmer. Perhaps he could help the old man. And from Zimmer he would at least learn the whole of his *gemütlich* waltz.

But the old German never came. For some unknown reason he did not return to the publisher's for his copy—perhaps he felt it was useless.

Despite his sentimental reaction to both young Wolff's arrival and the anticipated meeting with Herr Zimmer, Jacques indulged in no fanciful romanticizing of his birthplace. He still visualized clearly the poverty-stricken Street of the Bells. For Cologne he had only unadulterated loathing. There were too many memories of the buffetings and slights to the child of the ghetto ever to be effaced. And that last enforced sojourn there, when he had had to flee Paris with Herminie and the baby, had left an ineradicably bitter taste. So much so that when his German agents and personal friends, Bote & Bock, wrote him that Cologne had requested permission to put on *Orpheus* he replied flatly: ". . . à propos, *geben sie nicht Orphée nach Köln.*" ("Do not give *Orpheus* to Cologne.") The remainder of the letter was a mixture of German and his now more natural tongue, French: "You also know why. For that reason, I hope, if possible my operas will not be presented there; the inhabitants of Cologne have for their compatriots who acquire glory *so wenig übrig* and it is better to let them drink their beers in tranquility. . . ."

For most of his mature life Jacques had been an exile from his native land but, unlike Wagner who, also an expatriate, remained completely German at heart, Offenbach considered himself a Frenchman. His deepest desire had long been to make that an actuality. But although France—whether republic, monarchy, or empire—consistently gave asylum to refugees from other lands, her requirements for citizenship often made it an unattainable goal. It was not sufficient to have a means of livelihood, but a proof of adequate capital as well was required.

Until the advent of *Orpheus,* Offenbach had never been able to lay aside enough money to comply.

Even then, without the endorsement of his friend Count de Morny, the process might have been even more drawn out. Due to such influential backing Jacques received notification in the middle of January, 1860, that his application had been approved. For him another great ambition was achieved. No longer need he heed the sarcastic references of his enemies to "that foreigner" and "that fellow from across the Rhine." *He was a Frenchman.*

It was from the other side of the Rhine that the repercussions came. Many of his erstwhile compatriots couldn't forgive him for changing his nationality. This seemed to Offenbach absurd. Paris was his home, everything and almost everyone he held dear were in France, all of the happiness of his life was closely associated with France. It seemed only consistent that he was now a French national.

Among his French friends and associates there was honest rejoicing and they spontaneously decided to give a testimonial benefit for their confrere and new fellow-citizen. They arranged for the use of the Opéra Italien one night in April and even invited the Emperor himself to attend. Napoleon III readily agreed to be a patron—he was an Offenbach enthusiast—but he made one request. He had not as yet seen *Orpheus* and insisted that excerpts, at least, be included on the program. As if anyone could conceive of overlooking it.

To be sure, the creators of *Orpheus* were a little worried over this. Suppose the Little Napoleon should recognize *Orpheus* as a burlesque of his own *opéra-bouffe* regime? They found such fears groundless, as Napoleon III was a self-complacent Olympian monarch, not overburdened with perspicacity or appreciation of real satire.

It was a touching tribute, that gala. Actors came from various theatres to perform; the Bouffes of course was closed for the evening. Mlle Cico, the well-known boulevard star, sang songs from *The Violinist* as a curtain-raiser; Hortense Schneider came out of temporary retirement; the Comédie-Française troupe did a playlet; Offenbach's own company performed *Orpheus*.

The Opéra Italien, or the Salle Ventadour as it was sometimes called, was a large theatre and the price set for tickets to this benefit performance was high. In spite of this the house was quickly sold out and ticket speculators were offering fabulous sums for any procurable seat. Offenbach had agreed to look over the list of subscribers and was careful to see that only names known to him were permitted to make purchases. When two boxes and four orchestra seats were returned, ticket agents offered three thousand francs for the former and sixty louis for the latter, but Offenbach ignored them and consulted the list of those previously refused for lack of space.

Any man would have been deeply affected by the magnificent gesture his friends accorded him and Offenbach, replying to the ovation at the Opéra Italien, unashamedly wept. This night had given him all the recognition he had ever craved—as an artist, as an individual, as a respected citizen. The presence of Napoleon III added the official touch and the Emperor followed it by sending a bronze medal with the simple inscription, "The Emperor to Jacques Offenbach." This token was accompanied by a gracious letter from His Imperial Majesty saying he would never forget "that splendid evening." And the Emperor was reminded of it the next year when, with his concurrence, Offenbach was decorated with the Legion of Honor.

Jacques' detractors were, of course, enraged by the furor over him but their sarcasm over the testimonial gala was only too easily traceable to personal animosity. The most venomous of these proved to be Hector Berlioz who had once pretended friendship for Offenbach. That was long ago when Jacques was a struggling musician, for the bitter, self-centered Berlioz was incapable of tolerating success in another. As Charles Monselet observed of Berlioz: "Some people have been intolerant of him; he has been intolerant of everybody."

Berlioz had long been acclaimed as the great musician and

superb composer that he was, but he had suffered much before
winning recognition and in his bitterness he wanted to make
others suffer too. Again it was Monselet who stated succinctly:
"All his life Berlioz has had one irreconcilable and mortal enemy
—himself."

Berlioz detested Meyerbeer, Halévy, Gounod, and all the
others who had achieved any degree of fame. So Offenbach was
in exalted company.

The embittered man particularly resented the Emperor's
friendliness toward Offenbach since he, Berlioz, had been ignored by the Tuileries. To a less petty person, the answer to
that was a simple one—the Emperor's musical tastes were confined to light, easily remembered melodies. Berlioz' profound
works were beyond his comprehension and bored him. Offenbach he could understand and enjoy. Therefore Offenbach was
his favorite composer.

Offenbach, on his part, had the greatest admiration for Berlioz' musicianship and his comments on it would have done
justice to Berlioz' own estimation of himself. Offenbach, who
was a competent enough orchestrator, freely admitted that he
had more than once consulted Berlioz' treatise on instrumenta-
tion, "which is excellent."

Yet it would have been strange indeed had Offenbach not
been offended by the ill-tempered attacks of Berlioz. Berlioz
both sneered at him as a musical do-nothing and attacked him
personally. It was he and his coterie who most persistently
labeled Jacques a German and a foreigner. The animosity between the two men increased through the years but, in the heyday of his own success, Offenbach could generally afford to
ignore the comments of the older man.

4

Albert Wolff asked an acquaintance if he didn't think Offenbach had talent, to which the latter replied: "He has much
talent but an immense fault—one can never pay him a compli-

ment. When you are on the point of saying, 'You have talent,' he remarks, 'Haven't I genius?'"

To those who disliked him, Jacques' air of importance was infuriating. But to his friends this was a surface and somewhat comic mannerism which covered a basic goodness and decency. To them, his childlike vanity was actually appealing. Villemessant, an extrovert himself, could find only amusement in the letter which Offenbach sent him from Berlin that July.

Jacques had given up the summer theatre off the Champs-Elysées and closed the Bouffes for the season. Instead he was concentrating on road companies of *Orpheus,* playing the various metropolises of Europe as well as the French provinces, adding new laurels to the already fabulous success of his opera.

Jacques, reporting on the reception in Berlin, pretended that he was a "Monsieur Duval" (the classic French version of "Mister Smith") and through the medium of this mythical third person with mock modesty recounted his triumphs in detail. Beyond this comedy was the very real pleasure he took in referring to himself as a Frenchman. He wrote:

MY DEAR MONSIEUR VILLEMESSANT,

We have finally had the first performance here of *Orpheus* by Messieurs Crémieux and Offenbach, this work about which there has been talk for so long, perhaps too much talk, since the friends of the manager of the Friedrich Wilhelm Städtisches Theater where the work was played were afraid that the noise which has been made over it would harm the opening. Well! I am happy to be able to tell you that the success has gone far beyond what one dared hope. Monsieur Offenbach, who came here to direct the final rehearsals and to conduct the orchestra at the premiere, was greeted on his arrival at the podium by a triple salvo of applause; to tell you that Monsieur Offenbach was called back three times, that there were five encores, that the players had their share of ovations, will give you some idea of the enthusiasm with which the public received this

eminently French production. I must admit that my
Parisian heart was very flattered at seeing a work we
have applauded over two hundred times being sanc-
tioned by the top Berlin society. The Berliners have previously acclaimed several operettas of Monsieur Offenbach at their Grand Opera, *Pepito, The Marriage at
the Lanterns,* etc., etc. And Vienna, Breslau, Koenigs-
berg, etc., have also applauded *Orpheus in Hades.* If I
enumerate so minutely all Monsieur Offenbach's hits, it
is because as a *Frenchman,* I am proud to see the director of the Bouffes received so well in Germany. While
the ovations held Monsieur Offenbach in Berlin for
several days, his company was giving performances in
Brussels with great monetary success. I am told that
they are going to terminate their profitable run in Belgium shortly, in the midst of their triumphs, but a previous engagement undertaken by the director of the
Bouffes forces them to be in Lyon by the tenth. They
will be back in Paris the first of September and will reopen the doors on the Passage Choiseul with the inex-
haustible success of *Orpheus.* If anyone asks you from
whom I get these very exact details of their peregrina-
tions, I must tell you that it is from Monsieur Offenbach
himself, who was pleased to communicate them to me.
Hoping you will enjoy this altogether French epistle, I
am,

ALBERT DUVAL

From Berlin Jacques went to Ems, where, as in the previous
year, he supervised the brief season at the Kurpark. Then, in
August, he joined his family at the Villa Orphée.

He was glad to be home. He had traveled a lot, enjoyed his
succession of triumphs, but he was happy to be back in his
"own country." For a few weeks he rested at Etretat where, surrounded by good friends, he was able to recount in further detail the wonderful receptions which had been accorded Jacques
Offenbach throughout the Continent.

5

In spite of his apparent self-satisfaction, despite his popular acclaim, Offenbach nurtured a further ambition. This was to be accepted as a serious musician. Too often he had been dismissed by those whose esteem he valued, as a light and unimportant composer. While his capabilities were admitted—except by the extremely prejudiced—it was widely said that Offenbach craved monetary gain rather than artistic recognition. It was easy and thoughtless criticism, for when one had a wife and growing family, money was a desirable adjunct to comfortable living. And until *Orpheus,* Offenbach had never been far removed from the specter of poverty.

Since his phenomenal good fortune, he had been able to realize two great longings—citizenship and the satisfaction of being a property owner. In the autumn of 1860 he turned to the fulfillment of a third. He wished to write music which would stamp him as a composer of intrinsic worth.

Through Count de Morny's intercession, Offenbach was commissioned by the Opéra to do a ballet and, even more gratifying in a sense, the Opéra-Comique, that long-hostile institution, approached him to do an operetta. Recalling the many years when he had vainly stood on its threshold begging for entry, this request brought a special satisfaction.

Meanwhile *Orpheus* had resumed its merry career at the Bouffes, guaranteeing freedom from worry in that quarter.

Offenbach, never being one to keep his good fortune to himself, was soon being much discussed on the boulevards. Men like Janin and Berlioz were extremely indignant that he should be produced in the same sacred sanctums as Meyerbeer, Halévy and Rossini. Elsewhere there was argument as to how much talent he actually did possess.

Late in November *The Butterfly* was given at the Opéra and was well received. Even some of Jacques' erstwhile hostile critics treated it decently. Only Janin—seconded by Berlioz—was unfriendly and even he limited himself to sneers at Offen-

bach's "youth." (Jacques was forty-one.) *The Butterfly* saw
forty-two performances, one more than his years, quite respectable attention for the Opéra, and once, ironically, it shared the
bill with Wagner's new opera *Tannhäuser*. *The Butterfly* was
neither spectacular nor a great work, but it had charm and
from it came "The Waltz of the Sunbeams" which, in a later
metamorphosis became known as "The Apache Dance," the
hackneyed accompaniment of every adagio dancer since.

On Christmas Eve Jacques realized his further aspiration of
presentation at the Opéra-Comique. But this operetta was an
unmitigated failure, the worst of Jacques' entire career. The plot
of *Barkouf* was a stupid yarn about a dog who became Gover-
nor of Lahore. He barked his commands and at the finale the
whole chorus was shouting "bow-wow." The book was the work
of the first-rate librettist, Scribe, in collaboration with a man
named Boissaux and apparently it was the Opéra-Comique's
own choice, but it certainly did not lend itself to any fine musical interpretation. In fairness, it had to be admitted that Offenbach's score was also less than might have been expected of
him. *Barkouf* played only seven times.

His enemies enjoyed a field day. Berlioz, who persisted in
labeling Jacques as "the German," regardless of his naturaliza-
tion, coupled him with Wagner, whose music he admired no
more than Offenbach did, remarking that "the wind which blows
across Germany had driven them mad." Comparing Offenbach
with Wagner, he railed particularly against the dissonances
which were sprinkled throughout the *Barkouf* score, "grating
the teeth and nervous system."

It was a humiliating episode in Offenbach's life but it might
have been harder to bear if *The Song of Fortunio* had not
opened at the Bouffes ten days later. This was the same one-
act play of Alfred de Musset's, previously called *Le Chandelier*,
for which Offenbach during his tenure at the Théâtre-Français
had written the music. Through the years he had kept his beautiful love-song—the one he had been forced to lay aside at the
time—and as much because of his attachment for it as his recognition of the potentialities for the Bouffes of Musset's whimsy,

he acquired the rights to the play from the poet's brother. The half-mad Alfred had been dead almost four years.

Crémieux and Halévy had completely redone the playlet and Jacques had added several pieces, such as the frothy "Waltz of the Clerks." But "The Song of Fortunio" was of different calibre. Its exquisite simplicity, the crystal purity of its melody, made it rank as one of the best things Offenbach composed. Meyerbeer stated sincerely the day after the opening, "I should like to have done it."

To a degree Offenbach's own estimation of himself was vindicated by *The Song of Fortunio.* His was too mercurial a temperament to be long downcast by the disastrous affair at the Opéra-Comique. He dismissed it from his mind, turning to newer interests and resolving that on some future day he would prove his real musical worth. Meanwhile he gave his entire attention to the Bouffes, adding two other delightful acts to the repertoire that winter.

Financially speaking, the Bouffes had arrived at an impasse and, ruefully, Offenbach was forced to admit he had no talent as a manager. Although the books should have shown a substantial profit Offenbach had consistently dissipated the excellent earnings. Either he magnanimously raised everybody's salary or, deciding that some of the theatre seats were worn, had the entire place done over, or launched on a new and more extravagant production. Somehow he never could comprehend the advisability of keeping a surplus on hand.

Comte was not alone in his uneasiness. At a stockholders' meeting in March pressure was brought to bear on Jacques and this time, with good grace, he resigned as manager. When the theatre was reopened in September it was under the supervision of a man named Varney. Offenbach, freed of the financial responsibilities, continued as stage director and composer.

He toured as usual that summer, returning to Brussels, Vienna and Bad Ems. But in August he had turned toward Etretat for his annual vacation.

And there the catastrophe occurred. The Villa Orphée was burned. Some furnishings were saved, others charred, but the beloved house was left a shell. And many of Jacques' manuscripts—unpublished works, tentative ideas for operettas—were destroyed.

Offenbach was apparently ruined, for his bank account was overdrawn and now most of his personal possessions were gone.

The Offenbach family removed to the hotel at Etretat and there, after his first shock, Jacques' buoyant spirits reasserted themselves. He could write other music, he would make money again and they would rebuild their home.

Without Herminie it might have been different. Herminie, never complaining, was greatly responsible for keeping up Jacques' courage. From the practical point of view also she came to the rescue. Out from her secret hiding place she produced francs, several thousand francs, the steadfast, unobtrusive savings since the opening of *Orpheus*.

"Where did you get them?" demanded Jacques, astounded and even slightly suspicious, when she produced the fat roll of bills.

"From your pockets, my dear," she laughed.

It vaguely occurred to Jacques that she might have made a better manager of the Bouffes than he, even though she was a woman. But that was more than he could be expected to admit. He just beamed at her affectionately.

6

Count de Morny was not only an influential patron of Offenbach's but a good personal friend. Morny's relationship with Offenbach had grown beyond that of a wealthy and influential acquaintance. It had developed into genuine friendship. They presented an odd contrast, these two, somewhat reminiscent of the earlier team of Offenbach and the aristocratic Friedrich von Flotow. (Flotow had long since drifted out of the picture and in fact, now spent most of his time back in Germany.)

Like the aristocratic German, the Emperor's half-brother was a tall, handsome man of distinguished appearance. He towered over the scrawny, homely Offenbach. But they had much in common. Both were dandies, boulevardiers, only really at home in the world of the theatres and cafés.

Although the dignity of Morny's position deterred him from entering into the informal comedy of the Offenbach "Fridays," he was an occasional visitor to the apartment on the Rue Laffitte. He would drop in casually, hoping to find the family alone, and there pass an engaging hour of conversation and light gossip with Herminie and Jacques. They would sit in front of the fireplace with two red plush chairs on either side, the larger one occupied by Jacques, the slightly smaller one by Herminie, and between them a third chair for Morny.

The Offenbachs' two personal chairs were really quite regal. Although easy chairs, an impressive framework surmounted the backs and formed the arms. In a moment of affluence, Jacques had purchased them at a gallery sale of the effects of some decayed noble household. Morny, in his easy manner, used to insist they would do honor to the Tuileries, since they looked so much like throne chairs.

One day Morny bethought himself of this pleasantry and to the utter astonishment of Herminie and Jacques sent a note requesting that they lend the larger chair to the Emperor and Empress. A certain Shah, it seemed, was to be entertained by Their Majesties and the Palace officials had been unable to find a chair worthy of the visiting potentate's dignity and yet impossible to confuse with the throne chairs. Jacques, of course, agreed to forego his favorite seat for the next few days and the use to which it was being put amused him sufficiently to compensate for the possible discomfort.

While Morny's visits to the apartment were comparatively rare, Offenbach saw him often. Morny was a ubiquitous boulevardier and he was present at almost every new opening at the Bouffes. During the spring of 1861, however, his coach was noted regularly during daytime hours standing outside the theatre. Obviously, something unusual was afoot.

The many-sided Morny was a literary dilettante and one evening during an entr'acte had approached Jacques concerning a new aspiration. He sketched the germ of an idea for a

play he had in mind and since he was a novice at play wri
ing, asked Offenbach whether he could not arrange to have
put in shape. Also, of course, he wanted Jacques to do the mus
score.

Unhesitatingly, as Morny's wish after all was a comman
Jacques arranged a meeting with Halévy, already known
Morny, and with Crémieux. Halévy and Crémieux complied l
doing a scenario and any misgivings they may have had
Morny's amateur tendencies were soon allayed. Morny mac
shrewd alterations of the original, contributing a number
good suggestions and witty lines. When the play, to be call
Monsieur Choufleuri will remain at home . . . was put in r
hearsal, Morny appeared daily, supervising it throughout.

Late in March, just about the period Offenbach relinquish
the management of the Bouffes, that theatre closed its doors o
evening and the principals, along with a skeleton orchestra, r
paired to the Palais Bourbon for a private performance of *Mo
sieur Choufleuri* before the Count's select group of frien
Morny used the literary nom de plume of "Saint-Rémy" b
there was no serious intention of fooling anyone.

It was not a matter of fawning when Morny was congrat
lated on his amusing little play. It was unquestionably of t
standard of the regular Bouffes attractions, and Jacques' mus
as always, contributed the necessary extra spice. So much
that when the Bouffes reopened in the autumn *Monsieur Cho
fleuri* headed the billing, sharing the program with the *So
of Fortunio* which wound up the evening.

Monsieur Choufleuri had a profitable and commendable r

7

In the year 1862 Adelina Patti made her Paris debut in *T
Somnambulist*; the Count de Morny was made a duke; t
Prince Imperial, at the tender age of six, attended a theatre 1
the first time; and numerous happenings of note occurred
Jacques Offenbach.

The first of these followed the presentation of *M et M*

Denis, a one-act play of the usual Offenbach standard, but otherwise of no great importance. However, one of the actors, Potel, decided to add his own comic fillip at the end of the opening performance. Stepping to the footlights he announced that the authors of this masterpiece were Messieurs Delaporte and de Laurencin and "the music is by the maestro Offenbach."

This seemed harmless foolery but unfortunately no account had been taken of the presence of certain humorless critics. The editor of *Figaro-Programme,* Monsieur Cardon, felt called upon to sit in judgment. Just what rating did Offenbach deserve as a composer? Cardon's intentions were not suspect, as he had all along been one of the friendlier critics, but it was apparent that he was building the proverbial mountain out of the equally proverbial molehill. He seriously questioned the ranking of Offenbach as a maestro.

This contretemps entertained Offenbach. He was never one to overlook publicity and, besides, he enjoyed writing controversial letters, so in especially fine humor due to the success of *M et Mme Denis,* he penned an open reply to Cardon.

> Oh, Potel! Well-meaning friend, you have certainly got us into something! And now, what to do about Monsieur Cardon! Well, *Monsieur!* Please be calm and stop protesting your good intentions and learn that *maestro* is an Italian term which is applicable to all composers whether great or small, as *maître* in France is applied to all lawyers, from the most eloquent to the most stammering, as *monsieur* is used for everybody, as well for Monsieur Janin as for Monsieur Cardon. . . .

This clever, if impudent letter, brought a laugh from Jacques' well-wishers as well as renewed attacks from the opposite camp. His childish vanity inevitably made him a vulnerable target and many were easily convinced that Offenbach himself had directed that he be titled maestro. In fact, they said, it was understood in theatre circles that one could ingratiate onself easily with Monsieur Offenbach simply by addressing him as "Maestro."

No doubt Offenbach was being made victim of his own humor, since Potel had not delivered the little curtain speech without his director's sanction. Certainly, also, Offenbach was by no means so inflated as to believe he rated the appellation maestro in Monsieur Cardon's use of the term. At the same time he was patently flattered even if it *was* only used in jest.

Of far more outstanding import to Offenbach in that year of 1862 was the granting of his long-cherished wish for a son. It had been several years since the birth of his last daughter, the eldest girl was almost grown up, and Jacques had for some time been resigned to the idea that his family was complete. And now at last a son and heir!

The day after the birth Jacques completely ignored his business duties and occupied himself with a collection of hurried notes.

"It's a boy . . ." he announced to Nadar. "I have a son . . ." he wrote another friend. "I wish to be the first to tell you that I have a superb son. Congratulate me . . ." he stated more formally to an acquaintance.

He asked the Duc de Morny to stand as godfather to his son and, on that gentleman's acceptance, he proudly had the child christened "Morny-Auguste-Jacques."

He also gave himself over to daydreaming. Would his son be a composer like himself? Perhaps a far greater composer? But immediately he was beset by a contradiction of feelings. Naturally it appealed to him that his son would be like him, follow his career, even overshadow him, but when he thought of his own long struggle his paternal protective instinct demanded that the boy be saved from the same fate. Well, perhaps he could ease the way for him. . . .

In the days ahead he must concentrate on solidifying his own position. Which brought him up short by the fact that matters were at an unpleasant standstill. He was beginning to resent Varney, his successor as the Bouffes manager. Presumably the man had a better business head than he, but he had been instated with the understanding that Offenbach should con-

tinue as usual with his operettas. Now Varney didn't seem to
have room for anything like his accustomed output. Recently
Jacques had proposed another full-length operetta, similar in
conception to *Orpheus,* but Varney had brushed him aside, saying the Bouffes could not afford such large-scale enterprises.

Throughout that winter and spring only three small acts of
Offenbach's were put on the boards. His annoyance was somewhat assuaged, though, as summer approached, for Varney was
anxious for him to supervise the newly refurbished companies
of *Orpheus* which were once again starting their triumphal
rounds.

That done, Jacques repaired to Bad Ems, where he had a
contract to run the Kurpark theatre for the entire season. Here
he was allowed a free hand and it soothed his irritation over
relations at the Bouffes.

Bad Ems was a delightful spot, gay and fashionable. If the
clientele was international, the overtones were decidedly French.
There were four spas in Germany—Ems, Baden, Wiesbaden and
Homburg—which profited from the distinction of being the only
places at that time in Europe where gambling was unimpeded.
Napoleon III had prohibited it in France and, for that reason,
the livelier and well-to-do elements of Parisian society joined
the soberer followers of cures. Arsène Houssaye, still a fervent
believer in get-rich-quick methods, came to Bad Ems where he
wrote his wife: "I thought I would be lonely among the water-
drinkers but I have met many Parisians here—Aurélien Scholl,
Pontmartin, Albert Wolff, Villemessant. . . ."

Jacques, who was one of the water-drinkers, also enjoyed
the same convivial companionship as at home in "Eter-tat" or
Paris. This year, as for several past, he took the cure, as his gout
or rheumatism still bothered him; in fact, it seemed to have
grown worse recently. And it was here, at Bad Ems, that a new
person entered his life, one who almost—but not quite—estranged
him from Herminie.

On an excursion to nearby Bad Homburg in search of talent,
Jacques had discovered a lovely creature in a music-hall. Her

name was Zulma Bouffar and she was fair, with blue eyes and a fine voice. She was lively, coquettish and, as Jacques soon found out, had the temperament of a gypsy.

Her life up to the present—she was only twenty—had, as a matter of fact, been almost as nomadic as a gypsy's. She was French by birth, the child of traveling players who had brought her to Germany at the age of twelve. She had been earning her living in that country more or less ever since, periodically moving from town to town. For some years she had sung in taverns in Cologne and, Jacques learned, had served her apprenticeship in the very restaurant where he used to play his cello as a boy.

Albert Wolff remembered seeing her there. Her father, he said, was known as the "little Parisian" and used to be given his dinner by the tavern. Then, after Zulma had sung, he would pass the hat around.

This parallel to his own life endeared Zulma Bouffar immediately to Jacques. But her attraction for him went far deeper. She absolutely fascinated him—by her beauty, by her charming ways, even by her moodiness (for she was most unpredictable) —to a degree that no other woman had, including Hortense Schneider. As for Herminie, she was a being apart from this other world of his and, by the moral standards of the day, he considered this ripening affair with Zulma not as a betrayal of his deep love for Herminie, but as a separate compartment of his own life.

Jacques and Zulma shared the remainder of that summer at Bad Ems together. Her tempestuousness, her unpredictability, her almost pagan behavior at times, made this sojourn at Bad Ems less tranquil than formerly, but that year Offenbach experienced an infatuation such as had seemed impossible for a man of his mature years.

He introduced Zulma to the public in a delightful skit called *Lischen and Fritschen*, which had come into his possession at this time through sheer coincidence. One Saturday evening, just after the advent of Zulma on the scene, the director of the

Kurpark had given a small supper for Offenbach at the Casino. The entire party, including the director, was French and most of them were friends of long standing. Conversation turned on Jacques' prodigious facility in composing and how he worked best in the midst of turmoil, when someone asked him how rapidly he could do a score.

"Last year," Jacques responded smilingly, "Elie Frébault did a libretto for the Bouffes, but I didn't know until the day before it was to go into rehearsal that Frébault had a clause in his contract calling upon me to do the music. I did it—roughly— overnight. Not orchestrated, of course."

"How rapidly do you think you could produce a finished work?" someone else then asked.

Jacques reflected. "Oh," he said slowly, "if I were given an act I could write the music, orchestrate and rehearse it for presentation in one week."

A wager was thereupon proposed to him.

"All right," he answered, half joking, "if you'll find me the play, I'll put it on next Saturday."

At that Paul Boisselot, a playwright and one of the guests, announced he had a libretto in his trunk which had been laid aside to be put to music. There were cheers from several of the diners and the man who had offered to bet Offenbach slapped him on the back.

"Then it's agreed!"

"Agreed!" declared Offenbach, laughing.

And in one week exactly Offenbach presented *Lischen and Fritschen*. In that week, without any apparent effort, he composed the music, orchestrated it and rehearsed the new act.

It was a light, amusing little tale about an Alsatian girl and a good deal of its drollery depended on the piquant French-German speech of the heroine. Zulma, due to her background, spoke French with German overtones and German with a decidedly French accent. Actually, her accent was not far removed from Offenbach's. But while he was grotesquely comic, her feminine, more modulated equivalent produced a captivating effect.

Jacques won his wager on the production time of the play, and also won his bet with himself. Once again his professional instinct had been correct. Under his careful—if accelerated—direction, Zulma had shown herself of star caliber. Her fine reception at the little theatre in the Kurpark was a matter for rejoicing and Offenbach planned to put her on at the Bouffes next season.

When at the end of the summer he returned to Paris, Zulma Bouffar went with him. Jacques, who had conceived of their affair purely as a summer idyll, found he could not break the ties of infatuation which bound him to her. The passionate affair went on, but he still retained a sense of discretion. He kept a clear head about one aspect of it. He was more careful than ever to see that Herminie never learned that he was straying from the path of rectitude.

8

Even the emotional upheaval which Offenbach underwent that summer at Bad Ems did not distract him from his composing. Nothing, presumably, could bottle up the outpouring of melodies with which his mind always seethed. If there was no particular operetta on which he was concentrating, he simply jotted down a fragmentary theme, a waltz, a song, anything which occurred to him, but it was axiomatic that some new musical idea would inevitably present itself.

While at Bad Ems he had, in a desultory fashion, begun work on an opera for Vienna. The Vienna Opera House, no less, had commissioned him to do a work for presentation the following winter. This was a great triumph for Offenbach, particularly as the widely discussed Richard Wagner had simultaneously been rejected by them. Still feeling the smart of the fiasco of *Barkouf* at the Opéra-Comique, Offenbach was determined to retrieve himself, to show that he was worthy of the appellation "maestro."

A newcomer named Nuitter had temporarily replaced Halévy,

whose governmental duties kept him well occupied, as Jacques' favorite librettist. Nuitter and Tréfeu had gone ahead on the scenario of the new opera. While at Bad Ems, Offenbach made a further contract with a local librettist to do the German text. It was to be called *Rheinixe*, or *Rhine Pixies*.

However, when he returned to Paris the score of *Rhine Pixies* was still in a jumbled state. It was Jacques' curse, so to speak, that he worked best under stress and unfortunately he still had plenty of time to complete this new commission.

He had, for his tastes, too much time on his hands, as he found on his arrival in Paris that the reopening of the Bouffes had been indefinitely postponed. Varney had decided to renovate the theatre even though Jacques had had the interior redone when he was still manager. Jacques failed to understand, in the circumstances, why *he* had been considered so extravagant. Also, if he had been in charge, the theatre would at least have been opened on schedule. He remarked on this to Comte, who was inclined to agree with him.

With Nuitter, Jacques had a full-length operetta, *The Gossips*, ready for production; a one-act piece, *Il Signor Fagotto*, parodying Berlioz and his pompousness (replete with dissonances); and, of course, *Lischen and Fritschen*, Zulma Bouffar's vehicle. All of these had been tried out at Bad Ems so there was little polishing to be done.

After a brief stay in Paris therefore, Jacques, unobtrusively accompanied by Zulma, went off to Vienna to make final arrangements for *Rhine Pixies* and also for other works of his at the Karlstheater. Up to a couple of years before Offenbach had suffered through lack of proper copyright controls in Austria, so that, whereas his works had enjoyed considerable popularity in Vienna, until recently they had all been pirated. The new manager of the Karlstheater fortunately was thoroughly reputable and Jacques was only too glad to assist him as guest conductor.

He was back in Paris before Christmas, rehearsing Zulma and finally, in earnest, finishing *Rhine Pixies*. For some reason—

·it was after all a silly story for an opera—he could not work v
the proper enthusiasm for the job. Perhaps it had been hangir
fire too long. Much of the earlier music was discarded, one
two new things added. Then searching through previous co
positions, he resurrected the "Waltz of the Sunbeams" from h
ballet *The Butterfly*. Sunbeams, he told Herminie who tried
dissuade him from using old material, went well with pixi
Far less excusable was his insertion of the "Fatherland Son;
that cheap, bellicose piece he had done in Cologne in 1848. C¢
tainly he had taken no pride in it—on the contrary had be¢
ashamed of its jingoism—but, since *Rhine Pixies* had a Germ
setting, he deemed it suitable.

Just after the New Year *Lischen and Fritschen* reopen
the Bouffes. The renovation was still incomplete, the doors we
not yet rehung and the cold winds swept down the aisles. It w
a double triumph for Zulma Bouffar that she won her audien
over this handicap.

Immediately following the opening Jacques set off again
Vienna to supervise the final rehearsals of *Rhine Pixies*, leavi
Zulma behind to garner her laurels. It was noticed that he w
looking gaunt and tired and he was, in fact, suffering a go
deal of pain. His gout seemed not to have reacted to last su
mer's treatment at the spa and gave him serious discomfort. 1
long train journey should have been restful but Offenbach us
these hours of supposed leisure to work on some future proje¢
It was only in working that he forgot his pain.

In Vienna a third theatre was producing Offenbach so th
for the moment, he found himself more popular there than
Paris. The Viennese were very pro-French and the "offenba
iade" was to their taste.

"The war cry here is 'Offenbach Forever'!" Jacques inform
Halévy.

That was prior to the opening of *Rhine Pixies*, for with t
production, his high hopes once more collapsed. It wasn't
terrible fiasco that *Barkouf* had been but the consensus was t
he should not have strayed from his own particular domain

opéra-bouffe. While the libretto was a poor vehicle Jacques' music was uneven and, on the whole, far below the standard of the Opera House. (It was reported that the sour-visaged Richard Wagner went about smiling.) There were, nevertheless, several lovely things in *Rhine Pixies* which received recognition, the finest by far being "The Goblins' Song." One critic spoke of its "lovely, luring sensuousness." It attracted only passing consideration then, but it was destined to achieve immortality one day as "The Barcarolle" in *Tales of Hoffmann.*

The opening night of *Rhine Pixies* was altogether a most unhappy one for Offenbach. His health had not improved and the rehearsals had put an unprecedented strain on him. Terribly exhausted, he had collapsed just before the curtain went up and, instead of leading the orchestra as had been intended, he was forced to sit in the wings for the premiere. Any of his Paris friends, seeing him thus, would have been shocked for, bent over with pain and fatigue, he looked like a withered old man. Miserably, throughout the performance, he contemplated his swollen fingers.

But in a day or two Offenbach was bustling and bouncing about town as lively as ever. The Viennese journalists' club requested him to write a waltz for their annual carnival ball and Jacques, who never refused journalists anything, promptly complied with an airy bit he christened "Abendblätter." Johann Strauss the Younger, who had also been approached, followed Offenbach's lead and baptized his waltz "Morgenblätter." Throughout the evening of the celebration their two compositions received alternate attention and Jacques, meeting young Strauss, spontaneously observed: "You ought to write operettas. You have the ability."

No doubt young Strauss also had that consideration in mind and one day he was to seriously threaten Offenbach's position in this field, but tonight he was grateful for the older man's compliment.

Jacques remained in Vienna no more than a month and was back for the opening of *The Gossips* at the Bouffes the end of

February. With it, he regained the prestige he had held as the composer of *Orpheus*. *The Gossips* had the verve, the movement, the peculiar genius that was Offenbach at his best.

It also brought prestige and prosperity back to the Bouffes, both of which had been sadly lacking since Varney had taken over. Varney, the stockholders' choice to replace Offenbach as manager, had proven even less competent. His business sagacity was no better and his theatrical sense far poorer than Jacques'. On the excuse of needing more variety, he had limited Offenbach's output. Vainly, Jacques pointed out that he had been the founder of the Bouffes and that the theatre's particular appeal had been built almost exclusively on his own works. Varney seemed unable to comprehend the type of play needed and his own choices were playing to a half-empty house.

The Gossips ended Varney's tenure. For the first time in months, the Bouffes was sold out in advance and if the stockholders needed any further convincing, Offenbach's new operetta furnished the proof.

Another manager replaced Varney but it was early evident that his ideas were not far removed from his predecessor's. His watchword also was more variety, which meant less Offenbach. Jacques' protests were fruitless. For one full year no new work of his was put on the boards.

It was in March, 1864, when *The Georgians* was given and, like *The Gossips,* it revived an apparently dying theatre. By that time Jacques' disgust with the Bouffes management was complete and he decided to sever connections with it. He instituted legal proceedings to establish his rights to the various operettas held by the Bouffes and signed a contract with the Théâtre du Palais-Royal for his next work.

In lesser circumstances this breaking of relations would have caused him a wrench. Offenbach's name had for so long been associated with the Bouffes, "the theatre I founded" as he liked to point out, but since it no longer represented what its creator had conceived, it assumed the status of a disinherited brainchild.

9

The theatre at Bad Ems had replaced the Bouffes in Offenbach's affections. There he was given a free hand and there his own scores filled the bills. In the summer of 1864 he spent the season at Bad Ems, as usual and, as usual, was joined by Zulma Bouffar.

Zulma continued to enchant him, although they often quarreled outrageously. Jacques, who was used to an authoritarian role, found himself frequently defeated. He was helpless against the swift moodiness of Zulma. Often she was all sweetness and gentleness and then he was soothed and happy. But at other times she was a young fury. Or, that phase passing, she was sunk in an incomprehensible depression and it was Jacques who had to comfort her. But whatever the mood, she drew him to her like a Circe.

Despite this forceful attraction, Jacques remained spiritually bound to Herminie. Fortunately, he never was forced, nor tried, to defend himself since Herminie's preoccupation with her growing family left him much alone. She refused to accompany him on his trips, saying she could not leave the children. Her only annual excursion was to the rebuilt home in Etretat and Jacques' stays there, perforce, were limited. Even in Paris, Herminie still inclined to let him attend functions or visit the cafés unaccompanied, feeling her place was at home. She was quite aware of Jacques' fondness for the company of women. Nevertheless, Jacques' sense of decorum had never given her reason for complaint. He was, with all his amatory lapses, a reasonably uxorious man.

Throughout every one of his trips, Jacques unfailingly wrote Herminie daily. Once in a while he protested because she did not respond with the same constancy. She did not take to the pen with the ease he did and she always had the excuse of her household and motherly duties. Jacques had few moments of idleness himself, as he pointed out jokingly in answer to her naive query as to how he spent his time at Bad Ems. He announced that he was giving her his schedule for the day, not unlike all the other days.

At 6:30, I got up and drank the waters of the spa.

At 9:00, Désiré and Paul came for a lesson on *Jeanne*. [This was a play he was putting on.]

At 11:00, lunch.

At noon, rehearsal of *The Soldier*.

At 2:30, visit from Monsieur de Talleyrand, the French Minister to Berlin, who asked me to come with him so that he might present me to his wife.

At 4:00, my bath.

At 5:00, my daily letter to you.

At 6:00, I dine.

At 7:30, ensembles of *Jeanne* and *The Soldier* at my place.

Even so, it was a less crowded day than many, unless Jacques had simply neglected to mention the various scores he was working on. One in particular occupied his attention between plays at the Kursaal. This was the new *opéra-bouffe* for the Palais-Royal for the coming winter. As with *Orpheus* and so many of his other operettas, it was primarily his personal conception. It was to be a direct successor to *Orpheus*, another burlesque of the classics. This time it was *The Iliad* and Helen of Troy was the heroine.

Only Ludo could do adequate justice to this ambitious project and back in Paris he and a new collaborator, Henri Meilhac, were writing a rough draft. This is not to say that they were left undisturbed by Jacques, to work leisurely and tranquilly. A steady flow of peremptory notes flowed in from Ems. "Where is the second act?" "Please add another scene." Or, "Give me another couplet."

Jacques superstitiously believed that Ems brought him luck. Forgetting *Rhine Pixies*, he remarked in a letter to Villemessant: "It was at Ems that I did a large part of *Orpheus*, a little of *Fortunio* and much of *The Gossips;* you see that I have reasons for loving this charming spot."

He loved the place additionally because he believed it brought back his health. The rheumatism had grown steadily worse in the past few years but at Ems he invariably felt better. Possibly the cure helped for the time being; more likely, it was because he was particularly happy in this delightful resort.

"I admit," he went on to Villemessant, "that I have a special predilection for Ems; I find health and a certain inspiration at the same time. . . . Ems pleases me also because of the simplicity which still reigns here. Ems, to the spas of Baden and Wiesbaden, is what Etretat is to Trouville, Dieppe, Cabourg. Neither luxury nor idle youth have yet invaded it."

Jacques, notwithstanding the luxuries he was able to enjoy these days, still scorned pretentiousness. Etretat, unspoiled, remained his ideal summer home and any favorable comparison with it was a superlative compliment.

Even Ems did not deter him from longing to see Etretat. Nor could Zulma, with all her charms, hope to possess him for more than an occasional interlude. By August, the annual cure ended and, the theatre well established for the season, Jacques took the train to his rebuilt and always beloved Villa Orphée.

There Herminie and the girls, now becoming young ladies, and little Morny-Auguste-Jacques, already learning to talk, awaited him. In the tranquil surroundings of Etretat and the peaceful company of his family Jacques truly relaxed.

Never much of a swimmer, due to his rheumatism, he nowadays confined himself entirely to stretching out on the beach in the sun. Unconsciously a martinet, he forced the whole family to observe a punctuality and exactitude which was not apparent in his absence. At eleven-thirty sharp, at an indication from Jacques, they repaired to the Casino for an apéritif, the children, to be sure, confining themselves to lemonade. Promptly at twelve they rose and went to the waiting *charabanc* which Jacques had purchased a year or two before. Each member of the family had a particular seat in the coach. Jacques sat up front with the coachman, little Auguste on his knees and his pet dog at his feet. With everybody settled, a benign smile on his face, Jacques gave the signal and they were driven home. Rarely was the household limited to the immediate family. Jacques' friends and Herminie's in-laws made the house bulge. There were young Robert Mitchell and Georgina Mitchell, Herminie's half-brother and half-sister, respectively. There were Georgina's husband and Robert's wife. There were Gaston Mitchell and Uncle So-and-So and Cousin Thus-and-Thus. Jacques never could keep the relationships straight and was always asking questions. He would look around the dining-room table and, breaking up morsels of bread, roll them into little balls.

"This," he would say, pushing out one little ball, "is Georgina. And this is Pierre. Now what relation is he to Georgina?"

If someone answered "brother-in-law" he would discard that bread ball.

"All right, that one at least we won't discuss any more."

But on the next occasion he had forgotten again.

He didn't really care. He loved people so much he thought it ideal if the house swarmed like a hotel. During that August, Albert Wolff, Halévy, Georges Bizet, Nadar and his wife, all put in an appearance in the packed household. And Jacques, whether at the beach, in the jammed dining room, or working in his study with all the privacy of a railroad depot, was supremely contented. He even forgot the insidious charms of Zulma Bouffar.

10

Helen of Troy—or *La Belle Hélène* as she was officially christened—was a role made to order for Hortense Schneider. From the operetta's very inception both Offenbach and Halévy had pictured her, and her only, in the part. So, on his return to Paris from Etretat, Jacques' first act was to call on her.

She was living alone now, her lover, the wastrel Duc de Gramont-Caderousse, having left for Egypt. He was a consumptive and it was believed in those days that Egypt's climate was beneficial to the tubercular. Unworthy as he may have been,

Hortense Schneider's love for him was sincere and the enforced separation a sad one. She did not, however, give herself up to moping. Her own egoism, in any case, would have been a sufficient force to bring her back to the stage and she had been playing at the Palais-Royal for the past year. But when Jacques made inquiry he learned that there had just been a rupture between the star and that theatre.

If Schneider was never long absent from the footlights she nevertheless continually threatened to leave, and this was another of her crises. Not one to underestimate her drawing power, she had demanded the vast salary of six thousand francs a year from the Palais-Royal and, on their refusal to meet her terms, dramatically stated that she was through with them. She telegraphed her mother of her impending arrival in Bordeaux, gave up her apartment, and packed her trunks.

She was sitting on one of the already locked trunks when the doorbell sounded.

"Who's there?" she called sharply, without moving.

"Me, Offenbach," came the familiar voice, "and Halévy."

At that she got up and opened the door, but her pouting face revealed the mood she was in. Looking at her, Offenbach nevertheless thought that "only Cath can do justice to Helen."

Rapidly he told her of the new operetta, of the wonderful role for her. She gave him a quick smile and shook her head.

"Too late, my dear. I've given up the theatre. I am leaving tonight for Bordeaux. For home."

Halévy interrupted, sketching details of the play and, while he talked, Jacques sidled over to the piano. Lightly he skimmed through several of the contemplated tunes and, watching out of the corner of his eyes, saw Schneider ease herself back on the trunk. She began to hum softly to the music. But when the two men returned to the attack she was still adamant.

"No, no! It's too late. I'm leaving."

Nothing would persuade her and that night, just as she had threatened, she took the train for home.

It put Offenbach in a very bad situation. He could not contemplate the thought of *Helen* without Schneider. Just as his music was important and Halévy's couplets necessary, so its future seemed to him (and to Halévy) also to depend on Cath's creation of the leading part. He urged the Palais-Royal to reconsider her demands, which they flatly refused. Then he approached the Variétés. They agreed with Offenbach that Schneider must play the part. If, but only if, Hortense Schneider would be the star, they would produce *Helen of Troy.*

Back again Jacques went to the Palais-Royal and that management sourly promised to relinquish him from his contract. The Variétés promised to meet Schneider's demands. There only remained the matter of convincing the temperamental Hortense.

That night a telgeram went off to Bordeaux.

"Business with Palais-Royal finished but possible at Variétés."

Jacques had worded it cunningly, but Hortense Schneider was even more cunning. A week in Bordeaux and the humdrum life had begun to pall. She was already regretting her decision and beginning to feel jealous of the unknown who would inherit her role. In fact, the more she thought of the part the more she felt that she alone could do it justice. But her telegram was terse.

"I as!: two thousand francs a month."

This was fourfold the sum she had asked of the Palais-Royal and that had been outrageous. But, shrewdly, Cath realized that Offenbach was as dependent upon her as she upon him. Of course, she was certain no one would accept such a figure, but she could always bargain. To her utter astonishment, it was agreed to without argument.

Two days later Hortense Schneider was back in Paris.

11

Jacques made another of his flying visits to Vienna to supervise the opening of *The Georgians* but his "leisure" time was fully occupied with *Helen.* On October 6 he wrote Halévy:

"I will be back in Paris at 5 A.M. Monday. I will bring the complete first act . . . so we will be able to put it on immediately. The second act will be ready three days after or sooner, if necessary, since it is almost entirely composed. That leaves the third; as I cannot work too fast [sic] I ask at least three times twenty-four hours, and there we are."

Unable, of course, to refrain from mentioning his latest ovation, he went on:

"*The Georgians* was given here yesterday. . . . I was called back at least ten times, I no longer remember the number, the curtain had to be raised and lowered without pause after each act. . . ."

In his usual hurried, nervous way, Jacques was likely to neglect the rules of punctuation. Recalling the real reason for writing Ludo he added in the same paragraph, "Come Monday about ten o'clock."

Halévy, accompanied by Henri Meilhac, was at Offenbach's apartment at the hour indicated. Jacques liked Ludo's new collaborator, the good-natured, moon-faced Meilhac, although he did think him a trifle lazy. Nothing seemed to jog him into action (except girls, as Jacques early commented) and he was inclined to reveries from which it was difficult to bring him back to reality. But Ludo said he was adept at sketching scenarios whereas he, Halévy, only excelled in dialogues. Altogether a good team, that. Jacques appreciated it but in exchange it was Halévy who received the brunt of criticism and directions. Let him work it out his own way with Meilhac.

Within a short time the rehearsals of *Helen* were in full swing; the acts were being rewritten, Jacques' score was undergoing changes and the usual "bedides goupures" were being made. The Duc de Morny, for his own amusement, attended many of the rehearsals and, incidentally, contributed several witty lines of dialogue gratis.

Hortense Schneider was going to be superb in the role but it entailed numerous quarrels between Offenbach and herself before the rehearsals were over. Cath's temperamental outbursts were reminiscent of the early days at the Bouffes. She had never been one to accept criticism kindly. And Jacques, when angered, retreated from his first voluble fury to a dignified restraint.

"Mademoiselle Schneider," he would say, and there was an extra Teutonic hiss to the words as he sought to control himself, "*please* do that over."

Offenbach was sorely tried at moments, although when the play was produced these unpleasant contretemps would be completely forgotten. In his heart he still had great fondness for Hortense Schneider, whom he sometimes called "my child." Regardless of their early relationship, their attachment to each other had much of the quality of father and daughter, and Schneider, even with all her temperamental displays, was careful not to overstep this bond.

She knew too that Jacques was suffering a great deal of pain and on several occasions actually ignored his needling comments. His rheumatism was so bad that on the night of the final rehearsal he asked Ludo to replace him.

"Afterward come to me, please, and tell me how it went and if there are any further cuts to be made."

He was sunk in dejection that night and Herminie wrapped one of her shawls about him as he sat shivering in front of the fireplace. He wondered, sadly, if he would be able to conduct the next evening.

But with his marvelous recuperative powers, the hours of rest seemed to bring Jacques back to normal. The opening night he stepped agilely to the stand, conducted vigorously, and afterward jumped to the stage where, with his infectious grin, he accepted the plaudits of the audience. Herminie wiped the mist from her eyes and smiled happily too, because her Jacques had scored again.

Helen of Troy was more than a simple burlesque of *The Iliad.* It was that special concoction, an "offenbachiade," that delightful brand of light satire, set to music, which poked oblique fun at modern life in the disguise of Trojan days. As in *Orpheus,* it laughed gently at the frivolity of the Empire and the Court. As with *Orpheus,* the lines were full of innuendo and often risqué, but in their light vein they avoided the vulgarity of heavy humor. Offenbach's music touched the peaks reached by *Orpheus,* fitting the dialogue and the situations. The pure harmony, the occasional well-placed dissonances, the spirited dances and tender love songs all contrived to accent the action.

"Really," said one friend, "I do not know any music on earth which contains such a mixture of extremes. It is impossible to choose between the sentimental Offenbach and the other, or even to know them from each other, they are so completely fused."

As to Hortense Schneider, with her provocative voice and winsome ways, she was on her way to captivating Paris, the city, as truly as Helen captivated Paris, the man.

Only one minor flaw marred the perfection of the opening of *Helen of Troy*—after all, an exceptional record for any opening. Paris' song, on his first entry, counted upon to set the tone of the opera, drew no response from the audience. This had shaken the entire company but Dupuis, the popular tenor who was playing the part, was especially upset. Until now his career had been one of uninterrupted achievement and he was chagrined over the failure. The more he considered it, the more disconsolate he became over the future. He had done his best at the opening and the inauspicious first reception gave him no reason to believe that he could retrieve this fiasco. After a night of insomnia, he decided to ask Offenbach to release him from the part.

His mind made up, he was preparing to leave his home when a communication from Offenbach arrived, asking him to come and see him. Dupuis lived at Nogent-sur-Seine, in the suburbs, and he hurried to catch the train. It was afternoon when he reached the Rue Laffitte. As he started to speak Jacques forestalled him by informing him he had written three new songs to replace the original ill-omened number.

"See which you like best," said Jacques.

He went over to the piano and played them one by one.

"Well?" he demanded.

Dupuis, who had scarcely said a word, lifted the last sheet from the piano.

"I think this is the best."

"So do I," agreed Jacques amiably, and without further ado sent Dupuis on his way to practice it for that night.

The train back was crowded but Dupuis, wedged into a compartment, hummed, whistled and learned the words to the substitute song. One or two of his fellow passengers regarded him quizzically, but he seemed utterly unaware of them.

That night, following a quick practice with the orchestra, Paris made his entry on a new note. The house roared its approval. And the delightful tune, "The Judgment of Paris," written overnight, became one of the foremost songs of *Helen of Troy.*

12

In February, Offenbach's long-pending suit against the Bouffes was settled. It had resulted in a compromise. Originally the Bouffes had broken its contract with Offenbach by not producing his works. He had retaliated by attempting to establish his own rights to all his works, past as well as future. The suit ended instead in the Bouffes' guarantee to give at least two one-act plays of Offenbach's to which they already held title, and two new productions of his per year.

With this settlement, the manager, Varney's successor, was discharged and Jacques was asked to return to "the theatre I founded."

In spite of the legal battle, Jacques and Charles Comte (who after all was only one of the numerous stockholders) remained good, even close, friends. Jacques continued to tease him about his stinginess and Comte invariably contended that Offenbach was a reckless fool, but these declarations were forthright and had, in fact, become standard jokes between them over the years. Jacques considered no "Friday" complete without the presence of his trusted comrade, Comte, and was always ready to do him favors. But he was still unprepared for the request which Comte suddenly made to him.

For some time now the eldest daughter had been in evidence

at the weekly "at homes." The Offenbach family respected all
the strict bourgeois conventions and the children, until they
reached the age of sixteen, were relegated to their rooms. By
the same token, at sixteen, they were to be formally regarded
as young ladies.

Berthe, the eldest, had assisted her mother as hostess for the
last year. She was a rather solemn, not especially attractive-
looking girl, but the older men had always been solicitous in
their attentions to her. Jacques, if he reflected on this at all,
assumed this was a display of natural good manners, so that
when Charles Comte asked for Berthe's hand in marriage he was
flabbergasted. Comte was his contemporary and such an alliance was startling.

On thinking it over, though, he concluded that Comte was
as upright and decent a son-in-law as he could desire. True, he
was inclined to be parsimonious, but his virtues were many.
Jacques' long business association with him attested to that. He
was, too, a cheerful and smiling person, and extremely kindly.
On discovering that Berthe reciprocated Comte's affection,
Jacques was quite content. He welcomed the thought that
henceforth Comte would be one of his own family.

"I make the most magnanimous gesture I am capable of to
an old and good friend," he said simply.

He said it with a touch of sadness, for he had just lost a
good friend. The Duc de Morny had died unexpectedly in
March, as a result of bronchitis. Only a few days previously
he had attended another performance of *Helen of Troy*. So
closely had he been associated with this play that, when Jacques
gave the customary supper to celebrate the hundredth performance (this had been a ritual with him ever since *Orpheus*)
Morny's ghost hung over the otherwise joyous gathering. There
was not one member of the company who didn't recall the
presence of the charming, debonair gentleman either at rehearsals or seated in a box at one of the performances.

There were many in Paris who criticized the purity of
Morny's policies; there were those who, with good reason, dis-

trusted his politics. All this was outside Jacques' scheme of things. To him, Morny had always been a true friend and he missed him greatly.

Had he lived, perhaps the Duc de Morny would have graced the wedding of Berthe to Charles Comte. The wedding date was set for early August and Jacques rushed back from his annual sojourn at Ems just a few days before.

As it was, ninety-six Parisians descended upon Etretat for the occasion, as naturally the Villa Orphée was chosen for the reception. Comte being a Protestant, the ceremony was performed in the sacristy of the local Catholic church. Jacques, always viewing religion in its broadest sense, had no inclination to force conversion on his old friend. As for himself, he practiced his Catholicism sparingly, yet remained on excellent terms with the local *curé*. So much so that the latter was delighted when Offenbach announced he was composing his own mass for the nuptials and would undertake to rehearse the choir.

For three days the entire resort of Etretat was given over to the marriage celebration. Even the Villa Orphée could not contain the extraordinary influx of guests but, although they were housed throughout the village, they were served all of their meals in the Offenbach home. A table of mammoth length, or rather a succession of tables, stretched through the four main downstairs rooms and here everybody assembled for breakfast, as well as lunch and dinner.

Surveying this scene of his lavish hospitality, Jacques frankly commented on what a long way he had traveled from the crowded, miniscule dining room in the cramped house on the Street of the Bells.

For the wedding reception itself, the sun shone bright and warm so that the bride and her parents were able to receive on the lawn. On that day, brimming over with pleasure, Jacques even brought out his long-disused cello and, for the first time in many years and perhaps the last in his life, played on it while the guests danced.

Even such a solemn occasion as his eldest daughter's marriage could not conform to strict formality.

13

Returning to the directorship of the Bouffes should have been like returning home. Actually Jacques did not view it with the sentimentality of former years. Today he was the most important figure of the boulevard theatres and any playhouse would have been glad to produce his work on his own conditions. Scarcely a day passed when a caricature, or a mention—laudatory or disparaging—did not appear. Offenbach didn't particularly care which. As for caricatures, he loved them. Two of his close friends, Nadar and Gill, produced some quite savage ones at which Herminie complained. But Offenbach, for all his vanity, knew he was a perfect target for caricaturists and laughed as heartily over the results as anyone. He was not supersensitive and, when it came to publicity, he did not consider any attention, good or bad, as a personal affront.

As for the Bouffes, he was glad of a free hand again but otherwise he cared no more whether he was working for this, or for the Variétés, or any other theatre. He inaugurated the autumn season with a revue, a successful one-act play in November, and plans for a three-act opera in December, for all of which he did the scores.

He set forth his ideas for the three-act opera in detail to Villemessant. It was to be called *The Shepherds* and have the fragile charm of Dresden figurines. He wrote:

> In the first act, we are deep in antiquity and to show Mythology that I have no feeling against her, I have treated it as *opera-seria*—being understood (right?) that *seria* music does not exclude melody. . . . In the second act I have swum in complete Watteau and I have tried my best to remember (it is so good to remember) our eighteenth-century masters. In the orchestration, as in the melody, I have tried not to swerve from the Louis XV style, the musical translation of which so much beguiles me. In the third act," he continued

enthusiastically, "I have tried to realize the mood of our present-day Courbet, as far as possible, his pictures in which the women wear clothes. You will appreciate our reserve. I only continue to affirm to you that I have never written a score more lovingly, having to fill the most delightful frame that I could wish for; three epochs, three different colors united in the same opera.

Offenbach was once more attempting to do something "important," something which would establish him as a "serious" composer. But the very fact that the opera was not in the vein of what Offenbach enthusiasts might expect contributed to its doom.

The play was unhappily hoodooed from the beginning, and this was really unfortunate, as it did have charm. The staging was exquisite and the music of a melodic purity and delicacy of which Offenbach had every right to be proud.

But at the dress rehearsal something went wrong with the footlights. Just as the shepherds were prostrating themselves before the apparition of Eros, who was played by Zulma Bouffar, and who was to be bathed in an aura of gaslight, there was a ghastly explosion and the lights went out. Although, as was soon verified, no one suffered injury, the noise was hideous and the audience, in panic, stampeded out of the theatre. Backstage it was almost as bad and Zulma Bouffar, understandably terrified, fainted.

The formal opening was therefore postponed for a week and assurances that the accident was a minor one were given out through the newspapers. Offenbach also made a point of conducting the opening night, but none of these precautions could overcome the effect of the accident. The public simply refused to go near the theatre.

It was a bitter disappointment. Offenbach had counted on an artistic triumph but the merits of his work never had a fair chance of being proven. And the results of this misfortune had even graver repercussions. As so often before, Jacques had made *The Shepherds* a financial as well as an artistic gamble. The

Bouffes sorely needed a series of hits to put it back on its feet; instead, the cost of this production had very nearly emptied its coffers. Now it had to be written off as a total loss.

The net result was that Offenbach, after a very brief tenure, was asked once more to resign as director. Although in later years he came back to the theatre with individual plays, it was the end of his close association with the Bouffes.

The *Almanach de la Musique,* a publication at no time especially friendly to Offenbach, all but gurgled with glee at this turn of events.

"We announced last season that Monsieur Offenbach was again taking over the direction of the theatre. His new administration has not been of long duration . . . this *illustrious* musician is once more retiring. . . . At this moment we are assured that a great artist, Mme Ugalde, is going to take over the direction of the Bouffes-Parisiens. May she succeed and deliver us forever from Monsieur Offenbach, from his music and his absurd pretensions!"

Mme Ugalde was one of Jacques' numerous theatrical discoveries. It was he who had so brilliantly directed her and brought her to prominence. It was she, in exchange, who had contributed much toward the success of *The Gossips* and *The Georgians* by the brilliance of her performances. The point of view of the *Almanach de la Musique* was therefore a singular one.

There were others, of course, who joined the hue and cry against Offenbach. A few years ago, the debacle of *The Shepherds,* together with his enforced departure from the Bouffes, might have been disastrous. Today the effect was scarcely noteworthy. At the Variétés, after over a year of packed houses, *Helen of Troy* still reigned triumphant. Another Offenbach operetta, *Bluebeard,* was scheduled for early presentation there and it was only to make room for this that *Helen* was temporarily retired. In Berlin and Vienna, Offenbach was the vogue, and in the lesser capitals and the provinces they were begging for his works. Everywhere, from the Tuileries to the lowliest cabarets, they were playing Offenbach tunes and none of his detractors

could stem the tide of his popularity. Jacques Offenbach had
very nearly reached the apex of his career.

14

Offenbach, with his touch of wizardry, was the creator of
many theatre stars, but none of them—not even Zulma Bouffar—
was ever so closely associated with his works as Hortense
Schneider. Although there were several years, and profitable
ones too, when she was not allied with Jacques, it was after her
return to his directorship, and in his plays, that she scored her
biggest hits.

Her name had become almost synonymous with *Helen of
Troy*. Now, with *Bluebeard* about to replace it on the boards,
Schneider was the unquestioned choice. Offenbach had written
his music with her in mind and Meilhac and Halévy, writing
the libretto, had quite naturally conceived her in the leading
role.

Just before the contract was to be signed, the Châtelet theatre made Schneider an offer. If she would quit the Variétés and
join them they would pay her the stupendous sum of five hundred francs a night. It was then that Hortense Schneider made
perhaps the most altruistic gesture of her life. She refused.

Of course, before completely cutting off this opportunity,
she informed both Jacques and the Variétés of the offer. Jacques
pleaded with the Variétés management and, happily, unlike the
Bouffes, they had no need to be niggardly. They promised
Schneider the same salary the Châtelet had offered. Schneider's
hesitation had shown an unprecedented loyalty toward Offenbach and he, on his part, proved the worth of his friendship.

Bluebeard repaid them both. This delightful parody of Henry
VIII and his wives, in which the authors took the license of pre-
serving the latter from the fate of their original counterparts,
was in the best Offenbach tradition. The English tourists, who
were overrunning Paris these days, were particularly enchanted.

And now Jacques Offenbach was not only the toast of Paris,
but of all Europe.

CHAPTER FIVE

"La Vie Parisienne"

1

The rumblings of not too distant wars had echoed in Paris for most of the past decade. In Italy, in Austria and in the German Confederation the guns had been firing almost constantly, but the echo had been faint. Then, in 1866, came the Seven Weeks War between Prussia and Austria. Still the sounds of battle could not be heard distinctly, but a slight uneasiness was felt in the French capital. Bismarck, the Iron Chancellor, backed by the resurgent military might of Prussia, was steadily pushing, pushing onwards. Two years previously Schleswig-Holstein had been wrested from Denmark and now Austria ceded her influence over Hanover, Nassau, Hesse and various other German duchies and principalities. The German Empire was in the process of consolidation.

Napoleon III, blind to the trap being prepared for him, matched his wits against the Iron Chancellor's. In 1864 he had allied himself with Austria to keep a Hohenzollern prince out of Mexico, and gave his blessing to the ill-starred Maximilian.

Switching his allegiance following the Seven Weeks War he requested—and got, temporarily—Venetia from Austria. He then indicated to Bismarck his desire for the cession of the Left Bank of the Rhine to France, as additional compensation for his friendship. By the time Bismarck responded, the distant cannonade could be heard ominously clear in France.

Napoleon III, once so popular, was discovering the fickleness of humanity. No longer did the populace cheer him as he drove along the streets and there were renewed mutterings from the Republicans. The lesser Napoleon, in his way, like the first Napoleon, wanted to add to the greatness of France, but already the people sensed the fumblings of the would-be statesman. The murmurs were as yet faint, for France itself was still enjoying prosperity. The Bourse soared; unemployment was at a minimum; the building boom went on.

In Paris, huge modern department stores were opening, like Le Belle Jardinière, Le Printemps and Les Trois Quartiers, which were greeted by those who knew as "diminishing the number of costly intermediaries between the producer and the consumer." Everyone was pleased by the attractive new low prices they were espousing.

Baron Haussmann's ambitious project for remodeling Paris, giving work to thousands, was still far from completion. Many of the city's most cherished monuments had been restored, such as Notre-Dame and Sainte-Chapelle. The ramshackle shops hemming in the Tuileries had been demolished and the Palace itself connected with the ancient Louvre. Elsewhere fine new edifices had arisen but the biggest single undertaking—the new Opéra—would take another three years for completion. That strangely impressive hodgepodge was still in its rough stage, as were so many of the new boulevards. The half-finished streets and the defacing scaffolding everywhere, although they blighted the beauty of the city, nevertheless were not depressing. To the people they represented work and pleasure and progress.

Paris danced and drank and made merry. In the dance-halls and cafés they waltzed and polkaed to Offenbach tunes and the theatres were jammed with those in search of the Offenbach formula for entertainment. Numerous Offenbach imitators had sprung up, garnering their proportionate share of fame and fortune, but none did more than stimulate the apparently insatiable public appetite for the "offenbachiade." Offenbach, more than any other individual, had set the mood of the times. Or rather, Offenbach continued to be the mirror of carefree Paris.

When one of his own operettas was scheduled for production it was news of primary importance. His impending attraction, slated for October, had been the source of speculation and conversation in the salons and on the boulevards for weeks. This, it was rumored, was to be unlike all his previous presentations. It would not be a burlesque of mythology or history, nor would it be a fantasy. It was to be a satire of the times as its name, *La Vie Parisienne*, promised.

During rehearsals the production seemed, to all the participants except Offenbach, altogether dull and without sparkle. He, on the other hand, had unshakable faith in the *choses adorables* strewn throughout the piece. Still his own best publicity agent, Jacques announced to all who cared to listen that he was producing a marvelous and quite different operetta and with customary prodigality he dispensed handfuls of tickets to his numerous friends. Not the least of these was his "child," as he now thought of her, Hortense Schneider, who had just ended the first run of *Bluebeard*. Jacques' hurriedly scrawled note attested to his sincere affection for her:

MY DEAR FRIEND,

I know that Meilhac is taking care of your box—it is very necessary that you be at our premiere—a premiere of mine without my darling daughters, Helen and Boulotte [the latter was Bluebeard's favorite wife], would be an impossible thing. Tomorrow then, I hope you will use more than one pair of gloves in applauding the *choses adorables* which I have done in La Vie Parisienne.

Your respectful father,

JACQUES OFFENBACH

Offenbach's complete confidence in Vie Parisienne was duly rewarded. Like Orpheus and like Helen, to say nothing of subsequent hits, it was received with an acclaim bordering on delirium. The amazing thing about each new Offenbach success was that touch of spontaneity he injected, the fresh enthusiasm, never vitiated, which it invariably evoked from the audience. It was always as if he had just discovered, with each particular vehicle, a brand new formula for entertainment.

Actually, when one analyzed it, there was nothing very extraordinary to describe about Vie Parisienne. Its plot was slight, but bolstered by a veritable web of secondary situations. Its music was by no means of the caliber of Orpheus or Helen. But . . .

In its tempo Vie Parisienne surpassed everything of Offenbach's, from the opening on the crowded train platform at the Gare St. Lazare to the finale in the Café Anglais. The music, starting with the "Chorus of the Travelers" as the curtain went up, accompanied the rapid action throughout, setting an incredible pace of movement and timing. And if, as was true, the music lacked the lyric quality of his best works it possessed, to a greater degree than any, that ability to imitate everyday sounds, that special gift of mimicry, which was Offenbach's forte and without which there would have been no "offenbachiades." One heard, as much as one saw, the bustle and confusion of the railroad station, the popping of corks and clinking of glasses in the café, the rustle of crinolines and silk petticoats, the tapping of kid boots on the pavement. Implicit in the "Major's Song" was the precision and pompousness of the military, while that of Gabrielle, the little glove girl, echoed the lightheartedness and lightheadedness of her species.

Nothing is better guaranteed to delight an audience than to let it see itself, or at least the background in which its component members move, and this was the first and greatest appeal of Vie Parisienne. It reflected the life of the boulevards, of the café set, the international group. There was not even a mention of the Court. Among the chief protagonists were a Swedish baron, a wealthy Brazilian and an Englishman, all of whom could be seen in Paris almost any day, while the sets were faithful replicas of places they all knew—the Gare St. Lazare, the Grand Hôtel and the Café Anglais. It was the last-named which was the greatest sensation, including in its magnificent gilded setting the prototype of the headwaiter himself—correct, snobbish and condescending to the other waiters—a familiar character to the habitués.

Herminie and two of the Offenbach daughters were in the audience that night. Berthe, naturally, was with her husband, Charles Comte. But Mimi, seated beside her mother, had only recently attained that tenuous age described as "young lady" which permitted her to attend the theatre. It was still novel enough to excite her tremendously and her small, twinkling eyes, remarkably like her father's, darted ceaselessly from the stage to the elegantly clad audience.

Even this did not compare with the thrill when afterwards, the family, accompanied by a dozen intimates, repaired to a café to celebrate the successful opening. The café was, of course, the Anglais. There, in reality, Mimi beheld the splendidly gilded walls, saw the snobbish headwaiter bowing obsequiously to her father, listened to the babel of languages which marked the international set, and drank a glass or two of champagne.

Later she attended many other openings but this one, somehow, always seemed the grandest. And perhaps it was.

2

Zulma Bouffar, who played the role of Gabrielle, the glove girl in *Vie Parisienne,* had scored another triumph. Jacques had never for a moment doubted that she would, but had this by some mischance not been true, his situation would have been somewhat delicate.

His long affair with Zulma was drawing to a close. Following the debacle at the Bouffes the previous winter, he had taken her with him on a business trip to Prague. Zulma had been horribly frightened by that violent explosion at the dress rehearsal of *The Shepherds* and was in a bad nervous state. Jacques hoped that the trip would repair the damage to her frayed nerves.

He himself, however, was in none too good health. His rheumatism had grown worse and his worries, during that season with the Bouffes, had scarcely helped his own nervous condition. Never of a phlegmatic disposition, he found Zulma's temperamental outbursts a severe trial.

It astonished him that his infatuation had survived so long. He had never conceived of their affair as more than a transient relationship and he had no illusions concerning the depth of Zulma's love for him. That she was fond of him he felt certain, but considerations of her career markedly colored her affections. Jacques had never believed that she was constant and would have been surprised if she had been. He had his family (no one knew better than Zulma his deep devotion to it) and she had accepted a mere secondary role in his scheme of things. Moreover, in the theatre world wherein Zulma had grown up, constancy was not a cardinal virtue.

Zulma was young with a long future stretching before her, whereas Jacques, although still in his forties, had been greatly aged by ill health. Philandering had lost its charm. He thought with longing, during those days in Prague, of his tranquil, comfortable homelife with Herminie.

With his customary prudence, Jacques had early dispatched a strategic note to his close associate Nuitter.

"It is absolutely necessary that you render me a signal service. Look up, for me, Monsieur de Pène and ask him to insert [in his paper] this very same day these few words or similar ones: 'Several artists of the Bouffes who are not at present working, such as Monsieur Berthelier, Mesdames Bouffar [sic] and Marie, open this week in a series of performances at Nantes.' His paper is read at my home and these few words could come at no more opportune moment. I ask on your part and on that of Pène's the greatest discretion. . . ."

At no period would Jacques have willingly permitted Herminie to be hurt, but at this present juncture in his life it was more vital than ever to shield her.

This Prague dalliance with Zulma, it was obvious, would be their swan song. But in order to avoid the unpleasantness of any abrupt rupture, it was imperative that Zulma should have a new, a successful vehicle in which to return to the Paris stage. Again the toast of the boulevards, she would soon find consolation elsewhere. Jacques had never failed to retain a friendship, once the love affair was ended. It took a certain tact and appreciation of another's pride. He was not an especially tactful person but he was a thoughtful one and he awaited the moment when Zulma would take the initiative of the final rupture.

He could already see the finale when he returned from Prague. He arrived home bearing a set of exquisite Bohemian glasses of varying sizes—the largest for himself, the next for Herminie, and one each, in proportionately smaller sizes, for the children.

The next day, with Herminie near at hand, he had begun a new operetta.

3

"Herminie!" Jacques called. "Herminie!"

But already he heard her coming down the hall.

"Listen," he said, as she came into the study and, reaching over to the piano with his right hand, outlined the opening bars of the song he was composing. Herminie leaned on the piano, her dark eyes half-closed, just the way she had done twenty-two years ago when Jacques was courting her. She shook her head slightly when he stopped.

"Jacques, it seems to me that resembles something else. . . ."

Immediately Jacques stiffened.

"It's quite possible," he replied coldly, "but so many of my colleagues are inspired by me, or wouldn't hesitate to be inspired, that it shouldn't prevent me, I think, from stealing a little from myself."

Herminie said nothing and, as Jacques returned to his score, she went back to the living room. Offenbach could hear the sound of voices down the hall, because Herminie as usual had callers, and the noise soothed him. Since the children were growing up he was sometimes upset by the quiet of the household. Of course, Auguste was still very young . . . which made him wonder, where was the boy now? But, with a new harmony already faintly evolving in his mind, he was soon absorbed in his notations.

"Herminie!" he called a few minutes later.

Again she was at the door and again he indicated a tune on the piano. And again she shook her head. It was not good.

"Jacques, I'm sorry, but it's not up to what you can do. . . ."

Jacques regarded her icily.

"I thank you, my dear," he said, pompously. "I thank you and above all I am very sorry to have bothered you uselessly. . . . You understand absolutely nothing about it. . . ."

Once more Herminie returned to the salon but in a short while Jacques called out again.

"Herminie," he asked docilely, as for the third time she came into the study, "perhaps you would prefer this?"

As he played the latest attempt a slow smile spread across her face. Stretching her arm out before her in her characteristic fashion, she murmured, as if to herself: "Herminie, Herminie, you were right!"

Jacques looked up from the keyboard and started to grin. He looked like a small boy who had been naughty, had been forgiven, and then given a piece of candy. Smiling at each other for a brief moment, they both began to laugh. They laughed together until the tears came.

Offenbach often tried Herminie's patience to the utmost, but it always ended like this. He realized himself what a trial he could be but, of course, he knew Herminie understood he didn't *mean* it. Without her . . . well, he simply could not visualize such an impossibility. As he had written in a couplet (done to an air from *Orpheus*) for one of their Friday buffooneries:

> *Offenbach est insupportable.*
> *Il est toujours plein de manies,*
> *Et lorsqu'il est un peu aimable,*
> *C'est qu'il pense à son Herminie. . . .**

Herminie too knew Jacques' dependence upon her and it was this knowledge of her importance to him which gave her the greatest pleasure. Sometimes, when he went away on one of his numerous trips, she would guiltily sense a temporary feeling of relief but very soon she would begin to feel lonely. She would miss those calls from his study, the nightly hovering over his table as he ate his lone early dinner before the theatre. She would worry about his health and whether he was getting sufficient rest or whether he was eating enough.

Looking at him now, she was conscious of how much he had aged. His eyes, outlined with crow's feet, still sparkled merrily and his broad smile was that of an adolescent, but his hands were knotted with gout. It was by sheer will power that he controlled them at the piano. Nadar had once said he darted about like a "cross between a cock and a grasshopper." He still seemed like that, most days, but there were other days when the searing pain of the rheumatism made him a bowed old man.

Late that afternoon, as he did every day now when he was home, he came into the living room and slumped into his "throne" chair (the same one Morny once had borrowed) by the fireplace. The warmth of the fire soothed the pain in his legs and, while Herminie and her callers chattered together, he took a nap. Rather, he closed his eyes and rested. He needed this short repose and where could he rest better than in the midst of company? Alone, he would have grown too fretful.

Nevertheless a latecomer, seeing a flicker of the eyelids as he entered, was insulted.

---

* Offenbach is insupportable.
 He's always full of whimsies,
 And whenever he's a little amiable,
 That's when he thinks of Herminie. . . .

"Do you know," this person remarked later, "that Offenbach pretends to be asleep in order not to say good evening?"

But Herminie, furtively glancing at his emaciated form, knew otherwise. She knew he lived on nervous energy principally. He was always terribly thin and he still pretended to be proud of his slim "youthful" figure, but Herminie was concerned over his consistent lack of appetite. She was always trying to tempt him with a variety of diet but, since he was never really hungry, no food ever interested him. Once, Jacques having accidentally remarked that peaches were the most delectable of fruits, Herminie, in spite of the fact that it was midwinter, had rushed out to the de luxe Potel & Chabot establishment to buy some. Jacques, not remembering his chance remark, scarcely pecked at the expensive fruit and Herminie was conscience-stricken to think that she had paid the outrageous sum of twenty francs per peach for nothing.

This particular evening, awakening from his nap, he inquired: "Are you having sole tonight, by chance?"

"Yes," said Herminie promptly, as usual presupposing a bit of gourmet interest. Actually they were not but, excusing herself, she hurriedly dispatched the cook to the fishmonger's. Later, as she sat with Jacques while he ate his early meal, she distressedly watched him push the delicate and costly fish aside. His thoughts were elsewhere.

"Herminie," he asked tenderly, as he had so many times before, "would you care to come with me when I go to Brussels next week?"

When she quickly answered in the affirmative, he looked at her with surprise and pleasure. It had been a long time since she had accompanied him on a trip.

Herminie was a simple person, but she was by no means a stupid woman. Whether or not she knew of his relations with Zulma Bouffar, she must have suspected some of his affairs, but if she ever protested it was for Offenbach's ears alone. Indeed, it is doubtful if she seriously resented his peccadillos. Having early recognized Jacques' penchant for the company of pretty women, rather than sulk or exhibit jealousy, which she knew was the quickest way of losing a man, she had from the beginning of their married life made sure that their visitors included a fair share of feminine charm. Beautiful women adorned their "at homes" and graced the summer holidays at Villa Orphée.

Herminie was, in fact, often appreciative of the tranquilizing effect which lovely ladies exercised upon Offenbach. Their next door neighbor and friend at Etretat, Mme Thorallier, a daughter of the elder Dumas, was a charming woman who captivated Offenbach and sometimes, when he was exceptionally irascible, Herminie would send a hurried note over to her.

"Come over—come soon, please. He is impossible. You are the only one who can calm him."

While Herminie must have known that Jacques would find feminine company in his absences from her, she could not object strenuously, since she had so often refused to go with him. She disliked travel, preferring the familiarity of her own home to the strangeness of hotel rooms. When the children were small she had reasonable excuse for remaining home, but now all but Auguste were old enough to be left alone and, besides, the family was sufficiently affluent these days to afford a nurse to watch over the child. Herminie knew also that Jacques' need for her was greater than ever and as she said "yes" to the trip she was fully repaid by the look of joy on his countenance.

Jacques was, indeed, incredibly happy when they set off on their jaunt. It gave him a feeling of contentment to have her by his side and he was, as always, extremely proud of her.

"Your mother," he wrote in a letter to his small son, "is superb, in spite of her thirty-seven years. When she passes, people turn around in admiration which," he added slyly, "I at first took for myself."

Later in the year Herminie made another trip with him, but that summer Jacques spent more time than usual at Etretat. He did take his customary sojourn at Bad Ems and one or two trips to supervise the opening of road companies, but for the greater part he basked in the warmth of the summer sun and the enjoyable company of his family and friends.

When he returned to Paris in the autumn for the rehearsals

of *Vie Parisienne* Offenbach received notice to vacate the apartment at 11 Rue Laffitte. The building, in accordance with Baron Haussmann's plans, was marked for demolition in order to widen that great artery, the Boulevard des Italiens, around the corner.

The Offenbachs were at first distressed. It had been their home for ten years, ten very full years, and memories crowded in upon them—of parties, of visitors, of the growth of their family, of struggles and successes. But the apartment had long been too crowded. The family had grown and even at the beginning the "at homes" had been constricted by its lack of room. Today, successful as he was, Offenbach could easily afford a bigger place, one more in keeping with his position.

The scaffolding and excavations, the torn-up streets, temporarily marred the beauty of Paris but it was hoped, optimistically, that by next year when the new International Exposition was to be held, the lovely city would be completely rejuvenated. Many other families in the city already had been forced to move but few complained, because those who loved Paris felt about it as about an adored woman—she must be decked in her best. Jacques, the *vrai parisien*, fully subscribed to this concept. His own enforced move was intertwined with the spirit of the times.

La Vie Parisienne was a reflection of modern Paris, and the Offenbachs, when they moved to the handsome new building on the corner of the Boulevard des Capucines a few months after the play's premiere, felt themselves a distinct part of it. Besides, for Jacques and Herminie, it was a milestone of the new era (if never openly admitted) in their relationship with each other.

CHAPTER SIX

"Make Way for the Duchess of Gerolstein"

1

The winter of 1867 was bitter cold and the lakes in the Bois de Boulogne were frozen a good part of the season. There the Emperor, an expert skater, and the Empress were seen frequently gliding over the ice. The Empress, not being as good a skater as her husband, usually clung to the arm of a courtier, which stimulated gossip, especially since it was noted that Eugénie favored extremely short crinolines. Several times she fell on the ice and the prurient felt that the spectacle she presented was in bad taste.

Offenbach repaired to Nice for part of the season (as he had been doing for the past year or so) to avoid the rigors of the cold weather, but before he left, the family had already moved into their new abode on the Boulevard des Capucines. In spite of the snow and ice, laborers were working feverishly to finish the various civic enterprises before the Exposition opened in May. In the theatre world, plans were under way for numerous spectacles and new plays were already being tried out.

During the previous summer the triumvirate of Meilhac,

Halévy and Offenbach had begun preliminary work on *The Grand Duchess of Gerolstein*, scheduled for the Exposition crowds. To judge from the carping clinical notes which flew from Etretat to Paris, it did not go well, either.

"I have read and reread your second act," Jacques wrote. "It is extremely solid, but—it entirely lacks gaiety." Or, flatly, "The duet you have done has the same faults as the other bits. It is useless. The Duchess should be burning with love and you make her sing couplets that would freeze water in the month of August."

After several rough drafts, by mutual agreement, they laid the project aside. During the winter, though, Halévy resigned his ministerial post to give his full time to playwriting. His patron, Morny, was dead and politics had no further attraction for him.

As he remarked: "All I carry away with me from the seven years in the midst of the representatives of my country [he had spent many more in Government, if his civil service training were included] is the most profound political indifference. How much strife has raged over my humble head! But as for genuine convictions, there were none, none whatever, either on the Right or on the Left. There are only people who are nothing and who want to be something and that is all."

Jacques, like Ludo, like many Parisians, was also politically disinterested. What could one citizen—or subject—do about affairs of state, anyway? Strangely, since he lacked convictions, it was he who had suggested a political satire for the edification of the Exposition visitors. During January and February the triumvirate had returned once more to work on the *Grand Duchess*, this time exchanging copy and letters between Nice and Paris, and by the time Offenbach came back to the capital the work was ready for rehearsal.

The Grand Duchess of Gerolstein opened April 12, well in advance of the Exposition, but not without the usual difficulties with Hortense Schneider's temperament, as of course she was slated for the leading role. On the opening night, just before the curtain went up, she burst into tears of pique because the

Censor had interfered with her costume. He had forbidden her wearing of the Grand Cordon, an imaginary decoration but one which he considered resembled the bona fide variety too closely. The overture had already begun and backstage there was general consternation and hysterics. But, as she said later when she had reached the point of laughing at herself:

"Like a circus horse that hears the polka, I dried my tears and when the curtain went up I was smiling."

She could laugh easily then because, at the second performance, she had defiantly redraped the Grand Cordon across her voluptuous bosom. The Censor seeming not to notice this defiance, she gleefully sported the decoration to the end of the play's run.

Rumors had been extant far in advance of the operetta's opening that *The Grand Duchess of Gerolstein* was explosive with political allusions and it seemed that everyone in Paris was filled with curiosity to see the daring satire. But it would have been strange indeed had Offenbach turned to "serious" drama and this was no exception. Typically Offenbach, it was in lighthearted vein. Gerolstein, naturally, was a mythical duchy but with an obvious resemblance to several minor German principalities. The Grand Duchess sang, "Oh, how I love the military!" and the cocky little would-be conquerors—Nassau? Hesse? any one of them—were pilloried. Jacques' music was burlesque throughout, setting the tone with the mock solemnity of "Here is my father's sabre."

The Grand Duchess was definitely frivolous and the people were not only satisfied but relieved that this *opéra-bouffe* did not overstep the bounds.

That spring a defensive-offensive alliance had been concluded between Prussia and the South German States and the French did not like to be reminded of this threat to their theoretical European hegemony. This was, of course, Bismarck's answer to Napoleon the Little's request for the cession of the Left Bank of the Rhine.

There was just one line in the play that flustered the ostrich-like mood. It was when the victorious General sang to the

Duchess on his return from battle: "Your Highness, in eighteen days I have ended the war!"

As it had taken the Prussians exactly eighteen days to reach Sadowa in the recent conflict with Austria, the allusion was pat. No one cared for this reminder of Prussian might and cries rose from the other side of the footlights. After a repetition of this reception the line was changed in deference to the public's sensitivity. Now the General sang: "Your Highness, in *four* days," etc.

The anti-German sentiment in Paris caused some tension when the official Prussian contingent came to the Exposition. King William, the Crown Prince, Bismarck and Moltke all arrived together. Nevertheless the Iron Chancellor's white cuirassier's uniform and huge jackboots were the targets of ridicule rather than of more serious manifestations. Just the same, beneath this air of derision and, at its best, tolerant amusement, was a great uneasiness.

The Prussians came to see *The Grand Duchess* and were the focus of attention. To the general astonishment, the grim Bismarck laughed uproariously and it was even reported that he had slapped Moltke on the knee and said: "But it is exactly like that!"

Before the advent of the Prussians many other monarchs and heads of state had already viewed *The Grand Duchess*. Napoleon III himself had come to the play within a week of the opening. He was so thoroughly entertained that a short time later he returned with the Empress. Monsieur Thiers also went to see what the furor over *The Grand Duchess* was all about. With the opening of the Exposition, the foreign dignitaries flocked to the theatre. The Kings of Bavaria, Portugal and Sweden preceded the Prussian monarch; the Prince of Wales ("Oh, he's one of those *constitutional* rulers," Eugénie had observed) became an almost constant attendant; and the Czar of all the Russias telegraphed from Cologne en route his desire to witness a performance that very evening. Forewarned, the theatre management canceled all other reservations and turned the theatre over to the entertainment of the Muscovites. There was no doubt of the success of *The Grand Duchess of Gerolstein.*

It was an altogether gala season for the boulevard theatres. At the Gaîté, Ada Isaacs Mencken was playing in the *Pirates of Savannah,* Adelina Patti was singing in *Don Pasquale* at the Opéra, *Mignon* was introduced at the Opéra-Comique and the Odéon had revived *The Barber of Seville.* But the first demand of almost all the visitors was for Offenbach—and he was represented by no less than five successes. *Bluebeard* was playing again, *Helen of Troy* had been brought back to the boards, and *Vie Parisienne,* presumably ending its run, finally was booked through the summer.

The old Bouffes-Parisiens, anxious to share in the general Offenbach popularity, dickered to buy back or lease the rights to *Orpheus.* Still disgusted with their treatment of him Offenbach was in no mood to discuss it, but Cora Pearl, the famous Irish beauty—and trollop—had been seized with theatrical ambition and longed to flaunt her pulchritude as Cupid in *Orpheus.* As she was at this period the mistress of Prince Napoleon, it appeared the better part of discretion to accede to the request. Besides, Crémieux, whose name was signed to the libretto, was willing to give in.

Outside of her shape, Cora contributed little to *Orpheus.* Shortly after the opening a messenger barged right out onto the stage bearing a jeweled gift from her fatuous suitor. The sparkle of diamonds was noticeable from the audience and sarcastic cries of "Bravo, Cora!" mixed with hisses. The tough little cockney girl became so flustered she was scarcely able to stammer her song. When, the following evening, a band of students created a disturbance she was so perturbed that she decided to retire to what she thought of as "private life" forthwith. But *Orpheus* not only withstood, but long outlasted the brief contribution of Cora.

It was Offenbach's heyday and next to the Court personages themselves, his name was perhaps the most frequently mentioned in France.

2

Fashion, which so often unwittingly forecasts profounder changes, was showing a marked trend toward soberer clothes. The era of lavish crinolines had definitely ended and that of the straighter, less sumptuous skirt arrived. Moreover, the most stylish color was brown, its drab tone generally offset by the smart new coral jewelry. Ironically, this new color was called "Bismarck brown."

Fashion was somewhat in advance of the mood of the people, who accepted the new styles as evidence of the delightful luxury of new wardrobes. Like the legendary ostrich which hides its head in the sand, the people refused to recognize the portents. Paris was especially gay these early summer days.

Hortense Schneider was among the gayest. Nightly her dressing room was packed with the great and near-great and almost nightly some crowned head or princeling graced her audience. "Cath" had for some years reaped the pleasures of fame and acclaim, but nothing had been as fulsome as the attention she now received. The Prince of Wales had become so enamored that nearly every evening he could be seen walking her pet dogs outside the stage door as he waited for her to join him. Although he was her most assiduous suitor he was certainly not the only one, nor even the lone representative of royalty.

This august company in which she found herself was bound to create certain delusions of grandeur in Hortense Schneider's brain. As she was often banteringly addressed as "Your Highness" the illusion that she was, in fact, the "Grand Duchess" began to form. Before long she had so identified herself with the role that the metamorphosis was complete.

One day, in a fine carriage, she was driven to the Exposition. She was stopped at the gate with the explanation that this particular entrance was reserved for the royal visitors. Outraged, Hortense Schneider announced with superb hauteur: "But I am the Grand Duchess of Gerolstein!"

At that the abashed attendants drew back and Hortense Schneider swept regally into the fair grounds.

In no time the story had circulated along the boulevards. Added to it was a quip of the gay blades. The entrance to Schneider's dressing room was on the Passage des Princes, where the Prince of Wales was so often observed walking her dogs, and some unknown wit with a slanderous tongue christened Hortense herself the "Passage des Princes."

Hortense Schneider, more and more deeply involved in the society of royalty and, occasionally, lesser nobility, was unperturbed by the comedy at her expense. In the circles in which she moved, at any rate, she *was* the Duchess of Gerolstein.

Fortunately the "Duchess" was not forced to run the risks of other rulers. The day after the arrival of the Prussians in Paris they, together with the Russian Czar, were invited to review a military parade in the Bois. Sixty thousand men, bearing the campaign flags of Italy, Syria, the Crimea, China and Mexico, marched by in an attempt to overawe their European neighbors with this display of French might. The Czar was sharing Napoleon's carriage when, just after the parade was over, several shots rang out. Neither ruler was touched and Napoleon, the courteous host, suggested that the shots must have been meant for him rather than for his guest. Later however, a Pole, who had reason to bear the Czar a grievance, was arrested.

Not long after, on July first, the Sultan of Turkey joined the Imperial visitors but official celebrations for him had suddenly to be canceled. That very morning word had been received of the execution of Maximilian in Mexico and the French Court was thrown into mourning. This event seemed to cause considerable embarrassment between the French Emperor and his guests.

3

Jacques was away at Ems during the political excitement and that spa was unusually peaceful and quiet, many of the regular visitors having remained in Paris this year instead. His enforced solitude would have depressed Offenbach anyhow, even without his physical sufferings, but in his loneliness he grew panicky.

"I am not doing very well," he wrote Ludo. "The baths have done me harm, my palpitations and pains around the heart have come back strongly. . . . I do not know, even before I leave, if the doctor will permit me to take them (the baths) again. . . ."

He also worried that he would not be able to go to Etretat on his return as "the sea is not good for this type of illness" and begged Halévy "consequently not to say anything to my family that I am even thinking of going to Etretat at the end of the month."

After writing this he roused himself to dress for a rehearsal. Looking over his wardrobe he chose all the bright-colored accoutrements possible to cheer his flagging spirits, so that an acquaintance, seeing him coming across the park later, was rather startled. There was the ordinarily sartorially correct Offenbach wearing yellow trousers and waistcoat, topped by a light blue jacket, while on his head was a bright green hat. To finish off this extraordinary attire he sported a red umbrella.

Seeing someone he knew, Offenbach brightened.

"It's just gout," he confided. "You know, when one is as thin and sober as I am, there is a certain coyness in admitting to an infirmity which generally only attacks those who live high."

He hadn't even the release from pain of an occasional glass of brandy. He tried to drown his misery in work. There were still the nightly performances at the Kursaal, even if they were not so well attended this off-year, and between rehearsals he reverted to composing. As he said of himself: "I am soaked in music. What a wonderful douche music is! The only one, besides, which my rheumatism permits me."

Music was his consolation and he wrote continuously and inevitably. Much of it was forgotten, some was later destroyed, and much more simply aged in stacks of scores that might one day be resurrected for incorporation in an opera. Whether the music had any practical value or not was not a primary consideration in the compelling urge which possessed him.

Villemessant wrote Offenbach about a conductor he had just discovered. In a Viennese restaurant at the Exposition he had heard a rather exceptional man, an unknown to Paris, who impressed the publisher of *Figaro* to such a degree that he arranged with his paper for several articles on him. The man, he wrote, was young Strauss, son of the famous waltz composer. The *Figaro* articles, plus a *soirée* to which Turgeniev and Flaubert added their sponsorship, had seemingly launched the young man on a promising career. Offenbach remembered meeting the younger Strauss in Vienna and was interested to learn what he had accomplished since. This was among many threads he wished to pick up in Paris. He was homesick and glad at the end of July to return to his "homeland." Exposition or not, rheumatism or not, he was also impatient to join Herminie and the children at "Eter-tat."

4

The Société des Auteurs was an efficiently run guild. Its funds were ample and it was a powerful guardian against the pirating of its members' works. To keep its treasury full it levied a small percentage on the revenue from all members' output, although violations of the latter were frequent and often accidental due to the intricacies of bookkeeping.

The previous year Jacques had been called to an accounting. Because of his widely scattered royalties, including such items as fees from cafés and dance-halls playing his pieces, there had been some oversights. No one blamed Offenbach specifically and it was a routine matter, but naturally fines were assessed on the overdue payments.

Jacques paid his fines with good temper but some time later, chancing to pass an insignificant café-concert in the non-fashionable Château d'Eau working quarter where he heard familiar strains, he decided to have a little fun. As was his wont, he addressed a letter to the guild:

> Last year you reminded me so well as to my obligations
> that today it would give me pleasure to know my rights.

. . . I believe, among others, to have that of being protected by you and I also believed that I had confided
my interests to you in abdicating my independence
. . . but . . . for some time I have been played (without reimbursement)—God knows how or where—and
your duty was to stop this abuse or, at least, to inform
me of it. You have done neither. Your President, Gentlemen, is in a way our father; at least he has two principal prerogatives: he scolds and he protects! But if
all I know of him is the rod, I admit that I prefer to
become an orphan again. . . .

There was division among the directors over this communication—some merely laughed, others took it seriously, and a
few were irritated by Offenbach's levity. The payments of the
poor little Chateau d'Eau café would have done little more than
pay for his postage stamp. Offenbach, having entertained himself by the writing of the epistle, promptly forgot all about it.

Except for affairs of the immediate present, he had a singularly bad memory. During work on any given play he could
recall the minutest details, occasionally to the discomfort of his
co-workers. Once an operetta was produced, however, he forgot even its major features with the most incredible rapidity.
In all sincerity he would time and again ask, hearing someone
hum a refrain: "What's that you're singing? I know it's something of mine, but I really can't remember what it's from."

While he was far from underrating his own capabilities, with
the exception of one song he had no professional pride or sentimental feeling about any of his compositions. The only air for
which he had real attachment and which, therefore, he could
always recall, was the "Song of Fortunio." He still considered it
the finest thing he had done.

Jacques was always extremely absent-minded. He had, among
other unfortunate habits, that of forgetting to button his pants,
a failing shared by many other males, to be sure. This had long
been a source of embarrassment to Herminie who finally concocted a signal to be used when company was present.

"Jacques," she would say, "Monsieur Durand . . ."

Jacques agreed that this was an excellent invention for guarding his respectability. Then the occasion arose and Herminie, slightly clearing her throat, gave him his cue: "Jacques, Monsieur Durand . . ."

Jacques regarded her blankly. "What? What about Monsieur Durand? What's happened to Durand?" Puzzled, he watched Herminie's face flush from pink to crimson. Suddenly he recalled the signal and guiltily fumbled. "Oh, my dear . . ." It was always the same.

In the new building on the Boulevard des Capucines there was a very likeable couple, Dr. Menière and his wife, who lived on the fourth floor just above the Offenbachs. Jacques and Herminie found them delightful neighbors. Jacques, naturally, concentrated more attention on Mme Menière, who often played bezique with him, a game he was fond of. Secretly she was a little afraid of him but he, all innocence, thought she was simply shy and sweet.

One night, returning from the theatre, he unthinkingly ascended to the fourth floor. Unaware of his error, he put the key in a lock identical to his own. As it was late, he tiptoed in the dark down the hall and reached the bedroom silently. Opening the door he blinked. The room was lighted and Mme Menière, not Herminie, was undressing. Horrified at his stupidity, he turned around without a word and hurried out of the Menière apartment and downstairs to his own.

Mme Menière was not sure whether she had had hallucinations or not. She called her husband, who was in the back of the apartment, and said it was strange but she *thought* she had seen Monsieur Offenbach in her doorway. The Doctor laughed but she insisted upon his searching the apartment. Discovering no one, he too was inclined to believe that his wife suffered with delusions.

The next day Jacques, having confessed his error to Herminie, apologized. He hoped sincerely that Mme Menière had not been frightened. To prove that she held no rancor, he insisted that she come down that very evening for a game of bezique, which she did. Looking at his worried face she discovered that he was by no means the awesome person she had at first thought.

5

Henri Meilhac was lazy but he also possessed the pleasant concomitant of being easygoing. He was a bachelor, of modest means, and loved girls and a good time more than anything else. Whenever copy was late, Offenbach would ask Ludo: "Is Meilhac in love again? Get him away from the women."

Meilhac lived in a perpetual state of being infatuated and it usually fell to Halévy to rouse him from his amatory dreams. Jacques referred to Meilhac sometimes as *le grand dormeur,* partially because of his habitually vague, faraway look and partially because he never retired before dawn and consequently was unable to keep early appointments.

Although Offenbach frequently poked fun at Meilhac he was really quite fond of him. It would have been difficult to dislike the young man, whatever vagaries he might have, for he was never ill-tempered and accepted raillery with equanimity. Jacques' affection for Meilhac, of course, was not on a par with that deep attachment he held for Halévy and, in their collaborations, he instinctively addressed most of his communications to Ludo and let him thrash out things with Meilhac, or with "Meillac" as he was likely to spell the name. Jacques' spelling was frequently original.

As Ludo seemed best able to manage his love-struck friend, it was a practical solution as well. Meilhac never took offense, since such an arrangment thrust the main responsibility upon Halévy. And as Halévy never objected either, the collaboration was ideal.

It was Halévy who had discovered Meilhac. Eight years before, he, Ludo, had been commissioned by the Variétés to do a play with Lambert Thiboust when the latter abruptly resigned. (A propensity of Thiboust's apparently, since it was this same behavior which had originally brought Offenbach and Halévy together.) On the steps of the theatre Halévy saw a young man whom he knew slightly and who was trying to establish himself in the field of librettists. Halévy, in his predicament, asked if he cared to join forces with him. Meilhac so well complemented him that their permanent partnership was early consolidated.

Meilhac was clever and talented. Had he cared to, he could have been a successful cartoonist and his sketches of himself and Halévy "collaborating" exhibited a delightful sense of the ridiculous. His wit stamped much of the dialogue in their farces, although he and Ludo always worked on it together. On the other hand, Meilhac specialized in the outlining of the plot, leaving the contribution of the lyrics to Halévy.

They did not work exclusively for Offenbach, nor did Offenbach confine himself entirely to their output, but the greatest achievements of any one of the three during a long period of years seemed to be when they were united. *Helen of Troy, Bluebeard, Vie Parisienne* and *The Grand Duchess of Gerolstein* were all examples of their superb teamwork.

In the two years succeeding *The Grand Duchess* their names appeared together on four productions, but in that time Offenbach himself was represented by no less than *eleven* new operettas. Three of these were only single acts agreed to for the Bouffes when Charles Comte had at last taken over the management, but eight were full-scale productions.

In November, 1867, *Robinson Crusoe* was produced by the Opéra-Comique, the first opportunity Offenbach had been given to redeem his fiasco of *Barkouf* there. The subject seemed an ideal one for his genre, although it was regrettable that Halévy and Meilhac were not also assigned to it.

Jacques worked hard on *Robinson* while his enemies waited for an opportunity to sneer. Poor Jacques' gout was so painful that only a supreme effort kept him on the job. The days when he could not walk were becoming more frequent and on one occasion during rehearsals he was unable even to make the few steps from the carriage to the theatre. Attendants lifted him in.

But Jacques' star was still in the ascendant and *Robinson*

Crusoe profoundly disappointed his ill-wishers. Jacques had achieved his purpose because, as one critic put it: "The success of *Robinson Crusoe* signifies the return of the public taste toward the true medium of the Opéra-Comique."

It had a merited run even if, in retrospect, it did not have the enduring charm of *Helen* and *Orpheus*.

One of the older theatres, the Menus-Plaisirs, on the Boulevard de Strasbourg, had been failing and when Offenbach was asked to revive it with one of his *opéra-bouffes* he wasn't particularly interested. Then he bethought himself of *Geneviève of Brabant* which he had always intended to re-do. Eight years before it had been only moderately well received at the Bouffes, but when the new version appeared on the boards at the Menus-Plaisirs it wrought a miracle in that moribund playhouse. Jacques had prevailed upon Hector Crémieux to aid Tréfeu in writing the new edition and he himself scrapped all but one song of his original score.

Oddly, it was this very song which almost brought about *Geneviève's* downfall. A note from the Censor stated in no uncertain terms that "the duet of the gendarmes is impossible." The *gendarmerie*, the august personage declared, was not to be made the butt of ridicule. But gendarmes were an important element in the operetta and the song was vital to it.

Crémieux, seriously worried, called in person on the Censor. He was, he felt, making no headway as he argued that these gendarmes had nothing to do with modern times.

"But," pointed out the Censor, "a *brigadier* is modern. Such a rank was unknown under Charles Martel."

At this remark, Crémieux was inspired. A good Frenchman, he knew what stress his compatriots placed on exact wordage. If the offense was chiefly against the rank of brigadier, why then, why not simply give the character in question another title?

"Suppose we make him a sergeant?" he queried.

The Censor thought a minute. That, he agreed, would do.

French logic—*clarté latine*—had found a way.

So, the day after Christmas, the operetta opened—intact—

with Zulma Bouffar playing Geneviève. It was altogether delightful and the strains of its music, unlike that of *Robinson Crusoe*, in this case outlived the composer. For the *gendarmerie* song was destined to achieve immortality in the United States. It is Offenbach's rousing march from *Geneviève of Brabant* that you are hearing when the United States Marines step out to:

> From the Halls of Montezuma
> To the shores of Tripoli . . .

As to the happy collaboration of Offenbach, Halévy and Meilhac, it produced, in order, *Le Château à Toto, La Périchole, La Diva* and *Les Brigands*. All except *La Diva*, which was a silly sentimental notion for dramatizing Hortense Schneider's life, added up to an already firm belief in the infallibility of the three as a combination. But perhaps *La Périchole*, a romance with a Peruvian setting, had the greatest appeal. Although ostensibly a comedy, there was an overlay of pathos in this operetta which was epitomized by the "Letter Song" sung by Hortense Schneider. This tender adieu to a lover has a poignancy, a spiritual quality which never palls. Of the scores of songs Jacques had already written and would still produce—surely none was more exquisite. He himself still kept a preference for the "Song of Fortunio" but for most Offenbach followers the "Letter Song" had even greater charm.

Vert-Vert, a lovely light opera on which Meilhac collaborated with Nuitter, might be added to this worthy company. It brought Offenbach back again to the Opéra-Comique with a fine score.

There was a notable change of trend in Offenbach's works of this period which showed a predominance of the simple harmonies of his earliest days. The mocking, comic quality of *Vie Parisienne* and *The Grand Duchess of Gerolstein* was laid aside for the melodic purity of his eighteenth-century inspirers. This was not entirely accidental; it was, as usual, the outcome of Offenbach's keen sense of a change in the public mood.

After twelve years they were sated with satirical operettas and, as each of Offenbach's presentations had established variations of treatment, so now he recognized the time for a complete renovation of style. The frivolousness, the carefree spirit of the French which, for a decade, had set the tone of "gay Paris," was giving way to an unrest and uneasiness over the portents of the future. The Universal Exposition of 1867 had been their last gesture of defiance against the elements. Most people, in their hearts, were worried and frightened. They wanted no more political satires, no more burlesques of the now thoroughly distasteful Court. They wanted to forget and to pretend there was no threat from across the Rhine.

Offenbach offered them what they now craved—romantic musicals, fantasies into which they could escape briefly and forget their fears and worries. *The Princess of Trébizonde,* done on Comte's request for the· Bouffes, would have had a very slight appeal a few years before but now it too won the popularity which the Offenbach touch gave to that near dozen of operas and operettas in these years before the deluge.

Only *The Bandits—Les Brigands*—fell slightly short of the mark. Ostensibly a comedy about Italian bandits and their quixotic chieftain, the old Offenbach propensity for satire reasserted itself. When the bandits stole three millions from the Duke of Mantua their leader's philosophy was that "one must steal according to the position one occupies in the world," and the best song in the *opéra-bouffe* was that of the legendary carabineers who "always arrived too late." The "tramp, tramp, tramp" in this number, now loud, now soft, mostly off-stage, was like a ghostly refrain and the rhythm in the line *"le bruit de bottes, de bottes, de bottes, de bottes"* was little short of unnerving. In spite of this, or because of its superb handling, *The Bandits* was such excellent comedy that a deluded public accepted it as a genuine soporific. Jacques, conducting the orchestra at the opening, turned to the audience with his usual grin of pleasure at the ovation they gave him.

In those years of 1868-69 Offenbach crested on a fabulous wave of success. The period of *Orpheus* and *Helen of Troy* paled in comparison. Besides, in the former period he had been primarily a French, a Parisian figure. Now he was world famous.

All over the Continent—Vienna, Dresden, Milan, Berlin, Brussels, Madrid—his operas were playing continually. Hortense Schneider, exceptionally amenable since her princely suitor was still attentive, extended a long London season with a succession of Offenbach successes. Even in far-off New York *The Duchess of Gerolstein* was playing to capacity.

6

Other people changed but Offenbach, except for accommodating himself to the times, was little different from the young man who had created the Bouffes-Parisiens, or who had led the orchestra at the Théâtre Français, or who had been the darling of the salons, for that matter. Both his virtues and his faults had remained static. He was quite as didactic, quite as quicktempered, quite as conceited, quite as preposterous. He was also just as softhearted, just as thoughtful, just as gregarious, just as humorous as ever. Those who disliked him saw no cause for revising their opinion; those who were fond of him saw no reason for reconsidering theirs.

Since Jacques had always been perfectly confident of his capabilities, success brought him no need of readjustment. He had struggled, yes—but today he struggled against pain and illness.

He loved people and still retained a horror of loneliness. He was loyal and clung to his old friends, the while adding new ones. Of his own early family, he saw little. His sisters lived in Germany and as an outcome of their early separation there were only the bonds of clannishness to draw them together, but he never repudiated his background and when occasion arose he assisted his relatives. As for Jules, he remained a shadowy unknown, pursuing his mediocre career of violinist in one or another of the Paris orchestras. From time to time Jacques was forced to give him attention, to see that he had a job, but fundamentally he was one for whom Jacques felt little sympathy.

Physically Jacques had aged, but mentally he kept the same

boyish qualities which could be both so ingratiating and so annoying. He was one of those rare persons who saw himself quite clearly. He knew just how entertaining and just how infuriating he could be. He still scorned pretense and pompousness and his pleasures remained those of his earlier, less affluent years. Next to Paris, non-fashionable "Eter-tat" was the place he most adored. Here at the Villa Orphée, surrounded by friends, he and Herminie still presided over a succession of "impromptu" parties. He continued to derive pleasure from the lively, if not subtle, burlesques on which he would spend as much time and energy as on an entire music score. And the butt of a majority of them remained Offenbach himself.

In July of 1869 Jacques went to Baden, where the baths were equally good, instead of Ems. The year before he had taken over the direction of the Kursaal theatre there in place of the one at Ems, specializing in the one-act plays of the Bouffes variety. But in August he rushed back to Etretat for a very special event. On August 14 he and Herminie would celebrate their twenty-fifth wedding anniversary.

This called for more than the customary Offenbach festivities. The Villa Orpheé was filled with friends and relatives and the very town was jammed with colleagues and comrades come for the occasion. Like Berthe's wedding, tables were laid end to end throughout the downstairs rooms for the ample, if simple, banquet. It was truly a wedding reception, with Jacques and Herminie dressed for the affair in the peasant costumes of a Norman village bride and groom, and a special wedding march composed for the occasion by Jacques.

Herminie, like Jacques, had naturally changed physically over the years. Her face was fuller and her figure more matronly than that of the sixteen-year-old bride of twenty-five years before. But her hair was still the lustrous black of the Spanish beauty and her dark eyes, if somewhat shadowed, were as soft and luminous as ever. Looking at her, Jacques was as enraptured as he had been on their wedding day. With her beside him, he succumbed to that state of bliss which he could never find elsewhere.

7

France was far from enjoying that idyllic state which Etretat, and the Villa Orphée especially, exuded. The growls from
Prussia were becoming so menacing that to laugh at them was
patently bravado, while on the domestic scene there was an
equal lack of reassurance. Now that Baron Haussmann's gigantic
enterprise was nearing completion the evidences of unemployment were again manifest; yet the cost of living continued, in
spite of promises, to mount. Strikes broke out and talk of so-
cialism was again in the air.

The mutterings against the Emperor had changed to open
clamor; a public demonstration was held at the tomb of a Republican martyr of the *coup d'état*. When one of the group was
arrested as the instigator of the demonstration, Léon Gambetta,
the young defense attorney, boldly attacked the *coup d'état* and
the so-called constitutionality of the Imperial regime itself.
Wisely, Napoleon III and his beautiful Empress confined their
public appearances to a minimum of official functions.

Offenbach, who had never dabbled in politics, found to his
utter amazement that he too was a target of abuse in certain
quarters. Hadn't he been a close friend of Morny's? Wasn't his
the music most often played at Court? And hadn't the Emperor
showered favors on him? Jacques' works, which had so faithfully reflected the mood of an era, were suddenly mistaken in
the public mind as propaganda for the Empire. Jacques never
having been a part of Court circles, and his operas having been
accepted at the time as rather daring spoofing of the Court, the
present interpretation seemed odd. But diatribes against him
and what he presumably stood for began to appear in the press.

At first he was bewildered, then angered. Unfortunately, he
had no idea of how to cope with these unexpected attacks. His
friends advised him that silence was the best policy and to this
he adhered, at least to the extent of refraining from replying
in print. But he did not refrain from personal comments. Halévy,
for one, was vastly amused by Offenbach's ingenuous remarks,

but in other quarters they only furthered the harm being done him. Jacques confused personal indebtedness and loyalty with the broader scope of affairs of state, but his defense of his dead friend Morny and what he believed was the fundamental decency of the Emperor only confirmed the suspicion of many of his listeners that he was an Imperialist.

Moreover, his long association with Villemessant bolstered this conception. Villemessant was, and long had been, a frank Imperialist. Now, just as Napoleon had been forced to call a general election and when public meetings for the nominations of Parliamentary Deputies were turned into grievance riots, the publisher organized a youth league known as the "Gourdins Réunis" to combat these embryo rebellions. A *gourdin* was a short stick, and such a pugnacious symbol together with like actions did little to squelch the mounting fury.

Offenbach took no part in his friend's crusade. To him rioting, whether of the Right or Left, was equally abhorrent. Even had he been so inclined, his physical condition would not have permitted it.

Jacques was, in fact, spending the spring of 1870 at St. Germain. Overwork, plus the sufferings of rheumatism, had brought him close to collapse. He had been badly frightened, otherwise he would never have acceded to his doctor's order of three months' rest. Naturally, he was to do no work but this, for him, would have been tantamount to a prison sentence. He did work at a more leisurely pace and was soothed by the calm of St. Germain in contrast to fervid Paris.

He worked principally on an enterprise which the great Victorien Sardou had agreed to write. The combination of these two men was an extraordinary one. Sardou was a man of reserve and dignity, with a reputation as a serious, even a profound, writer of drama. Temperamentally far apart from him, Jacques nevertheless had the greatest admiration for Sardou and exhibited it early by "tutoying" him. Sardou was not the sort of person with whom most people grew familiar quickly but to everyone's astonishment he reciprocated by "tutoying" Offenbach. He had taken a liking to Jacques and their strange collaboration ran marvelously smoothly.

In his naive appraisal of France's political situation Offenbach had recognized some truths. It had long been general knowledge that the pretty, if brainless, Empress meddled in state matters. In his own desire not to malign the Emperor—who had always been so kind and friendly to him—Jacques subconsciously transferred blame, when necessary, to Eugénie.

Jacques had read and reread the *Tales of Hoffmann*, a popular classic in France as well as in his native Germany, many times. He appreciated, of course, the allusions concerning him as an evocation of a certain character from one of E. T. A. Hoffmann's famous stories. (Perhaps because of his extreme fondness for them he had been formed into an image!) Now he saw the application of at least one of the *tales* to another personage. With a longing to fix blame where it was due, he recalled "The Heroic History of the Celebrated Minister Kleinzach" which, with careful moulding, could be made to fit the case of Eugénie.

When he first vaguely, only vaguely, sketched his idea to Victorien Sardou the latter was incredulous.

"I! Do a political fantasy!" he exclaimed.

Then he reflected.

"For a long time," he said slowly, "I have dreamed of doing a startling resurrection of Pompeii . . . if these ruins could only be revived. . . ."

Offenbach remarked that, while he had no objection to a Pompeiian fantasy per se, he thought the framework of Hoffmann's story better fitted to a satire on the Empress. He visualized a burlesque on the order of *The Grand Duchess of Gerolstein*.

Sardou promised to give "The Heroic History of the Celebrated Minister Kleinzach" consideration. Nevertheless, Offenbach was unprepared for the grave import which Sardou injected into his interpretation of the tale.

"Here is the subject in a few words," Sardou announced at their next meeting. "To give the horoscope of the Empire's approaching end."

Jacques was speechless. He was, actually, distinctly upset. This was going far afield from his conception of fantasy. His plays always held to the delicate touch of satire, not the heavy hand of polemics.

He said nothing as his friend further dilated his idea, but his brain was actively digesting many facets of the situation. For the first time Jacques began clearly to grasp the potentialities in the present political circumstances and Sardou's gloomy prediction shocked him. If, however, the country really faced this dire prospect an allegory such as Sardou advocated might be doing the nation a service. Sardou was a man of brilliant intellect and a fine playwright. Listening to him expound his thesis, Jacques grew calmer. To be associated, to work with such a man was an unusual opportunity. It was a new field for Offenbach, but in its timeliness the play held magnificent possibilities.

It was on this ambitious project that Offenbach worked at St. Germain. Sardou lived at Marly and correspondence was carried on constantly back and forth. Then, early in the summer, Offenbach joined his collaborator in Paris and there, in Sardou's study, his legs covered by a blanket despite the intense heat, he listened as the playwright read the finished outline. On the skeleton of Hoffmann's story Sardou had built a fantasy all his own.

"The King, Fridolin, had married a foreign princess, queen of style and fashion, to whom he confided, for no reason at all, the reins of government. . . . A bad fairy, a sworn adversary of the royal family . . . went into the vegetable garden of the palace and pulled up the roots . . . among them the Red Carrot, leader of the *radix* [slang for Radicals and a pun on the word for radish]."

Sardou, oblivious of his listener, read as if he were describing a vision. The allegory unfolded—the King, leaning on the bourgeoisie, has called the radical element to his aid, which dethrones him and usurps his power for itself. (Sardou, while criticizing the Emperor, held no brief for the Left.) His approach was that of the moralist and he ended his play with the return of the repentant King Fridolin, who has learned his mistakes, as savior of the nation, and with the defeat of King Carrot who is returned to the vegetable kingdom.

Offenbach was hypnotized by Sardou's intensity of purpose. He devoutly hoped Napoleon would heed the warning. Deep within himself he was skeptical of any such far-reaching effect but under Sardou's spell he considered the play a vital one. The era of *The Grand Duchess of Gerolstein* had passed and that of *King Carrot* had arrived.

But the time was more advanced than either Sardou or Offenbach knew. On July 14, 1870, when the opera was only three-fourths done, the Franco-Prussian War broke out. In lieu of the traditional celebration of that symbolic day of French independence, Napoleon III signed the Declaration of War.

Though the threat from Prussia had long been visible, the actual cause was a mere diplomatic manoeuvre. A Hohenzollern prince was candidate for the vacant throne of Spain and on France's protest the famed Ems telegram had been sent. The Prussian King had couched his rejection of France's demarche politely enough, but Bismarck, with no intention of forestalling the conflict, edited his words so as to provoke the holocaust.

By coincidence, Offenbach was at Ems when the telegram was sent. With horror and dread he learned the news and hurried back to his beloved France. Her fate—and his also, in a lesser sense—was about to be decided.

King Carrot had certainly come too late.

CHAPTER SEVEN

Flight From the Prussians

1

The collapse came so terribly swiftly. One day the popula
was bravely cheering the departing army with cries of "To B
lin!" and almost the next they were preparing to receive t
returning wounded. While Prussia had long been training
the conflict, no serious attempt had been made to properly equ
the patently inadequate French forces. The French General St
had assured Napoleon III that his troops were "ready to the l
gaiter button." Yet within seven weeks the Emperor, at the he
of his poorly trained soldiers, had capitulated at Sedan.

That night of September 2, the lesser Napoleon was te
porarily incarcerated in the empty castle of Bellevue. Like o
in a trance, he sat silent and stiffly erect in a chair, refusing a
light as darkness fell. Outside, a German regimental ba
marched by. At the sound of the music he turned his he
slightly. They were playing—Offenbach. Hearing the fam
strains Napoleon's reserve crumpled. Burying his head in
hands, he wept.

Two days later, in Paris, the Third Republic was proclaim

and the pretty, meddlesome, brainless Empress stole into exile. Those others who had devoted themselves to the Empire—deputies, senators, civil servants—vanished from the scene. Offenbach, with his family, also took flight. Because Offenbach, like the deputies and senators, was called an enemy of the people.

From Ems he had gone direct to Etretat, where Herminie and the children awaited him. It was quieter there, away from the hostile crowds of Paris, where some had so lost sense of proportion as to accuse the *Duchess of Gerolstein* of having contributed to the disaster. That Offenbach's publisher had with the best of motives, when war was declared, immediately reprinted his patriotic song, "God Save the Emperor," written eight years before, did not assist his case.

Many things were held against Offenbach now, not the least of them the fact that he was German born. Even Etretat was only a temporary haven and when Sedan came he, with Herminie, the younger girls and Auguste, fled to Bordeaux.

Jacques was mentally and physically near prostration. The national catastrophe, plus the personal vituperation against him, engulfed him in an abyss of sorrow. Just after their departure for the south the last rails linking Paris with the rest of the country were cut. The Emperor had capitulated but France still refused to accept defeat and the Capital was under siege. Jacques' old friend Nadar, that droll fellow whose hobby was ballooning, put his experimentations to practical usage. By this modern means he got Gambetta out of Paris to set up a government at Tours. Nadar had always been an ardent Republican— let those who accused Offenbach of associating only with Imperialists remember that! For, through all the years, Nadar never vacillated in his friendship.

Herminie was distraught trying to find means of consoling Jacques. In Bordeaux there was not even work to occupy him. Fortunately, in Italy his popularity had suffered no setback and, at her instigation, Jacques went to Milan to supervise some rehearsals while she, with the children, crossed the nearby border to Spain, visiting relatives in San Sebastian. Altogether a wise move in these parlous times.

Even in Italy Jacques found no surcease. There he received word of the capitulation of Paris and its occupation by the detested Prussians.

"I hope that this Wilhelm Krupp and his dreadful Bismarck will pay for all this," he wrote pathetically and naively to Nuitter. "Alas, what terrible people these Prussians are and what despair I feel at the thought that I myself was born on their side of the Rhine and am in any way connected with these savages! Ah! my poor France, how much I thank her for having accepted me among her children."

But the bitterest hurt was that they no longer *did* accept him, that he, so absolutely French in all his sympathies, was being repudiated. In February, Comte had tried to revive the Bouffes by putting on the innocuous *Princess of Trébizonde*. For answer, the hostile crowds assembled in front of the theatre, protesting the work of "that Prussian" and the play had to be withdrawn.

"I know about *Trébizonde*," he added to Nuitter. "I find it hard to forgive the miserable comrades who hope, because I have had a great deal of success, to injure me by saying I am German when they know very well that I am French to the marrow of my bones. They will suffer for their baseness. I hope you and I will get back to work again and although, alas, I was born in Cologne, you will still deign to give me your confidence."

Yet it scarcely seemed feasible to return to Paris for a while and Herminie urged that they go back to peaceful Etretat.

"Jacques is in Milan," she wrote from San Sebastian to a friend early in March, "on a trip throughout Italy. He will be back at Etretat in two weeks, where I plan to go shortly. His health is seriously altered and for three months now he has not had one week without pain. I am hoping that return to the surroundings he loves and for which he has so much need, will restore him."

Instead of Etretat, though, he returned to Bordeaux. Only a few days after Herminie had written her hopeful letter, the Communards, the extreme radicals, had taken over Paris. Jacques was so overwrought by these tidings that Herminie feared for his very sanity. She watched him anxiously as, isolated in Bordeaux, he feverishly composed music—not music for publication, simply music for consolation.

Day by day the news grew more ominous. Details of excesses seeped through. Paris, defeated by the foreigner, faced civil war. By May there was fighting in the streets, Frenchmen killing Frenchmen. Jacques wrote a hymn, "God Save France." Then he composed a prayer which was never published, but the depth of his feeling was expressed in the lyrics of Victor Hugo to which he had set the music:

> *Dieu, si vous avez la France sous vos ailes,*
> *Ne souffrez pas, Seigneur, ces luttes éternelles.*°

2

By the arrival of June the Commune had been suppressed and order restored, but Jacques still hesitated over returning to Paris. He had not yet the calm and strength needed to face the latent hostility he might encounter. He dreaded, too, the sights of destruction which awaited him. The lovely Hôtel de Ville was gone, the Tuileries reduced to rubble, the Palais de Justice badly burned, many other monuments desecrated. The Rue Royale was a shambles, but the damage had spread over most of the city.

While he hesitated, the decision was made for him. In Vienna they were putting on *The Bandits* and asked him to come for the rehearsals. It was a sensible solution because, at best, it would be a month or two before the Paris theatres resumed activity. (The very Variétés where *The Bandits* had been playing when war was declared had just a few weeks ago been used as a first-aid station.)

Jacques wrote Nuitter and Tréfeu: "Write me in Austria (not Germany, I will never set foot in that accursed land). . . ."

Austrians, to Jacques, were not the same as Germans. The Viennese in particular, he sensed, drew their cultural inspira-

---

° God, if you have France under your wings,
Do not suffer, Lord, these eternal struggles.

tion from Paris which, he always maintained, was in no way akin to the *Kultur* of the Prussians. With the knowledge that peace, albeit a sad one, had returned, Offenbach seemed to have revived and he finished off his hurried letter impishly: "Nuitter, you hug Tréfeu for me; Tréfeu, you hug Nuitter; and I will hug my dear Tréfeu's wife."

In Vienna he appeared to have recovered completely, moving about agilely, as of old. One day, driving in a carriage through the Vienna streets, he passed a crowd in the center of which he glimpsed a prostrate figure. People were gaping idly and making no effort to relieve the unconscious man on the pavement when Offenbach, leaping out and pushing into the circle, demanded information.

Someone volunteered that the man was an elderly employee of a nearby dance-hall, a musician named Rudolph Zimmer. (Zimmer . . . Zimmer . . . In the back of his mind Jacques heard his father saying wonderingly, "Do you still remember Zimmer's waltz?") Without further ado Jacques ordered him lifted into his carriage and drove him to a doctor's. The man was clearly suffering from undernourishment and Jacques, slipping some money into his pocket with a note to come and see him when he was better, left him in the doctor's care. If it were really the same Zimmer perhaps he would finally hear all of the waltz.

About a week later Herr Zimmer, apparently recovered, came to his hotel. Jacques greeted him warmly and offered him a drink. The old man, obviously impressed that his benefactor was the famous Offenbach, remarked that he himself had once been a music teacher and composer.

By way of answer Offenbach jumped to his feet and, striding over to the piano, played the eight bars of the waltz which had for so long haunted him.

"So there is still someone who remembers me and that someone is you!" murmured the old man, for it was, indeed, his composition.

Jacques, explaining how all these years the fragment had persisted in his memory, asked his visitor to play it.

"At last I shall hear it all!" he exclaimed.

But when poor Herr Zimmer sat down he too played the same eight bars, then stopped. He also had forgotten the rest.

"That waltz is my history," he remarked cryptically as he rose slowly from the piano stool.

Jacques was forced to leave Vienna unexpectedly that very night, but he returned a month later. Awaiting him was a parcel containing a sapphire ring and a copy of Zimmer's waltz. Herr Zimmer had died a few days after their meeting, presumably a victim of age and starvation, but not before he had written instructions to deliver this box to Offenbach. Attached to the ring was a note explaining that it had belonged to his dead fiancée. This and the waltz were all that he possessed of value.

Jacques vowed to have the waltz published. And he did, guaranteeing it himself, when Paris returned to normal.

3

In the middle of the summer Jacques went to England, where he found that he was still in vogue and detested by no one. This gave him courage for his re-entry into Paris the end of July.

It was quiet in the capital, the passing scars of occupation gone. But the marks of the civil conflict were evident. The Rue Royale was still a shambles, in the Place Vendôme there was a great emptiness where the Column had once stood, and a few stones marked the erstwhile elegant Tuileries. And in the Place de la Concorde the granite female figures representing Alsace and Lorraine were shrouded in black. After two centuries these proud provinces, in conformity with the harsh peace treaty, had been handed over to Germany.

Paris was sad, but already one sensed the resumption of activity, of life, there. Along the boulevards the theatres were reopening and, within a few days of his arrival, Jacques was seated on the stage of the Variétés directing the revival of *The Bandits*.

It was not like Offenbach to sit quietly in a seat, but he was again crippled by gout. Halévy, who was present, watched him anxiously, noting the trembling beneath his thick fur coat. As Jacques explained, he had not slept and felt depressed.

He could hear the members of the company gossiping of their war experiences and it was plain from their chatter that they considered the operetta outmoded. They rehearsed listlessly and at the finale of the first act—a supposedly lively drinking scene—the chorus danced like wooden puppets on strings.

Suddenly, forgetting his pain, Offenbach leaped to his feet.

"What do you think you are singing, ladies? Start all over again—the whole finale right over again from the beginning!"

He strode rapidly to the piano, motioned the conductor aside, seated himself and took over. His miraculous hidden forces of energy had again asserted themselves and his ardor soon communicated itself to the company. He started singing and shouting, stepped frontstage to put life into the supers, flung off his overcoat, and grabbing his stick beat time with all the force he had. He hit the piano so hard that he broke the baton in half but, with an oath, he threw it to the floor, grabbed a violin bow from a nearby member of the orchestra and went on beating time with astonishing vigor.

As Halévy put it: "He was no longer the same man, they were no longer the same players, the same singers. Offenbach had communicated his vitality to them and the finale suddenly bubbled with gaiety and cheerfulness and went with tremendous swing."

When it was finished Offenbach sank back, exhausted.

"I've broken my stick, but I've saved my finale," he remarked.

There was a spontaneous burst of applause and, as he looked up at the now genuinely enthused troupe, a faint sparkle came into his eyes. Offenbach had returned to the boulevards.

4

Offenbach was back on the Paris boulevards, but there was something lacking. His name again prolifically adorned the billboards, sometimes with revivals, often with new works, and while few were failures and most made money, they were not greeted with the wild enthusiasm of former years. It was not that Offenbach had changed—but the public had. Offenbach, who had always had an uncanny sense of the devious currents of public requirements, today was floundering.

He decided to revive an old show. The stupid *Barkouf* of away back was revised for the Bouffes-Parisiens. This time it was called *Boule de Neige* and sufficient charm had been injected to make it palatable, but it was unquestionably far removed from the great "offenbachiades." Meanwhile, Offenbach and Sardou finished the pre-war libretto of *King Carrot*, both of them refusing to recognize (although Sardou had slight misgivings) that its theme was *passé*.

Practically simultaneously with the presentation of *King Carrot* a feeble adaptation of Alfred de Musset's comedy *Fantasio* was given at the Opéra-Comique. Despite Jacques' music, particularly his "Ballad to the Moon," this boring play expired with commendable rapidity.

Offenbach, aware that he was not recapturing his old standing, conceived an idea more nearly resembling his erstwhile burlesques. He approached Halévy and Meilhac, who frankly didn't care for it, likewise Nuitter and Tréfeu. Stubbornly, Jacques himself wrote both score and libretto of *The Black Corsair*. It had its premiere in Vienna and later was put on at the Variétés, but neither in the Austrian capital nor in Paris could it charitably be called even a modest success.

In Vienna, as in Paris, Offenbach found a disconcerting drop in interest for his works. New composers were beginning to elbow him aside. In Vienna, the younger Strauss was realizing the predictions Offenbach had made for him and, in Paris, Charles Lecocq, that none-too-gracious young man who had split the Bouffes' prize fifteen years before with Georges Bizet, was making inroads against the older composer.

It was unpleasant medicine and Offenbach, characteristically, refused to swallow it tamely. He again felt the urge to run a theatre of his own. If he could give himself proper presentation he was sure he would recapture his popularity.

A year after his return to Paris he started dickering for the tenancy of the Gaîté. Many technicalities hindered his progress (one was to re-establish his rights to various operettas) and it wasn't until June, 1873, that he received clearance.

Once this was settled Jacques set to work on the new organization with the enthusiasm of the old Bouffes days. The present Gaîté was a comparatively new playhouse, having been entirely rebuilt after a fire in 1861. Nevertheless, Offenbach decided to completely renovate the theatre. In three months the interior was not only redecorated from top to bottom but the entrance changed from the Boulevard du Temple to the Square des Arts et Métiers, reversing the dressing rooms and ticket office. On top of this he hired a double troupe of players to accommodate all eventualities.

With alarm, his friends observed that Offenbach was spending with his oldtime profligacy. But being in a better financial position than when he had inaugurated the Bouffes-Parisiens, he installed both a resident manager and a director. His old friend Etienne Tréfeu, the librettist, was his choice for the former and Albert Vizentini, his orchestra leader, was to undertake the functions of the latter when Offenbach was absent. He had worked with Vizentini for many years and the man was not only a conductor of the orchestra but, more important, having once been a journalist as well, had a flair for publicity. Both Tréfeu and Vizentini were trustworthy and Jacques' choices seemed commendable.

He had so much confidence in them that late in June he departed for Aix-en-Provence, as substitute for Bad Ems of pre-war days. He had given Tréfeu and Vizentini detailed instructions to carry out the décor and preliminary arrangements for the first production.

Jacques' arthritis, which was the term now given his previously labeled rheumatism, kept him in almost constant agony. Yet in spite of his often intense pain, his daily worries, he displayed an extraordinary good temper. Instead of being allowed to relax in the warm sun of Aix, he was immediately and continually beset by queries from Vizentini. As if the man had never received directions, he demanded what he should do about this,

what about that, cautiously seeking authorization from Offen
bach for every move he made. Jacques, bedeviled, managed to
reply with good humor. France was in the grip of a heat wave,
Aix being one of the hottest spots, and Jacques' comments upon
it were generously sprinkled throughout the letter.

Tuesday, July 8, '73
What heat!

SIR,

Since my departure you have received about thirty
letters, 245 telegrams, and you complain! I understand
nothing (oh, how hot it is!) about the Pinard affair (oh,
what sun!). You have never spoken about it before. I
understand nothing about the business of Prevel, Barie
Duporti, having read nothing about the event. You must
have received the telegram for the Gilbert girl [the
actress, Mlle Elvire Gilbert]. I am going to hold everybody responsible! Everybody! Everybody! What a quaking if everything isn't ready—the hall restored, the chandelier in place, the costumes for *The Gascon* finished,
the sets delivered to the theatre. I expect the play to be
ready the day after my arrival. What quaking! What
quaking! We are cooking here! My health is improving.
I am thinking it might be better to rehearse the play
next Saturday even without my being there. I am suffocating, suffocating, suffocating!

My regards to all who want them.

Yours,

J. O.

Across the page this postscript was scrawled:

43 degrees Réaumur! Stifling heat!

Tréfeu sweats ⎫
Vizentini sweats ⎪
Jacques sweats ⎬ The Sweat Family
Eugene sweats ⎭

Don't write me any more! *

---

* This was a heavy play on words, the surname of the popular mystery
writer, Eugene Sue, being the same as the French word for *sweat*.

Gloating over his childish comedy as he sealed the letter, Jacques nevertheless hoped it would forestall any future barrage from Vizentini. When, a few days later, he was handed another epistle in the latter's handwriting, he sighed. On opening it, however, he found that Vizentini was merely announcing receipt of a communication from London, requesting a three-act *opéra-bouffe* for English production.

"Tell your English friend," replied Offenbach, who considered that he had enough commitments, "that I am sick and that, besides, all my time belongs to *Mme l'Archiduc.*" (This was a production promised to the Bouffes for early autumn.)

Not in the least dismayed, the English agent sent a second appeal through Vizentini.

"Tell him I ask 100,000 francs," Offenbach directed. "It's the only way, I think, of having peace."

In response to this the agent appeared in person in Paris, telling Vizentini he was still set on acquiring an original Offenbach operetta but making a counteroffer of 60,000 francs. When this intelligence was reported to him Jacques concluded it was time to reconsider. Such a sum was not to be lightly brushed aside. That night he wired that he would return to Paris. The contract was concluded for 75,000 francs, a counterbalance against the heavy cost of the Gaîté not to be ignored. It was a comforting thought, too, for when *The Gascon* opened it was little short of a fiasco.

5

Jacques was exhibiting an uncanny predilection for repeating history. He had gone on to "Eter-tat" after only a few weeks in Paris and, as the weather continued exceptionally hot, he began to reflect on the unhappy lot of those destined to remain in the capital.

A one-act piece, *Pomme d'Api,* was in rehearsal for the Renaissance, and it occurred to him how much pleasanter it would be to work on it at the seashore. True, in ordinary circumstances he would be called upon to return to Paris himself, but this was a secondary consideration, particularly in view of the far greater expense he now contemplated. After consultation with Herminie he felt that to install the troupe for a few days at the Villa Orphée would give these poor hard-working souls a nice holiday. Also they could put on another gala for the benefit of the widows of Etretat's fishermen, serving a doubly deserving purpose.

Settled on the scheme, Jacques sent meticulous instructions to Vizentini concerning the arrangements for the expedition:

> . . . The actors will leave Friday at six-thirty [in the evening] from the Saint-Lazare Station for Les Ifs. You will get first-class return tickets. Tell them that at Beuzeville, third station before reaching Havre, they change trains and take the one for Fécamp. Two stations before Fécamp is that of Les Ifs. There they will find a small bus which will bring them to Etretat. . . . I will send a servant to show them the way. I have received a package but not yet the one with the scenery nor the case of costumes and other things. . . . Don't forget to warn the actors not to fall asleep before Beuzeville or Les Ifs. They'll be there at 11.20. . . . Tell them to wrap up well, the women especially, for it is cold here at the seashore at midnight.

No one caught cold and it would have been surprising if the participants had shown themselves less than enthusiastic. For Mlle Théo, an unknown whom Jacques was launching in this vehicle, this kindness was beyond her wildest hopes. Perhaps as a token of their appreciation, all the actors made an extra effort with the little play. At any rate, when *Pomme d'Api* opened in Paris it was well received.

But Jacques' profit from it was *nil*.

6

Mlle Théo was blonde, with no particular voice, but with an ingratiating manner reminiscent of Hortense Schneider and

Zulma Bouffar. Jacques, very pleased with the reception she re
ceived, announced: "I think that Théo is ready for three acts."

In the next seven weeks he supervised the writing of, com
posed the score for, and produced *La Jolie Parfumeuse*. Neither
it, nor *Mme l'Archiduc* which had opened meanwhile, got more
than passing attention. Not so Théo, who was launched as a star.
Jacques promised her a worthier vehicle in the near future but
at present he was naturally primarily concerned with the estab
lishment of his theatre.

He was essaying something different. Today's public consid
ered him not simply old-fashioned but, in the moralistic atmos
phere of the Third Republic, inexcusably frivolous. Very well.
He had always intended, eventually, to turn to more serious ef
forts and now that he had passed the half-century mark, the
time had arrived. He would show them that he merited their
further consideration.

The Gascon, a drama with incidental Offenbach music,
had failed dismally. His next venture, *Joan of Arc,* for which
Gounod had done some fine music, was already in rehearsal
when the old Paris Opéra on the Rue Le Peletier burned down.
It was especially bad luck that the fire broke out during a per
formance of Mermet's *Joan of Arc.* Everyone was superstitious
and when the Gaîté production, which deserved better, was put
on, it was confined to a *succès d'estime.*

These misfortunes did not discourage Jacques too much, but
if he were not to become bankrupt he must take his chances
with his next choice. Experimental ideas were laid aside and he
turned to the opera which had always brought him luck—
Orpheus.

Naturally, it had to be more than a mere revival. After all,
almost everyone in Paris had seen it once. Besides, Jacques'
conception of his new theatre put the accent on *production.*
Orpheus was transformed into a great spectacle. He planned a
chorus of one hundred and twenty, a ballet of sixty-eight and
an over-all orchestra of one hundred. He added two acts and
eight more scenes, but it was the sets which astounded everyone.
To do *Orpheus* on a grandiose scale had always been Jacques'

dream, and now he was making up for the enforced niggardliness of the Bouffes-Parisiens days. His breath-taking Olympus was of marble and gold and his Hell was equally dazzling. The designs were Doré's originals, now treated with opulent justice.

Possibly something was lost in this extravaganza wherein the décor was so distracting that the brilliant music did not always receive full attention but, if so, the audience that February night of 1874 didn't regret it.*

The reception of this new version of Jacques' old stand-by was phenomenal and in a few short weeks he had recouped all his losses. This *Orpheus* proved to be the worthy vehicle he had promised Théo, who was the most captivating Cupid of all. At the customary banquet celebrating the hundredth performance it was announced that official receipts for *Orpheus* to date totaled the stupendous figure of 1,400,000 francs, an almost unbelievable sum.

That supper represented something outstanding to Offenbach. Even though *Orpheus* was not a new play, the renewed acclaim helped his ego. If *Orpheus* still appealed he was not a has-been.

He looked over the assembled group with a keen eye. Théo and the other principals were in decided evidence, but Jacques soon noted that several of the minor players were absent. This disturbed him, and the next day he made inquiry of the house manager. The latter, seeing that Offenbach was quite irritated by this presumed indifference, answered frankly:

"Maestro, the poor souls hadn't evening clothes."

Jacques stared at him, at first incredulous, then suddenly touched with pity. Everyone knew that theatre people had had a thin time of it since the war. His mind flashed back to his early salon days and the constant struggles and deprivations that went into obtaining his necessary attire. For these people evening clothes weren't *necessary* but their very lack had deprived them

---

* In the early nineteen-twenties, Max Reinhardt staged an *Orpheus* in the Grosse Schauspielhaus in Berlin which was so *kolossal*—a cast of *two hundred,* a ballet of *eighty,* an orchestra of *one hundred and twenty* players—that only the impresario's name was discussed and scarcely anyone seemed to register that the score was by Jacques Offenbach.

of the little pleasure which he had intended offering them. Here
he was on the upsurge again, feeling secure in his position . . .

"Tell them," he said brusquely, "tell them immediately, that
I am raising their pay by a third, *starting tonight.*"

7

The resurgence of interest in his work had a magnificent
tonic effect on Offenbach. Herminie watched with approval the
energy with which he bustled about and which for so long had
seemed lacking. Before nine in the morning he was off to the
Gaîté for the business of the day; late in the morning he was
back home, working on his scores and off again to rehearsals
in the early afternoon. He supervised a new version of *La Périchole* at the Variétés; did a successful act for the Bouffes; went
to London for the opening of his one strictly English production, *Dick Whittington and his Cat* at the Alhambra; put on
The Barber of Seville at the Gaîté and arranged with Victorien
Sardou for the right to set that playwright's best drama, *La
Haine,* to music.

He was so busy that he gave up any idea of going to Etretat
that summer. In July, faced with a recurrence of his arthritis,
he moved to nearby St. Germain again. Ludo Halévy was staying there and while Jacques pretended that his primary purpose
was to be alone for his work on *La Haine,* this was accepted
merely as theory.

For the first day or two he seemed content enough to work
alone, although Ludo looked in on him in the evening and usually stayed long enough for a few games of bezique. Jacques
was an inveterate card-player—it was almost as satisfying as
work. At the end of a week, however, as anyone but Jacques
could have foretold, he grew weary and depressed with his enforced solitude and would send Ludo notes, concocting some
flimsy excuse just to insure his friend's appearance.

"My dear Ludo," he said in one, "I'm afraid that you won't
come this evening after winning so much. Here is the telegram
I have just received. If, by chance, you are at home, come to

my place during the morning so we can talk it over or, better yet, come this evening to win some more. . . ."

Ludo, always devoted, certainly would have come anyway. An evening with Offenbach was an evening spent in good company, but he also was fully aware of Jacques' propensity for gloom when left alone.

The score for *La Haine* went well and Jacques was pleased later by Sardou's appreciation of it. The friendship of this strange pair continued, with the deepest mutual respect. Jacques told him of his plans for staging *La Haine*. The Florentine scene of Guelphs and Ghibellines must be faithful fourteenth century; then there would be another set, showing a replica of the Cathedral of Siena; there must be a constant marching of soldiers, not just three or four supers, but enough to give the illusion of an army. And the costumes must be of the best, accurate in period details and made of silk and velvet. Also . . .

Sardou protested. Accuracy of detail was an excellent goal, but the fineness of materials would not be appreciated across the footlights.

Jacques disagreed. *Orpheus* had gained by the recent spectacular sets. Sardou's—his friend's—great play would surpass it.

Regrettably, Sardou's fears were justified. It was bitterly cold that December and the night of the opening a terrific snowstorm blanketed Paris. Jacques pointed out that this was the cause of the disastrous first night and that they must wait for weather conditions to improve. Yet even when the snow melted the people did not come.

Offenbach directed that the theatre should be kept filled by every means. Given time, it would establish itself. He gave away seats to his friends and told Vizentini:

"If you and Tréfeu have friends you can count on, give them tickets—first balcony and orchestra. But fill them up, fill them up. I don't want an empty seat. . . . This evening the theatre must disgorge people."

Ten days of this and still the musical drama was far from attracting crowds. Sardou had been right. *La Haine* was indeed a magnificent spectacle, but the drama had been lost in the refulgence of the production. Recognizing the inevitable, Sardou suggested withdrawing the play.

Jacques protested but, following another week of fighting against odds, he had to admit defeat. The cost of keeping the production going was vying with the initial expenditure and that had been exorbitant. However, Vizentini shrewdly pointed out that the costumes at least could be salvaged as they would serve in the revival of *Genevieve of Brabant* with which Jacques was considering replacing *La Haine*.

Offenbach tolerated his personal loss in this enterprise with greater equanimity than his shame in having failed with Sardou's worthy play. When Sardou wrote him, graciously releasing him of responsibility, he was deeply touched. Sentimentally, he decided to publish the letter in the newspapers. Sardou had written:

> MY DEAR FRIEND,
>
> What I learn about *La Haine* is very sad. If one could have predicted that a play written with such care, such love and such conviction . . . applauded the first night with such extraordinary honors as the recalling of the actors after each act . . . and the next day the almost unanimous approbation of the press . . . that this play, at its twenty-fifth performance, does not bring in receipts capable of covering its expenses . . . we would not have believed it, neither you nor I. I am too proud of my work to allow it to trail along with receipts unworthy of it. And I like you too much to have you associated any longer with its unjust destiny. I beg you to stop the performances of *La Haine* and to reassure the spectators who do not find this prose tragedy *amusing enough* that I promise never to do another.
>
> With affection,
>
> VICTORIEN SARDOU

To Offenbach's astonishment, although it was not premeditated, Sardou's letter proved good publicity. The public began to interest itself in *La Haine*, although unfortunately not sufficiently to warrant continuing it. One line in Sardou's letter seemed particularly pertinent. The audience did not find his play *amusing enough.* Offenbach's name was associated with laughter and this obstacle still hindered his attempts to be "serious." He was in the position of the traditional clown who aspires to be a tragedian.

Geneviève could not be accused of being solemn and therefore seemed suited to fill the bill momentarily. Offenbach had not the money—nor quite possibly the inclination—to transform it into an extravaganza, as with *Orpheus,* but he did refurbish it with a few additional songs and sets. Nevertheless, it merely limped along, just paying its way and in no wise lifting the weight of debt with which *La Haine* had loaded him.

8

By spring, Jacques had to face the obvious. He was bankrupt. The unrecovered expense of *La Haine* was the immediate cause but other factors were involved. His choices of Tréfeu and Vizentini as director and manager had not proven as sagacious as anticipated. They were both of them honest and decent and devoted to Offenbach, but temperamentally they were incompatible. Tréfeu was phlegmatic, Vizentini impetuous, and the result was nugatory. As for Jacques, he had clung obstinately to his extravagant notions, for instance contracting for a topheavy troupe and then refusing to lease any of its members to a rival theatre.

The humiliation at any period would have been awful, but for Jacques, who had once reached the peaks, who was now ill and aging, it was devastating. He was utterly sincere when he stated that his first worry was for those who had lost because of him. Offenbach, whatever else was said of him, had always been scrupulous and even his worst enemies at this vulnerable moment could not accuse him of dishonesty.

Jacques declared that he would pay back every franc owing. On May 15 the holding company was dissolved and Jacques declared the sole proprietor of the Gaîté. He then assembled the entire troupe and reminding them of their triumphs to gether, of his affection and appreciation, said firmly:

"My children, you will be paid to the last centime. If I have been imprudent, at least I have retained my honor."

His was no idle promise. In June he sold the Gaîté to Vizentini, including the rights to a forthcoming play. In the next month he sold all his foreign rights to realize cash and pay his immediate debts. And from that day onward he guaranteed that everything he earned, over and above his actual living costs, would be used to wipe out the remainder of the deficit.

Offenbach's sense of fair dealing was to lead him into what proved to be a bondage of seven years. Perhaps one small item was most revealing of his sacrifice—he rented the Villa Orphée that summer, giving up his own much-needed vacation.

On March 4, 1875, Offenbach's friend and onetime protégé, Georges Bizet, awoke to find himself the most currently discussed man in Paris. The night before, at the Opéra-Comique, his extraordinary new opera *Carmen* had had its premiere. Bizet had previously received quite a bit of attention over *L'Arlésienne*, being hailed by some as the outstanding young composer and railed at by others as too "Wagnerian." The heated debate over the earlier work, though, was as nothing compared to the immediate furor over *Carmen*. This stark drama which had been made of Mérimée's tale, together with the realism of Bizet's music, offended many aesthetes but others regarded it as a revolutionary advance in the field of opera.

Jacques was an ardent advocate of the latter school. He refused to couple Bizet with Wagner, pointing out the far greater attachment to pure melody in the former's fiery music. He went rarely to any theatre outside his own but he was conspicuous in the audience of that first night of *Carmen*.

There were several reasons for his special interest in this opera, apart from Bizet. Meilhac and Halévy had written the superb libretto and Zulma Bouffar was singing the leading role. While her voice was not great it had a peculiar timbre which fitted Bizet's unusual music, and the character of the gypsy, Carmen, seemed designed for her interpretation.

The initial mixed reception bitterly disappointed Bizet, but in a very short time it was apparent that this radically different type of opera was being accepted at its true value. In May, Vienna took it for production and from Berlin, Brussels and London negotiations were already started. Yet when in June, three months to the day after the opening of *Carmen,* Bizet unexpectedly died of a heart attack, the superstitious and sentimental attributed it to a broken heart.

Jacques was horribly shocked by the sudden death of his thirty-seven-year-old friend. Coming as it did on top of his personal misfortunes, in the midst of renewed attacks of illness, it was doubly grievous.

Reaching his fifty-sixth birthday on the twenty-first of the month, Jacques had no inclination to celebrate. It passed quietly and gloomily, and in the evening he went downstairs to visit an elderly neighbor who was incurably ill, which scarcely improved his frame of mind. But, unknown to him, his associates were preparing a special tribute.

At midnight, or thereabouts, he was quietly relaxing in his favorite chair when an apparent explosion occurred in the courtyard. There was a burst of fireworks, shouts and the sound of brasses, then suddenly the strains of the "Hymn to Bacchus" from *Orpheus* came loud and distinct through the window.

Quivering with emotion Jacques started to rise, but already the musicians were mounting the stairs and Vizentini, leading, was entering the apartment. Herminie, not saying a word, smiled broadly. She had been in on the secret from the beginning, when the entire company of the Gaîté had planned this gesture toward the man they loved, the maestro who was ill and temporarily broken. At the close of *Geneviève* that evening, fourteen buses had lined up at the stage door to transport chorus, orchestra, scene shifters, administrators, everyone in any way connected with Offenbach and his theatre. Now to the tunes from *Orpheus,* they marched into the apartment. Vizentini placed a crown of gold laurel leaves (a relic of *Orpheus*) on the *Maître's* head and one by one the company passed by to shake his hand.

Jacques was profoundly touched. He might have failed, but

he knew now that there were people who still valued him fo himself.

Herminie, thinking of the old lady ill downstairs, was rathe worried about the disturbance so late at night and made a poir of calling on her the next morning. The feeble old lady ros nobly to the occasion.

"Don't worry about me," she said. "I would rather die t the music of the cancan than anything I can think of."

9

Herminie was superb through the whole ordeal of the bank ruptcy. The way she behaved one would have thought it mad no difference. She was both tranquil and sympathetic.

"Tell your mother," Jacques wrote his daughter Mimi fror St. Germain, where with Halévy he was putting the finishin; touches to a forthcoming operetta, "that I embrace her and tha I absolutely insist on renewing a thirty-one-year lease of con stant happiness with her."

Herminie did not complain over her enforced stay in Pari but by August Jacques felt that the loss of the Villa Orphé was more than he could bear. Actually they both longed for a glimpse of Etretat and late in the season they improvidentl) decided to spend a couple of weeks at the hotel there. Witl them went Jacques' favorite, the boy Auguste, now thirteen and a *lycée* student.

Albert Wolff, learning of their impending arrival, gatherec together some of Offenbach's friends for a hilarious reception When the bus from Les Ifs drew up to the hotel the welcom ing committee was waiting to receive them, dressed up as *opéra bouffe* soldiers and ready to accord Jacques full military honors Solemnly Wolff stepped forward and offered him his hotel ke) on a silver platter.

Auguste laughed raucously and Herminie joined in, but the implicit kindness unnerved Offenbach.

"This is too much, too much," he murmured, with a catch in his voice.

Just the same it was helpful to be in this congenial atmos phere and the stay in Etretat had its tonic effect. He worked, of course, as hard as ever, but not with the desperation of a few weeks back.

Jacques' greatest joy was the company of his son. Always his favorite, Auguste reciprocated his father's devotion and looked up to him with admiration. Whereas the girls had all shown musical gifts of varying degree, Auguste exhibited the potentialities of genius. For the last year or two, when at Etretat, he had played the organ at mass. In the little country church there was not much formality and often Auguste would arrive early to indulge his own pleasure in the pipe organ. Then the strains of some very inappropriate music were sometimes heard as Auguste, a devotee of his father's works, would try out the *galop* from *Orpheus* or the quadrille of *Vie Parisienne*. So softly did he play, modifying the rhythms, that the early worshippers were inclined to think everything proper and correct. Whatever the priest thought, he kept his own counsel, but Offenbach, turning up early for mass one Sunday, was highly amused—and secretly flattered.

When, during their stay at Etretat this summer, Auguste was thrown from a pony, cutting his face badly, Jacques was frantic. It was fortuitous that one of France's leading surgeons was vacationing at Etretat and he was able to save Auguste from disfigurement. The boy had, however, lost a quantity of blood and was suffering from shock. To Jacques, hovering over him, other misfortunes seemed trivial compared to the threatened loss of this boy. These fears were unwarranted but for one nerve-racking night Jacques refused to leave his bedside, watching through to daylight as the boy sank into welcome sleep.

10

The bleak future which Jacques faced, with no prospect of profit for himself for years to come, was ameliorated from a most unexpected quarter. He did not immediately recognize this blessing in disguise and, indeed, for the next few months was inclined to view it as a further tribulation.

It was while he was staying at St. Germain that the stranger had come to call on him. The day was a pleasant one and Jacques was seated in the hotel garden basking in the sun. His three grandchildren—the two little sons of Berthe and Charles Comte and the year-old daughter of Mimi, who had married two years previously—were playing about his chair. Hortense Schneider had come out for the afternoon and was seated beside him. Altogether he was feeling happy and relaxed in the cheerful surroundings. He therefore resented the strange man who intruded upon them. But the man was apologetic.

"I will not detain you long, Monsieur, as you will only have to answer yes or no."

"I am listening," replied Offenbach, mollified.

"I am commissioned to ask, Monsieur, whether you would like to go to America."

Jacques stared unbelievingly at him, then glanced at Cath. Her face reflected equal amazement. He burst out laughing. Surely this was some kind of joke. America! Why that was miles, weeks away—the other side of the world! Such a voyage seemed to him almost as far-fetched as the Jules Verne opus on which he was working, *Voyage to the Moon.*

But the man was serious. In Philadelphia they were having an Exposition the next spring and they wanted Offenbach to conduct some concerts. There would also be others in New York. The agent hinted at a sum of money which also sounded to Jacques like a figure out of Jules Verne.

Once Offenbach realized the proposition was serious he was miserable. He was frightened of the idea of an ocean voyage, dubious of the strange civilization across the sea, dreaded the long, enforced separation from his family. It gave him many sleepless nights, but he always arrived at the same conclusion. In his present financial condition this had to be accepted as a way out.

The knowledge of his impending departure haunted him all

that autumn and winter. It depressed Herminie too, especially since Jacques was in such poor health. Then she considered, perhaps the voyage, the rest and change, would help him. Ordinarily he liked the excitement of travel, was always full of curiosity and so would find the new land interesting.

Meanwhile he was working at his customary frenetic pace. *Voyage to the Moon* based on the Jules Verne yarn was produced in October by Vizentini. As this has been included in the sale of the Gaîté, Jacques got no profit from it. Besides, it did no better than its immediate predecessors.

At the Variétés the old triumvirate, once more reunited, put on *The Baker Has Money*. Hortense Schneider had been scheduled to play Toinette, *la boulangère,* but when she read the part she took offense. Although it was the best part, it was not the biggest, and Schneider could not conceive of playing a secondary role.

"Either I am Schneider or I am her shadow," she stormed. "Then treat me as before and speak frankly and I will retire."

This time it was the mild Halévy who opposed her, flatly stating that the part could not be tailored to her desires. The meeting was thoroughly unpleasant and Cath left in a huff.

The next day, as was always the case, she had got over her anger. Not so Halévy and, with Offenbach's concurrence, another actress, Mlle Aimée, was given the role. Somehow the Variétés was not informed, or some underling made a mistake, because when the rehearsal notices were dispatched Hortense Schneider received one. In the best of moods, she appeared— but Mlle Aimée was also there. Schneider's fury on discovering this apparent double-dealing reverberated down the Passage des Princes, but Mlle Aimée had already been signed.

In the final analysis it was really the triumvirate who suffered. Aimée, generally a capable actress, unfortunately played Toinette "with the authority of Justice," a fault of which Schneider would have been incapable. With her lighter touch, *The Baker* might have succeeded; as it was it brought forth a minimum of interest despite some of Offenbach's pleasant tunes.

It seemed especially sad because, as it happened, this proved to be the last work of the triumvirate and it was the only one of their combined efforts to fail to win acclaim.

Two other pieces by Offenbach followed in quick succession—*The Creole* and a one-act piece for the Bouffes, *Tarte à la Crème*—neither of which made any notable impression, although *The Creole* later had a decent run in London.

It was openly said that Offenbach was finished. People pointed instead to the Viennese, Johann Strauss, who had become the rage of Paris. Following this new composer's *Ali Baba and the Forty Thieves*, *Die Fledermaus* was enjoying a success commensurate with Offenbach's great days of *Orpheus* and *Helen*.

There was a remarkable resemblance between the gay Court of Franz Joseph, in whose shadow Strauss lived, and the erstwhile Court of Napoleon III. That Strauss was an importation no doubt added to his stature in the eyes of the Parisians, but that his operettas were in the style of the Empire, the style which the new Republic repudiated in Offenbach, they failed to observe.

The Viennese operetta had simply replaced the "offenbachiade" but few paused to consider how much Strauss owed to the original inspirations of Offenbach. *Die Fledermaus* was essentially French in conception. It was based on a libretto by Meilhac and Halévy and was played by Zulma Bouffar. It was witty and satirical and its music was reminiscent of the delirious pace and style set by *Vie Parisienne*. Yet it was *not* as witty nor as satirical as the best "offenbachiades," nor did the music compare in deftness and variety to Offenbach's plenitude of tunes. Offenbach was the godfather of the Viennese operetta but the latter never quite achieved the scintillation of the "offenbachiade."

Jacques wanted very much to see *Die Fledermaus* but, as it happened, he was one of the few Parisians who never did. He was confined to his home with renewed violent attacks of rheumatism-arthritis when it opened, and by the time he was able to get about he was engrossed in preparations for his departure for America.

The enormity of that undertaking was apparent as the train pulled out of the Gare Saint-Lazare. Trunks and suitcases had already been loaded in the baggage car but the overflow of steamer rugs, pillows and extra coats was strewn throughout several compartments. His party actually took up most of the car because, whereas he bade Herminie and the girls goodbye in Paris, his two sons-in-law Charles Comte and Achille Tournal (Mimi's husband), his brothers-in-law Gaston and Robert Mitchell, Auguste, the faithful Albert Wolff and several other friends accompanied him to Le Havre, where they all passed the night. It was an entirely male party (including Mr. Baquero, his American manager) with the exception of Mlle Aimée who, traveling quite distinct from Offenbach, had been hired for a touring season of various of his operettas.

Offenbach was positive that he would be seasick. They said that the new fast liner would only take eight and one half days, but in eight and a half days . . . Moreover, he would be eight and a half days' journey away from all whom he loved.

Yet when he saw the spick and span new liner, the *Canada,* he was somewhat reassured. It looked pretty sturdy and once one stepped aboard it was like a luxurious hotel. Jacques was, in fact, quite cheery as he said goodbye. He was off to a new unknown land, but a land where the name of Offenbach was well known and admired, a land where the name of Johann Strauss had not yet been heard.

Those on shore waved until the frail figure by the rail grew dim. And then they waved some more, just to be sure. Offenbach remained immobile. Until his eyes became misty he could make out the bright gleam of the brass buttons on Auguste's school uniform.

CHAPTER EIGHT

Boulevardier on Broadway

1

Although Offenbach was still a little shaky from the terrible crossing, he had recovered sufficiently to go out on deck when the *Canada* came into New York Harbor. The sea was still quite choppy and the pilot had difficulty at the Narrows climbing up the flimsy rope ladder on the side of the liner.

But Offenbach really had to laugh as the small steamers, bearing reporters and the Welcoming Committee, drew near to the ship. Once his mind was diverted, he forgot his own ills.

Of the dozen or so ship-news reporters, several were being frankly and violently seasick. The others, more seasoned greeters, were fighting off their occupational hazard with frequent swigs from the bottle. The members of the sixty-piece welcoming band were almost all in sorry shape. As their rocking craft approached the big new liner they tried manfully to harmonize the stirring march from *Geneviève of Brabant,* but the brasses found it difficult to reconcile key and pitch. Offenbach later learned that the Welcoming Committee had grown tired of waiting off Quarantine and had ventured out farther than was wise.

Flags and Venetian lanterns bobbed up and down as the small boats drew alongside the *Canada*. From one of the tugs a great pennant whipped in the wind so violently that all the passengers on the liner could decipher its message with ease:

GREETINGS TO JACQUES OFFENBACH

While one of the reasons, no doubt, for the reporters' trip out to the *Canada* was to record the completion of her maiden voyage, Jacques accepted the entire affair as a tribute to himself. In any case, he was the star passenger and the first one interviewed.

The whole fantastic arrival enchanted him. Mr. Baquero saw to it that both he and Mlle Aimée were hustled through Customs with a minimum of formalities and the next thing Jacques knew he was being deposited at the splendid Fifth Avenue Hotel. Without time to rest he was whisked to a matinee, rushed back to the hotel for dinner, and then hustled off to another play.

It was on his return to the hotel that night that Jacques was completely overwhelmed when he saw a sputtering band of arc lights across the balcony of the building spelling out:

WELCOME OFFENBACH

A crowd had gathered in front of the hotel and as he stepped from the carriage, shouts of "Hurrah for Offenbach!" went up and a band struck up music from *Orpheus*, to be followed by more from *The Grand Duchess of Gerolstein*.

Offenbach went to the balcony and responded to the cheers from below with the only English phrase he knew.

"I zank you, my vriends. Long leef America!"

Before retiring, he sat down and wrote his usual daily letter to Herminie:

MY DEAREST WIFE,
   They welcomed me with continuous cheers! . . .
I was forced to appear on the balcony of the hotel, like
Gambetta, and I shouted a tremendous 'Thank you,
Gentlemen,' a polite utterance which I trust will not be
suspected of subversive intentions. . . .

(When interviewed on the ship, he had adroitly dodged political
queries.)

Herminie had guessed right. The trip had done him good.
True, he had been seasick during the crossing, just as he had
feared, but so, it turned out, had been almost everyone else.
Even the Captain said it was the worst crossing of his experience and Jacques had quickly acquired the old salt's pride in
being able to support the rough seas better than most. Mlle
Aimée was not seen during the entire voyage, the young ship's
doctor was violently seasick, and Offenbach only succumbed
when the Captain suggested that he and the few other hardy
passengers share the salon instead of sleeping in their cabins
that particularly stormy night.

By the time they had reached Quarantine Jacques had completely recovered and was alive with interest. His curiosity and
excitement over this strange new land were so great that he even
temporarily forgot his rheumatism.

In the days that followed he sent Herminie further reports
of his keen observations. The Fifth Avenue Hotel to him was
one of the wonders of the world, like something out of the
Arabian Nights.

"This hotel," he told her, "is an immense bazaar. It houses
everything that one could want or need—a druggist, hatter,
hairdresser, bookshop, etc. One might arrive as lightly dressed
as Adam before the fall, as long-haired as Absalom before his
tresses were caught in the tree, and depart as respectable as
the famous Count d'Orsay of fashionable memory! Everything
is provided here, except someone to speak French."

This latter lack troubled him everywhere in New York (in
England he had found they generally understood French) and

he set to work immediately to pick up a little English for himself.

The cost of living was so high that Offenbach was appalled and in a few days, on Baquero's advice, he moved to an apartment on Madison Square. At the expensive Fifth Avenue Hotel his suite—bedroom, sitting room and bath—had cost him twenty dollars a day. True, this had also included "the right to eat all day long." The hotel dining-room had fascinated him even though American eating habits upset him.

"There is one thing worthy of note in America," he said. "It is that of all the fifty tables in the room, there is not one upon which anything but ice water is to be seen."

The custom of placing a glass of water upon the table before anything had been ordered seemed very odd. Abstemious though he was, Offenbach discovered that his request for a glass of wine was regarded as one of those strange French customs. To him, though, it was equally comical that, whatever meal one ordered, it was all brought at once.

"You suddenly find yourself surrounded by thirty dishes," he remarked. (Herminie, thinking of his peculiar diet, wondered—and worried—about how much he ate.)

The swank Madison Square apartment impressed him equally, where there were "hot air stoves in every suite, gas in every room and cold water always at hand." But also, "in a room on the ground floor are arranged three little buttons of great importance—one is to call the police, another in case of fire, the third to summon a servant!" One could have a telegraph installed in any room, just as in restaurants or shops, and get the news on the ticker tape as well as stock market quotations.

Surrounded by all this luxury and efficiency, Jacques was nevertheless happiest sitting quietly looking out his window at the activities in the streets below him. Streetcars crisscrossed the Square and the number of rails dissecting the streets distressed him, but he came to the somewhat original conclusion that they had been planned the same width as ordinary vehicles so that these latter could drive on the rails and thus make for speedier traffic. On the other hand, he loved the gay appearance of the gigantic parasols which were covered with advertisements and which shaded the streetcar drivers as they guided their teams. The American women, he thought, were the best looking, the best dressed, the most *séduisantes* in the world. Just the same, he could not get over his astonishment at the freedom accorded them, as he watched them walking, shopping, and even entering streetcars alone.

All that first week in New York, Offenbach was gathering impressions, making acquaintances. On Saturday, a dinner was given for him at the Lotus Club, a gathering of artistic and professional people which he found pleasing. On Monday he was guest of honor at the Press Club. To his delight, most of its members either spoke or understood French, "many of them having been war correspondents during the late sad business when the unspeakable Prussians invaded us," as he explained to Herminie.

On top of this entertaining, he was being taken to the theatre constantly. The mechanics of theatre production in America surprised and puzzled him. It seemed strange that the average playhouse had only half a dozen boxes as against the whole tiers of them in France and that, furthermore, the Americans seemed to prefer the orchestra seats. He was completely baffled when he learned that American playhouses rented by the period, that is, for a week or month or season, according to the success of the particular show, unlike the annual basis accepted in France. He felt that there was much to be said in favor of state subsidy, as there had been in France under the Second Empire, because then an entrepreneur knew where he stood, at least for a year. And when he learned that an American manager went into bankruptcy several times without losing face he thought it indeed an odd land, this land that he had come to only to make a little money in order to wipe out his own bankruptcy debts in France.

Nor did the theatrical fare here appeal to Jacques especially. True, he was well impressed with *Henry V* at the Booth Theatre. But at the same playhouse a week later, Meyerbeer's *L'Etoile du Nord* appeared to have been insufficiently rehearsed, a failing for which he could find no excuse. As he put it in a letter to Halévy: "The chorus and orchestra came in one after the other. . . . I thought I was listening to something mediocre out of Wagner."

Unfortunately, both the Grand Opera House and the Academy of Music were closed for the season. To Offenbach it was indeed strange that in eight months only sixty performances of opera had been presented in the repertoire of both houses combined.

Early in the second week Offenbach settled down to work. His contract called for two weeks of concerts at Gilmore's Garden in New York City, before moving on to the Exposition at Philadelphia. Gilmore's, as he was soon able to verify for himself, was the last word in establishments of this type. It had a stage centered in the midst of grass plots, tropical plants, flower beds and shrubbery intertwined with walks. Facing the entrance was a remarkable miniature imitation of Niagara Falls which ran during the interludes and in each corner of the garden were little Swiss cottages which served as boxes for six or eight. People had the choice of either walking around the garden during the music, sitting in the large gallery, or renting one of these de luxe Swiss chalets. Over all this huge garden—for Gilmore's had the incredible capacity of nearly nine thousand—hung festoons of brilliantly lit colored glass.

Before he attended his first rehearsal, Baquero had explained to Offenbach that the New York musicians had an organization of their own, a sort of union, and that generally the orchestra leader himself was expected to join it but that, since Offenbach was a visiting foreigner, they were willing to waive the usual requirement. Then and there, Offenbach made up his mind that he would ask for membership.

One hundred and ten musicians had been engaged for him, a formidable number, and they gave him a gratifying ovation as he stepped to the podium. Shortly, they began work on *Vert-Vert*. After about sixteen bars, Offenbach stopped the orchestra abruptly.

"*Excusez-moi*, Gentlemen," he said haltingly, in a mixture of

French and recently acquired English, "we have scarcely begun and you have already failed in your duty."

His eyes twinkled as he watched the consternation on their faces.

"What!" he continued after a pause. "I am not a member of your Guild and you allow me to lead!"

The men began to break into chuckles.

"Since you have not mentioned it to me, I must myself request to be admitted to your Association."

Immediately, several of the musicians protested that in his case it was not necessary, but Offenbach was insistent. As he well knew, he had already won—and intended to keep—their friendship and co-operation.

Gilmore's orchestra was an excellent one, composed of first-rate musicians, and Jacques found deep satisfaction in working with them. Never forgetting his own humiliations during his youthful orchestra days, he remained unfailingly considerate of the dignity of the individual. Conversely, to the men at Gilmore's, his handling of them and his music was a revelation and, thanks to this spirit, Jacques enjoyed days of achievement and adulation such as he had not experienced since the fall of the Empire.

When he cashed his first check he abstracted a silver dollar, which he sent to Auguste—his first dollar earned in the United States. Auguste, far from being spoiled by Jacques' inevitable continual sentimentality, reciprocated in kind. Writing his thanks from across the sea, the fourteen-year-old boy added with tender devotion: "When I am old, very old, I will sing your airs to my grandchildren in a trembling voice, and they will say, as in the 'Song of Béranger,' speaking of the great Jacques, 'He knew our grandfather. . . .'"

Reading this missive, Jacques was profoundly touched. He carried the letter with him in his wallet and even after he had answered it he did not destroy it. After his death it was found laid away among his papers, one of the few letters he had ever saved.

It arrived at a moment when the first excitement over the new country had worn off and he was growing homesick. He had met numbers of people, made friends with many, was entertained constantly, but all his close associates, his family, above all his adored Herminie, were far away.

Fortunately, at this low ebb he had to move on to Philadelphia, where it seemed probable that new sights and interests would rouse him from his momentary apathy.

But Philadelphia was a grim, depressing city. He arrived late on a Saturday night and in the morning when he went out for a stroll he was struck by the dour puritanism of its sabbath. Shops, theatres, cafés, everything appeared closed except the churches with which the city seemed "swarming" and, as he reported home, all he met were "people coming out of church with their bibles and funereal vestments." Offenbach had never been an ardent churchgoer but neither had he felt that the Catholic Church treated Sunday with an air of mourning, the way these foreign Protestant sects did.

When, in the afternoon, he expressed a desire to visit the Exposition and to see where he was to conduct and he was informed that it too was closed, he was astounded. When, the next morning, he read in the papers that some restaurant waiters had been arrested for serving liquor on Sunday, he was horrified.

"What an odd country and ditto its liberty," he observed. "One is so free that on Sunday one is absolutely forbidden to take a glass of brandy either in a café or elsewhere. . . ."

The proprietor of the Garden where he was to conduct seemed to share his general view. He was outraged that regulations forbade the maestro to give a Sunday concert in his establishment. Mulling over the matter in his mind, he thought he saw a way to circumvent the Blue Laws. Saying nothing to Offenbach until he had made all preparations, he appeared one day with a wise smile on his face. He had, he explained, received permission to hold a concert of "sacred" music.

"I rely on you," he informed Jacques, "as I have already had handbills printed." He handed one to Jacques who read:

OFFENBACH   GARDEN

Cor. Broad & Cherry Sts.

Sunday Evening, June 25th,
at 8 o'clock p.m.
GRAND
SACRED
CONCERT
by
M. OFFENBACH
And The
GRAND ORCHESTRA
in a choice selection of
SACRED AND CLASSICAL MUSIC

Admission   50 cents
ledger job print. philad.

Jacques roared with laughter. His sense of humor was so
tickled that there was no fear of his spoiling the scheme. Indeed, he sat down at the desk and proposed the following program:

"Deo Gratias" from *Le Domino Noir*
"Ave Maria" by Gounod
"March Religieuse" from *La Haine*
"Ave Maria" by Schubert
"Litanie" from *Helen of Troy* ("Dis-moi, Venus")
"Hymn" from *Orpheus in the Underworld*
"Prière" from *The Grand Duchess of Gerolstein*
("Dites-lui")
"Danse Séraphique," polka burlesque
"Angelus" from *Le Mariage aux Lanternes*

Regrettably, someone in authority must have realized the
hoax because at the last moment, permission was withdrawn.
And, happily, Offenbach was not forced to pass many Sun-

days in Philadelphia. His actual public appearances were confined to a half-dozen at "Offenbach Garden"—a place similar in design to Gilmore's and to which they had complimentarily given the maestro's name—but naturally this had entailed a week of rehearsals. To Offenbach's delight, part of Gilmore's Band had been lent for his use. This limited him to seventy-five men rather than the full complement, but they served him brilliantly and he received acclaim comparable to the furor in New York. A young music critic named James Gibbons Huneker attended one performance and summed it up succinctly: "Offenbach is a genius."

2

By June 20, Offenbach was back in New York with two weeks to spare before sailing and he therefore planned a sightseeing trip. First, though, Mlle Aimée, who was leaving for Chicago, persuaded him to accompany her part of the way and conduct performances en route, to which he cheerfully agreed. On his return, he set out for a visit to the fabled Niagara Falls.

Going up the Hudson he was thrilled and overawed.

"What a beautiful country we pass through from New York to Niagara!" he reported to Herminie. "We pass along the admirable Hudson River. I search my memory in vain for any European stream which can compare with this American river. There are some parts which recall the finest places on the Rhine. There are others which surpass in grandeur and charm anything I have ever seen before. . . ."

It remained for Niagara itself to spoil his pleasure. The Falls, of course, were impressive, but it was here he encountered vicious anti-Semitism. At the Cataract Hotel he was informed that no Jews were admitted. He had been faced with nothing like this since his childhood and, in fact, had almost forgotten that man still carried on his inhumanity to man. Now he was a minor victim.

Accommodations were found for him at another hotel, of course, but the incident embittered him toward much of America. He philosophized again on the meaning of liberty in this land of the free, where the Jew was set apart as a second-class citizen, where emancipated Negroes, only recently freed, were still not permitted in public vehicles and theatres and "in restaurants only as waiters." He thought back again to the Sunday Blue Laws in Philadelphia where, he mused, a laborer who only had Sunday in which to relax found most avenues of pleasure closed to him. He thought, ironically, of the fund-raising campaign in France for the proposed Bartholdi Statue of Liberty which the French intended to present to this country. As far as he could judge, there was only one great freedom notable in the United States, as compared to France, and that was the freedom accorded to women.

"I have a notion," he once observed, "that when Lafayette fought for American liberty he had in view the ladies of the United States, as they alone are truly free in America."

It was an unhappy phase he was going through and although his judgments were on the whole correct, they were sharpened by his homesickness. Ending a letter to Halévy, filled with such observations, he added: "Oh, my pretty Paris, my loved boulevards, my adored theatres, where are you?"

Yet, back in New York, the day of departure approaching, he again revised his opinions. Here no anti-Semitism touched him, personally. Everyone was friendly and he was entertained at theatres and dinners, lionized wherever he went, if somewhat overcome by the mania for autographs—being stopped frequently in public—and secretly a trifle scared by his mail. (Some of these letters were rather personal in their requests and, to be on the safe side, he answered none.) Yet, on the whole, he was pleased by the friendliness, the simplicity, the informality of most Americans.

Having felt that the country was too commercialized, lacking in the field of the arts, and with a preponderance of second-rate orchestras, he was also more than willing to give utterance to his deep respect for the musicians at Gilmore's.

On the night before he sailed, July 7th, he readily agreed to conduct them at a benefit for the New York Society of Musicians.

The ovation given him by the orchestra itself, as well as the applause of the audience, stirred him so deeply that he rashly promised to return the next year. During his two months' sojourn he had made considerable efforts to learn English and the result was that he actually delivered his farewell speech to them in that language.

Offenbach's own natural friendliness and his evident tact (unlike Dickens, he confined his criticisms to personal letters), had endeared him to almost everyone he encountered in the United States. As he departed, the New York papers vied with each other in friendly editorials, but perhaps the *Courrier des Etats-Unis*, one of the two French dailies, summed up most charmingly the impression he was leaving.

> Few European artists have been as much feted in New York as the composer of *The Grand Duchess*, it declared. One must also add that Jacques Offenbach has without doubt received from the good fairies the precious gift of pleasing everyone. . . . His cordiality, his modesty, his brilliant wit which, while always ready with a rejoinder never oversteps the strict rules of courtesy, his affability without pose, have made everyone his friend. . . .

Jacques thoroughly appreciated this tribute.

Back on the *Canada* again, homeward bound, as he watched the skyline of New York receding in the distance, he experienced a sense of regret at saying farewell to this land he had begun to grow fond of, this land of contradictions and extremes, but a land mainly of kindly people. Before he left, he composed a piano piece, "Les Belles Américaines," the best gesture he could make to his erstwhile hosts.

3

At Le Havre the entire family was on hand to greet him, Herminie and the girls, as well as the male relatives. In addition, the welcoming party included most of his friends from

Etretat, which was after all not far from the big seaport. It was such a reception as Jacques most loved and he was again blissfully content as they all made their way back to "Eter-tat" and the Villa Orphée. This year he had *not* rented the house.

During his stay in the United States Jacques had contributed an article to *Figaro* which had delighted its readers. Now, as he recited in further detail his experiences across the sea, Villemessant interrupted to suggest that he incorporate them in a book. Jacques pretended to laugh off the idea but, secretly, he had already considered it. Afterward, he always pretended teasingly that it was Herminie who had forced him to do it.

Jacques was a capable reporter and wrote in an amusing, brisk style. The basis of the proposed book was already at hand in his letters to Herminie and his friends, all of which they had saved. Adding to them factual comments, a little history, a sprinkling of anecdotes, the result was a thoroughly entertaining book. It was a singularly unbiased and, on the whole, accurate account. Only in a few instances could the innocent foreigner be observed as the victim of American joking. For instance, he remained to the end of his days convinced (as so many other Europeans had been) that all American males carried revolvers in their hip pockets.

Offenbach in America was published later both in France and in an English translation in the United States and it bore this charming dedication to Herminie:

To My Wife

DEAR FRIEND,

It was you who wished me to make up a book from scattered notes and random utterances of my heart. It is the first sorrow you have caused me. I bear you so little grudge, however, that I beg you will allow me to dedicate this volume to you, not for what it contains nor for what it is worth, but because I love to manifest in every way my esteem and my affection for you.

CHAPTER NINE

Grand Finale

1

Upon his return to France, Offenbach delivered himself of one of those sweeping statements he was so fond of: "Now I have become Offenbach again!"

While it was true that he had felt uprooted in America, nonetheless it was in the United States that he had again enjoyed the illusion of being the musical pacemaker of the glittering Second Empire. Back in his own world, try as he would, he seemed unable to recapture the glory of bygone days.

He was obsessed with clearing his debts at the earliest possible moment and while the financial gains of the American venture had been of great aid, it would need another year to get himself out of the red. The calm return voyage had enabled him to finish the music for *La Boîte au Lait*, Mlle Théo's new vehicle. In rapid succession he finished the scores of three other musicals, but none of them attained the goal he had been striving for.

It was not that Offenbach had written himself out. All of these pieces contained music of considerable charm, but some ingredient seemed lacking. As one critic hazarded: "Offenbach is no longer a prophet—yet Offenbach has never had more talent than today."

The unfathomable lack mystified many of his admirers and well-wishers. Perhaps it was the mere course of time. After all, he had belonged to the era of the Second Empire.

Renewed attacks on him had recently appeared in the papers, furthering this conception. On the return voyage Jacques, who had so shrewdly parried political queries when in America, was so indiscreet as to unburden himself to a fellow-traveler who happened to be a French Senator of the Left. While Offenbach simply availed himself of a citizen's presumable right to criticize his own government, the Senator translated it in terms of latent Imperialism. Actually Jacques' primary complaint was against the venomous diatribes to which he had been subjected in the Republican press, but it may have been that he had been foolish enough to draw invidious comparison with the papers of the Empire. It was this assumption, in any case, which drew the Senator's ire and he was instrumental in starting the revival of attacks against Offenbach.

The producers who were bringing *Helen of Troy* back to the boards worried over the possible effects of this slanderous campaign, but their fears proved ill-founded. After an absence of ten years, a new generation fell in love with *Helen* just as deeply as their elders had before them. For all that it represented the epoch of the Empire, it had a timeless appeal.

It was followed by a revival of *The Grand Duchess of Gerolstein*, with a new Grand Duchess—Hortense Schneider having shrewdly sensed that she, if not the play, had grown older. Like *Helen*, it seemed as fresh as ever and with this encouragement, *The Bandits* and *Orpheus* were brought back.

Offenbach was not insensible that all his present triumphs were holdovers from the past, but the full impact of this was not realized until the new Universal Exposition of 1878.

In January a strange hiatus was noticed on the marquees of the Paris theatres. For the first time since the birth of Bouffes-

Parisiens, Offenbach's name was missing from the billboards. It was only a temporary lapse and Jacques, thinking of the approaching Exposition, was unperturbed. But its subtle poison was already affecting negotiations. The Variétés cancelled its earlier plan for presenting an Offenbach operetta at the Exposition. Thereupon Meilhac and Halévy, who had been the logical choice as librettists, were commissioned by Charles Lecocq. Hurt, Jacques wrote them a note accusing them of deserting him in favor of "the Meyerbeer of the Renaissance," the Renaissance being the theatre which was producing Lecocq's operettas.

No one, it seemed, was any longer interested in him. When the Exposition opened, his name—the name of Jacques Offenbach which had always gleamed in as bright lights as those of the Exposition itself—was nowhere on the boulevards.

Jacques looked glumly out of his corner apartment window onto the brilliantly illuminated Place de l'Opéra (which was lighted for the first time in honor of the Exposition) and felt more alone than ever before in his life.

2

All his life Jacques had intended, eventually, to do something of "serious" value. He had tried, tentatively, with the Opéra-Comique and with the Vienna Opera, but he was perfectly aware himself that these were only halfhearted attempts. Someday, he always promised himself, he would have the money and leisure to devote to pure artistry. Now, here he was, nearing sixty, all his savings gone—and still nothing of lasting worth accomplished.

He knew that he could not postpone the effort much longer. The shock of finding himself passed by in the preparations for the Exposition challenged him to prove that he could not be ignored, to show those who laughed at his claim to the title of "maestro" that he deserved it.

Even so, it was the lesser reason. The ravages of illness had aged him beyond his actual years and he was faced with the fact that he was *old*. Nowadays when friends asked how he was feeling he invariably replied: "I am just a little tired."

His sufferings from arthritis had so depleted his extraordinary vitality that he sat longer and longer hours in the old worn easychair. At rehearsals he no longer exhibited the quick flashes of temper, but an amazing—and not quite natural—gentleness, which perturbed those who knew him well. On the wonderful "Fridays," although Jacques still manifested a childlike glee in the burlesques and clownish games, he no longer took an active part. Instead, he sat hunched with pain in his armchair or, at most, joined in a game of cards.

The American trip had seen his last real spurt of energy. In the two years since his return he had rarely been free of pain and, as it slowly and inexorably increased, as he was forced by inaction to be more and more alone with his thoughts, he was confronted with frightening reality.

Some day, not so very far off, the disease would kill him.

It took an unwonted courage for him to face this terrible truth. He, who could never bear to be alone, found himself isolated. Even religion gave him small comfort. Jacques had never been a devout person and while he gave passive allegiance to the Catholic Church, he was often beset by doubts. Yet the latent craving of every human being for immortality gripped him. His excessive devotion to Auguste was mixed with the egocentric longing for some sort of reincarnation through his son. Auguste would carry on the name; the son, with his own musical talent, might surpass the potential genius of the father. Auguste, to a greater degree than any of the girls, seemed an offshoot of his own body.

Therefore, added to Jacques' horror of his own impending doom, was worry over Auguste. The boy showed a tendency to sickliness, a frailness which Jacques, in spite of his thinness, had not evinced at the same age. As Auguste grew older he spent more and more time in his father's company, but the joy which their affinity of interests and mutual affection gave Jacques was tainted by a morbid foreboding that his son would not long survive him.

If only he could bequeath to Auguste what remained of his own waning strength! Instead, all he could do was imbue the boy with his aspirations for him.

In their intimate talks together, Jacques confessed his preoccupation with immortality and with the twin facets of his hopes—continuity through Auguste and apotheosis through his music. Young though he was, the boy comprehended his father's obsession and equally appreciated his choice for his monumental work. For what could be more appropriate than Jacques' favorite *Tales of Hoffmann*.

A great showman, Offenbach had long ago declared that the *Tales* provided the proper medium on which to make his exit. Then it had been half in jest. Now he said it in earnest. These bizarre, macabre, and at the same time comic stories which he had absorbed into his very being, which either accidentally or in some curious mystic way had formed him into a likeness, were the perfect vehicle on which to take his departure from the world's stage.

Once Offenbach had been an exuberant, mischievous, earthy spirit such as abounded in Hoffmann's magic stories, but now he more nearly resembled Hoffmann himself. He, like Hoffmann, was fated to die and it was the terrifying ghosts, the destructive spirits which also peopled the *Tales,* that now kept him company at night. The incessant pain either prevented sleeping or roused him in the still hours before daylight. Hoffmann had written:

"Everybody must have experienced being awakened at night by the slightest noise, which returns at intervals and drives away all sleep and increases one's inner fear until all one's senses are distraught. It has often happened to me to be suddenly awakened, whereupon I have felt an indescribable terror, as though I had had some awful experience. It is as if some strange power has suddenly penetrated within us and taken possession of our hitherto clear senses."

Offenbach, like Hoffmann in his terror of the unknown, lay often in a cold sweat longing for daylight and the warm reassurance of companionship. These frightening hours made him conscious of his transitory importance in the world and urged him along on the task of creating his legacy—an enduring opera. His debts were cleared and nothing material save his actual illness seemed to stand in his way. He would do other works, popular operettas to make necessary money, but while there was still time he would begin his masterpiece.

Some years before Jacques had casually mentioned his remote dream to Jules Barbier, the librettist of *Faust*. Barbier had been interested in the *Tales* and now Offenbach sent for him. To his dismay, he learned that Barbier not only had already completed a libretto but that Hector Salomon, chorus master at the Opéra, had begun a score.

This news was catastrophic. Jacques had come to associate himself so closely with the *Tales* that they had acquired a cryptic significance which made his long-cherished desire to write the score far more than idle choice. In his mind it represented a spiritual fusion, and that this fulfillment of his life should be denied him was heartbreaking. In his desperation he appealed directly to Salomon who, sensing that there was more than whim in Jacques' request, gracefully relinquished his own interests.

When the matter had finally been settled a remarkable tranquility came over Offenbach. He *knew* now that he was going to do a lasting work, a work of pure love and art, and his spirits rose. He even showed an echo of his oldtime gaiety and verve and once, risen from a sickbed to attend a rehearsal of *Mme Favart*, he actually joined in with the chorus at the end of the third act to execute a graceful fandango. Astonished and delighted, everybody applauded what seemed like a miracle. But it was simply a temporary renewal of life in the knowlege of a definite job to be done.

Mme Favart itself reflected this regeneration, redeeming the dismal parade of failures which had marked these last years. Its sprightliness was evidence to all that Offenbach's musical source had not dried up.

3

In April, 1879, Jacques' very old friend and associate, Villemessant, died. Offenbach's circle was narrowing, his world was disappearing, and more vividly than ever he saw Death creeping toward him. He no longer tried to evade it, but accepted its closeness and inevitability, fighting only for sufficient time to finish his masterpiece. He was working slowly and patiently —with a patience he had never before manifested—composing and rejecting, giving of his best. In his mind he made an analogy with Antonia of the *Tales* who, if she sang, was doomed to die. All that he now desired was to be allowed the time to sing, and then he, too, would die.

Early in May he went out to St. Germain to be alone (although Halévy still lived there) and concentrate, undisturbed, on the composition of his opera but, as was inevitable, he quickly fell victim to loneliness, and the nameless terrors of sleepless nights piled up on him. In his misery he exaggerated what he transposed in his mind as the indifference of his family. For several mails now there had been no letter from home and he wrcte Herminie indignantly:

> It is eight o'clock in the evening. I am alone. Absolutely alone. Halévy dines in Paris. . . . You give me little news. You have a half dozen hands at your service who could surely write me and tell me every day what is the state of your health. I admit that I am very hurt. . . . They [the children] find it entirely natural that their father completely isolate himself to work day and night. They have nothing to do but sing, take a walk, put on pretty dresses (I except Auguste, who wears trousers). I am not a very demanding father, but certainly their indifference goes too far. So much the worse for them.

Who thinks little of me—I forget completely. You, you
have an excuse for not writing, *you have pains in your
legs.* Ever since yesterday I have been suffering with
that also. Which does not hinder me, even though ill,
from being at the piano the entire day and of still finding the means of writing you this evening to say good
night and to embrace you.

As much because of his need for company as because of his
ostensible purpose to hold an audition, Jacques returned to town
the next week. He wished to play "three or four finished bits"
of his opera and invited not only a few intimates but several
theatre directors and some music critics as well to come to his
apartment Friday evening.

In the enjoyment of their companionship he seemed to regain
a modicum of vigor and, although this was the first test of his
efforts, he wore a confident smile as he sat down to the piano.
Within the group, on the contrary, there was a tenseness, an
uncertainty as to whether Offenbach would fulfill his promise
of many years for, despite his surface heartiness, they too knew
the sands were running out and that this was his last chance.

Softly and tenderly Offenbach began playing Antonia's "Romance," the music rising more impassioned as he led into Da-
pertutto's aria. Then, swiftly shifting the mood, he started the
"Doll Waltz" and ended his little recital with the lovely "Barcarolle," once the "Sirens' Song" of *Rheinnixe,* but rewritten and
burnished to a shimmering patina. In spite of his crippled fingers Offenbach was still a superior musician and, as he made
the transitions, he interpolated an explanation of the scene, weld-
ing the isolated fragments into an understandable whole.

As he finished there was a momentary silence and Jacques,
startled, turned toward his small audience. What he saw on their
faces told him he need not worry. Indeed, it had never occurred
to him that he might fail, but he wanted reassurance.

For the assembled group, the occasion was a supremely emotional one and the impact of Offenbach's music had momentarily
unnerved them. Their applause followed quickly but Albert

Wolff wiped his eyes, and there were others who were also near to tears.

All present knew that they had just listened to music of exceptional beauty and none need any longer question the breadth of Offenbach's genius. All the endearing qualities which Offenbach personified were present in this music—the *joie de vivre* and the tenderness inherent in every one of his scores—but there was also a finesse, a touch of passion, an emotional depth which lifted this work to a height of artistry he had never previously attained.

Among those in the drawing room that evening were the directors of the Opéra-Comique and of the Vienna Ringtheater. When the spell cast by Jacques' music had been broken both men asked the privilege of giving the opera its première. The music center of the world was shifting from Paris to Vienna but Jacques, appreciative of the tribute, did not hesitate. He belonged, first of all, to Paris.

4

Jacques had intended only a transitory stay in Paris, then to return to St. Germain to continue his work. But a day or two after the audition he was stricken with exceptionally violent pains and was confined to his bed. It was there, in the utmost misery, that he began the score of *La Fille du Tambour-Major,* (*The Daughter of the Drum-Major*) which the Folies-Dramatiques was putting on the coming winter.

As so often during his sufferings, he composed music that was gay and lilting, but it was in just such compositions that he found solace and escape from the reality of his torments. And today, added to his physical pain, was a terrible depression.

Memories crowded in upon him of the days when he was young and healthy, of his childhood, the devotion of his parents, and the happy home life on the Street of the Bells. In his nostalgia the poverty, the anti-Semitism, all the unpleasant aspects grew dim and, as he lay in bed recalling his boyhood, he was seized with a longing to revisit those early scenes.

As soon as he was able to leave his bed Jacques decided, rather than St. Germain, to go to the little German spa of Wilbad, hoping that the waters there would ease his sufferings, but even this pretense scarcely obscured his real motivation. He knew it was foolish, and he was ashamed of his weakness, but an urge beyond his control impelled him to carry out his little plan. After only a perfunctory stay in Wilbad, he went on to Cologne.

But when he visited the Street of the Bells he found the old home torn down. All that remained was the perennial drabness of the ghetto. Determinedly he searched out the companions of his youth but most of them, too, were gone. He saw his sisters, aged like himself, and found them strangers.

Such a sentimental pilgrimage could not have ended otherwise. Even his memories were now spoiled and more vividly than ever he was faced with the inescapable truth that not only he, but his whole world, was passing.

He fled back to Paris and Etretat, to the comfort of the present. Back home, although bedridden again, the nightmares were temporarily shut out by the boisterousness of his grandchildren. Cheered by the racket they made as they played by his bedside, he completed *The Daughter of the Drum-Major.*

5

Jacques had never thought of himself particularly as a man of courage, but in the now many years of pain and suffering he had rarely faltered. There was within him a driving force—call it a zest for life—which, quite apart from any conscious effort, had helped him surmount the gnawing pain, kept him working and pushed him into action at times when only will power could avail.

He was, also, a man of the theatre and lived according to its traditions. Somewhere, subconsciously, the tenet that "the show must go on" spurred him to almost superhuman efforts.

A contemporary described Offenbach in these last years as

looking like "a transparent, pale, sadly smiling ghost" out of one of Hoffmann's *Tales*. When he had gone to America his thinning hair, mutton chops and moustache had been only brushed with gray. Now, three years later, he was white, very white, his skin as white as his hair and his always thin figure skeleton-like. His eyes still crinkled when he was amused and he smiled often, but some of the sparkle and liveliness were missing.

He tried hard to regain his buoyancy of spirits, hoping desperately that when the final curtain was rung down he would still be in character. But the pain was beginning to subdue him and he had not the strength for laughter. All he could manage was a smile.

There had been much advance publicity concerning the fact that *The Daughter of the Drum-Major* marked Offenbach's hundredth score, but actually this was an understatement. It was simply the hundredth score he had composed for Paris production and even this lesser total excluded incidental accompaniments, not to mention individual waltzes, ballads, etc.

Jacques was anxious that *The Daughter* be a merited milestone, but surpassing any ordinary incentive was his desire to make his exit on a note of enchantment. Possibly he would be able to write another operetta, but he knew the time left him was becoming very short.

Even he, however, had not dared hope for the wonderful reception *The Daughter* received. In the verve and seductiveness of this music there was no hint of the physical torment in which it had been written. It was Offenbach at his most winsome, a worthy competitor of *Orpheus* and *Helen,* and the audiences received it enthusiastically. Again the name of Offenbach was blazoned over the theatre marquee and, if it only shone from one playhouse instead of many, there was no doubt but that Jacques had recaptured his former standing on the boulevards.

Immediately offers came for the rights to produce *The Daughter* in Vienna and Brussels. In Paris, the house was sold out well in advance and there was a general revival of interest in all of Offenbach's works. Earlier operettas were engaging the attention of more than one producer and even his none-too-

friendly rival, Charles Lecocq, approached him to do an operetta for his theatre.

"You know," Jacques remarked to Herminie, "our grandchildren are going to be rich."

He added shrewdly that he foresaw a slackening of interest
for a few years after his death but that one day his operettas
would again be appreciated at their true value. Maybe none of
them was a "great" work but he felt that he could justifiably be
proud of most of them.

Nowadays he frankly discussed his fate with Herminie and
it brought him a certain consolation that she too faced the hard
fact with frankness rather than with any false optimism. She
was fortunate in possessing the strength of absolute religious
faith but, if Jacques could not share this, at least her magnificent
calm helped him to face death in his own way.

The recrudescence of public esteem wiped out the humiliations of recent years and Jacques wanted, if possible, to follow
up the success of *The Daughter* with another, but nowadays he
could not work at his accustomed speed.

He was growing much feebler and even though that winter
of 1879-30 was a frightfully cold one, he knew that alone did
not explain his own chill as he sat before the fire wrapped in
a fur coat, a rug around his feet. It was as if the blood had been
drained from his veins.

Slowly he began the composition of *Belle Lurette* for Lecocq
and then, the score partly finished, he laid it aside to complete
the *Tales*. There was still much work to be done on the latter
but only his sense of urgency forced him to the task.

"Make haste and produce my opera," he said to Carvalho,
the director of the Opéra-Comique. "I have not much time left
and my only wish is to see the first performance."

Carvalho promised that it would be put on in the autumn.
Jacques nodded his head slowly. Yes, if he were lucky, he might
last till then.

He had hoped to go to Etretat once more but when June
came he was too weak to make the journey. Later on, when he

was rested . . . Meanwhile, he was taken by carriage to nearby St. Germain.

Herminie wanted to accompany him but Jacques was obdurate. In order to accomplish his task he must be alone but, as a concession, he agreed to permit Mimi, his favorite daughter, to visit him every two or three days.

But Meilhac, Halévy and Albert Wolff slipped in quietly to occupy the rooms above him at the Pavillon Henri IV. These three devoted friends intended to keep vigil. His doctor, too, looked in on him frequently.

"It is terrible," the doctor told the three men. "There is nothing left of him. His body is completely exhausted. I do not know what keeps him alive."

The three friends, though, knew. His overwhelming desire to finish *Tales of Hoffmann* gave him the strength.

"I have made a pact with Death," Jacques explained to Ludo. "I have said, 'If you let me finish my work in peace I shall be ready to follow you.'"

Every morning beneath them they could hear the lovely strains of music as Offenbach forced himself to his self-appointed task.

"Do you hear him?" Meilhac—the once lighthearted Meilhac —said in awe. "Listen! The musician is at work. What an artist!" And he added bitterly, "When he is dead they will appreciate him."

Jacques' fingers were so cold and crippled that only with the greatest concentration could he control their action on the piano, as the summer sun could no longer bring him warmth. Yet every day he returned doggedly to his work, slowly and patiently building his monument. This, his masterpiece, his legacy, could not be hurried. Many times, though, he doubted if Death would grant him the extra days he wanted. Stroking his pet dog, the Russian deerhound he had named "Kleinzaches" after the legend of the first act, he would murmur:

"Poor Kleinzaches, poor Kleinzaches. I would give everything only to be present at the first night."

Even his will power failed him at moments, his terrible fatigue overcoming him. Then he would lie back in his chair, wrapped once more in his fur overcoat before a log fire, Kleinzaches comfortably pressed against his feet.

The three vigilant friends, aware of the silence, would then come down to him. The *Maître* needed their company badly now. Motionless in his chair, staring into space, his white hair and face gleaming in the firelight, his eyes feverish, he seemed more than ever a shadowy ghost. Seeing them he would smile, stir slightly, and try to banter with them.

"What a lovely article Wolff will write after my death!" he once exclaimed.

6

All along, Jacques had kept up his hopes of going to Etretat before the summer was over, but as August drew near he realized that it would be impossible.

"The strings of the articulated doll shrink now at the slightest fatigue," he wrote Pepita. "Just going to Paris one day upset me a lot and yesterday and the day before I had a fever."

Pepita was running the Villa Orphée household that summer and, with a glimmer of his oldtime humor, her father addressed the envelope:

> Mlle Pepita Offenbach,
> "Chief Cook,"
> Villa Orphée,
> Etretat, Seine-Inférieure.

He longed to see the Villa Orphée once more. The fourteenth of August would mark his and Herminie's wedding anniversary and he had wanted so much to celebrate it together there.

"I am truly upset . . . but I realize the folly of such a trip. The doctor has warned me against it and I myself know he is right."

In another letter, he voiced his particular fears: "If I should fall seriously ill at this moment it would be a disaster. . . . I

have just a month left to do the third act of *Belle Lurette*, orchestrate all three acts, to do the finale and all the fifth act of
Tales of Hoffmann (I am not speaking of the orchestration which
will come later) and to do the act for the Variétés. Will I succeed? . . . Let us hope so. . . ."

He was returning to the Boulevard des Capucines ("Capucines House" as he jokingly called it), because it was too expensive to remain on at the Pavillon Henri IV.

When Pepita read the letters to her mother, Herminie said
little. In her heart she had known all along that Jacques could
not come to Etretat. Now there was no reason to hesitate. Her
place was beside Jacques and quietly she took the train for
Paris.

7

Jacques was so feeble that only by leaning on Herminie
could he get from his bed to his study, yet he continued his
work. By September *Belle Lurette* was finished, if not entirely
orchestrated, and *Tales of Hoffmann* was almost completed.
Really, it too was done, only there remained a little change
here, a bit of perfecting there. Carvalho continued to promise
the premiere for late in October and feverishly Jacques returned
to its orchestration.

First he annotated the score throughout, in case he should
not hold out long enough to do it himself. The extreme fatigue
never left him now and death no longer seemed terrifying. He
would welcome the release from suffering, only—only let him
see *Tales of Hoffmann* produced.

On October second the first full rehearsal of the *Tales* was
held and there was a distinct sense of relief when Offenbach,
his poor emaciated frame tenderly laid on a stretcher, was carried into the Opéra-Comique. So many had feared he would not
last until this moment.

The terrible weariness had seamed his face. His eyes, their
sparkle almost extinguished, were sunk in their darkly shadowed
sockets. But as the assembled company sang his opera through

for the first time, his face lighted in a happy smile. Once, in his excitement, he even propped himself up on the couch on which he reclined at the corner of the stage.

It was beautiful. Beautiful. Already Jacques could visualize the finished production and he was content. As the audition ended he gathered his strength to say a few words of thanks to the players for whom he felt such gratitude.

That evening he was greatly relaxed. It would not be long now, the struggle was almost over and he was resigned to the inevitable. He still hoped to see the premiere of the *Tales* but should that be denied him he would be satisfied with today's rehearsal.

He would, though, like to finish the orchestration and the next day, with renewed incentive, he returned to it. Herminie was sitting close by, ostensibly embroidering, when suddenly Jacques had an attack of suffocation and, as she hurried to his side, he fainted.

When he came to a short time later, Jacques looked at the group gathered around his bedside and said quietly:

"I think tonight will be the end."

Mere breathing took all the effort he was capable of and while he did not lose consciousness again, he spoke little. Nor did he fight off the darkness which surged toward him. He had warded it off so long and he was very tired. The doctor did what he could, but by nightfall a priest was sent for.

All night long Herminie and the children kept watch, Auguste looking almost as ghostlike as his father. Toward morning there was a slight rustle of the sheet and they saw Jacques lift his hand, touch first his head, then his heart, as if to make sure himself, then simply stop breathing.

With a cry, Herminie fell on her knees, her face pressed against Jacques' lifeless hand.

8

On Thursday, October 7, the funeral services were held at the Madeleine. The Madeleine was one of the larger churches but even so it was not big enough to hold all of Jacques' friends. Nor had anyone foreseen the press of the mere curious. Although it was a grey day, crowds were clustered in the square around the church and the more forward pushed into the basilica itself. Paris was overrun with English tourists and many of the sightseers filled the pews. Three of Jacques' closest associates— Crémieux, Halévy and Tréfeu—arriving late, were unable to make their way inside and were forced to remain under the portico.

They could not hear the priest, but they could hear the organ. It was playing the "Dies Irae" and "Agnus" adapted from fragments of *Tales of Hoffmann*. And later, as the small casket was carried out of the church and they stood with heads bared and bowed, they heard the familiar strains of the "Song of Fortunio." This lovely lyric, tender and sad, Jacques' preference among his works until the *Tales*, seemed altogether fitting.

By now the rain had begun to fall but as the cortege made its way along the Boulevard de la Madeleine few of the bystanders moved on. Burial was to be in the Montmartre Cemetery, but first there was to be a long detour.

Down the boulevards the procession moved slowly. This was Jacques Offenbach's final journey along the streets he loved so dearly and, as his coffin was carried past the Opéra-Comique, the Variétés, and finally the Bouffes, the cortege halted before each in symbolic farewell.

At the grave, Victorien Sardou was expected to say a few words but he was so overwrought that he was unable to carry out his intention. Others spoke instead, feelingly, eulogizing Jacques' "intrepid soul," "the true and devoted friend," "the man of unimpeachable honesty"—but they could not evoke the spirit of the valiant Jacques.

Jacques Offenbach had left the scene.

9

Yet Jacques Offenbach had not really left the boulevards. On October 30, just as originally planned, *Belle Lurette* opened at the Renaissance. Jacques had never completed its orchestration but his admired fellow-artist, Léo Delibes, had been designated to finish it. *Belle Lurette* was Jacques at his most infectious, eternally young and laughing. And, as the gay music sang out in the theatre with its quick rhythms and witty phrases, so uniquely Offenbach, one half expected that when the curtain fell the comic, ugly, but lovable figure of Jacques Offenbach would turn his back on the conductor's stand and, with his impish grin, his eyes crinkling and sparkling, accept the plaudits.

A sadness hung over the audience, but *Belle Lurette* was the delightful testament of the man who was the most Parisian of them all.

Two weeks later, *Figaro* organized a memorial program to Offenbach. All his "children"—Hortense Schneider, Zulma Bouffar, Lise Tautin, Théo, Mme Judic, Berthelier, and others—who had attained stardom under Jacques' guidance, came to pay their last respects on the Variétés stage. It was a very emotional evening, but only one among them broke down utterly. Hortense Schneider, the fond "Cath," was to sing the "Letter Song" from *La Périchole*. As she stepped to the footlights it could be seen that she was trembling violently. Bravely, however, she began the nostalgic aria—and then her voice broke. Sobbing, she was led from the stage.

It was Hortense Schneider's last appearance. Although she lived forty years longer, dying at the age of ninety in 1920, she never again sang in a theatre.

10

The premiere of *Tales of Hoffmann* had been postponed. With Jacques gone, there was no need to hurry and there had already been delays with the scenery and costumes. Besides, Jacques had not lived to do the orchestration. Auguste had become head of the family and on him devolved the responsibility of arranging his father's affairs. Already showing traces of the illness which would carry him off within three years, the nineteen-year-old boy nevertheless faithfully carried out his father's instructions and, in accordance with his last wishes, Auguste designated Ernest Guiraud to finish the opera. With Jacques' annotations, it was a simple labor of love.

Finally, four months after Offenbach's death, on February 10, 1881, *Tales of Hoffmann* had its premiere. Prominent government officials, mingling with members of the social world, gave an official stamp to the audience, while the ornate gowns and headdresses of the ladies added *éclat* to the gathering. There was a festive air about the audience, just the sort that Jacques Offenbach most loved.

He had been gone long enough so that one could think of him without the imminence of tears and, as the curtain went up and the music pervaded the theatre, it seemed as if the spirit of the gay, smiling, witty Jacques had again joined them.

But, in short order, they recognized a new quality in this music. This was not Offenbach of the carefree laugh but rather one who felt the oppression of unknown terrors, of evil spirits and of supernatural forces. Allegorically, one could read into the libretto and music the frailty of the human being fighting against fate. One danced, like a doll, or one sang, in order to give one courage or to hide one's fears.

Tales of Hoffmann was fantasy but into the music Offenbach had poured a passion and compassion such as he had never before exhibited. *Tales of Hoffmann* retained much of the familiar Offenbach, but it reached a greater height of dramatic beauty.

"When he is dead they will appreciate him," Meilhac had cried. And tonight Offenbach posthumously gathered the laurels he had so long striven for. No longer could his claim to the title of maestro be gainsaid. Jacques Offenbach had joined the immortals.

Yet, as the years passed, there were many who found they could not forget the persuasive charms of *Orpheus* and *Helen of Troy* and even Offenbach's lesser operettas continued to give off a gemlike sparkle. New generations, far removed from the era these operettas had satirized, nevertheless found they contained an ageless appeal. *Tales of Hoffmann* was a worthy monument, one with also a perennial appeal, but it joined the ranks of "just another opera" while no one else ever managed to produce an "offenbachiade." Many searched for the secret formula, and the Viennese operettas frankly owed their inspiration to Offenbach, but no one ever attained the full complement of wit, sprightliness, intoxicating rhythms and variety of melody blended into an "offenbachiade."

Jacques Offenbach, who only faintly suspected it, had long before carved his own niche of immortality.

Bibliography

Cafés et Cabarets de Paris, Alfred Delvau, 1862.

Mémoires du Boulevard, Albert Wolff, 1866.

Mémoires d'un Journaliste, 2 vols., Henri de Villemessant, 1867, 1872.

Foyers et Coulisses, Vol. 1 *(Histoires anecdotiques des Bouffes-Parisiens),* Henry Buguet, 1873.

Offenbach en Amérique (avec notice biographique par Albert Wolff), Jacques Offenbach, 1877.

Offenbach: Sa Vie et Son Oeuvre, André Martinet, 1877.

Airs Variés (M. Offenbach, critique: sa profession de foi musicale), Adolphe Julien, 1877.

Les Confessions, Souvenirs d'un Demi-Siècle (1830-1890), 6 vols., Arsène Houssaye, 1885-1890.

From the Tone World, newspaper essays, Louis Ehlert, English translation, 1885.

Petits Mémoires Litteraires, Charles Monselet, 1885.

Notes et Souvenirs, 1871-1872, Ludovic Halévy, 1889.

Paris Pittoresque: 1800-1900, La Vie, Les Moeurs, Les Plaisirs, Louis Barron, December 5, 1899.

"Lettres Inédites de Jacques Offenbach," Marie-Charlotte Croze, *La Nouvelle Revue,* September, 1910.

Steeplejack, 2 vols., James Gibbons Huneker, 1920.

The Second Empire, Philip Guedalla, 1922.

Offenbach, René Brancour, 1929.

Carnets (avec une introduction et des notes par Daniel Halévy), 2 vols., Ludovic Halévy, 1935.

La Vie Parisienne: A Tribute to Offenbach, Sacheverell Sitwell, 1937.

Orpheus in Paris: Offenbach and the Paris of His Time (translated by Gwenda David and Eric Mosbacher), Siegfried Kracauer, 1938.
Offenbach: Mon Grandpère, Jacques Brindejont-Offenbach, 1940.

Also French and American newspapers and periodicals of the times, librettos, and music scores.